NO

DOUBT

About It

NO
DOUBT
About It

The Case for Christianity

Winfried Corduan

BROADMAN
&HOLMAN
PUBLISHERS

Nashville, Tennessee

Library of Congress Cataloging-in-Publication Data
Corduan, Winfried.
    [Reasonable faith]
    No doubt about it : the case for Christianity /
Winfried Corduan.
        p   cm.
    Originally published : Reasonable faith, 1993.
    Includes bibliographical references and indexes.
    ISBN 0-8054-1647-1 (pbk)
    1. Apologetics. I. Title.
[BT1102.C615   1997]
239—dc21   97-8569
                                                    CIP

To Bruno and Ursula Corduan,
my parents,
who taught me to love the truth

Table of Contents

Preface

At a time when it is becoming fashionable to question whether there even is such a thing as truth, this is a book about the truth of Christianity. It is based on the idea that truth continues to be an indispensible commodity. No matter how much our culture disparages truth, people now, as always, must live by the objectivity of truth. What you accept as true does make a lot of difference. Christianity teaches that your eternal life depends on it.

The defense of the truth of Christianity is called *apologetics*. The term is derived from 1 Peter 3:15, in which we are exhorted to be prepared to *give a defense* for our hope. The Greek word *apologia* (*defense*) is the word that would be used to defend one's case in a court of law. Thus the Christian should be able to state *what* he or she believes, and *why*. Apologetics helps the Christian mount a credible case for the truth of Christianity.

This treatment of apologetics is based on some assumptions that should be given from the onset.

1. *Evangelical Christianity is true.* One way of making a case for Christianity would be by watering it down so that it will be acceptable to anyone. Thus in the twentieth century we have seen versions of Christianity doctored up to suit atheistic, pantheistic, Marxist, secularist, and existentialist presuppositions. The interesting thing about that phenomenon is that, even though the intent was to make Christianity more plausible to the non-Christian, it really did not sell. It simply confirmed people in their atheistic, pantheistic, Marxist, secularist, or existentialist presuppositions without converting them to Christianity. The lesson is that Christianity, devoid of its own core, is really not worth defending. Thus the only version of Christianity we are interested in mounting an apologetics for is what I consider to be biblical (conservative, evangelical, some would say fundamentalist) Christianity. Only here do we find the fulfillment of our spiritual need.

2. *It is possible to defend Christianity.* More and more the philosophical world, even among evangelical Christians, is shying away from apologetics. Christians are being told that, even though there is nothing irrational about their beliefs, they ought not to look for an actual defense of them. I consider this approach to be insufficient. In the face of an onrush of arguments critical of Christianity, it may not be rational to hold on to Christian belief apart from evidence. I am convinced that the evidence is there.

3. *Apologetics is possible for the non-specialist.* This book has for its primary intended readership an undergraduate college student not majoring in philosophy. The student will hopefully find that these arguments are manageable and effective, without providing pat answers.

Acknowledgments

Thanks need to go to:

Dr. Paul House, my colleague, department chair, and friend, for suggesting that I approach Broadman Press with the idea for this book and for his continuous encouragement;

Dr. R. Douglas Geivett, my colleague, for helpful comments and many good discussions;

Mrs. Joanne Giger, department secretary, for pitching in cheerfully whenever asked;

John Mark Adkison, a student, for directing me to Metallica's lyrics, just when I was afraid I was going to lose touch (my own sons are more into rap);

Dr. John Landers, Dr. Vicki Crumpton, and the rest of the editorial staff at Broadman & Holman, for their upbeat and competent work on this project;

Dr. Norman L. Geisler, teacher and friend. In many ways my work here needs to be seen as an extension of his;

Dr. David Wolfe, former professor, who encouraged me to struggle with the philosophical approach to truth more than anyone else. He will recognize many of the patterns he has taught me in chapters 3 and 4—and undoubtedly he will decide that I still do not see things the way I should;

Nick and Seth, my sons, who have encouraged my writing. Only a parent can understand the joy of having their children come to a firm knowledge of Christ. Only an evangelical philosopher can fully appreciate what it means for both of them to select apologetics for their nighttime reading;

June, my wife, for reading through the manuscript and gently pointing out deficiencies. She paid me the ultimate compliment of laughing at all the right places (and at none of the wrong ones); and

Bruno and Ursula Corduan, my parents, for bringing off the improbable. They nurtured me in a Christian environment while at the same time encouraging me to embrace truth wherever it is found. Both of them, in many conversations from early childhood on, taught me that an open-eyed faith in Christ is the only desirable one. May their ministry continue through this work.

1

Faith, Reason, and Doubt

Forbidden Questions

Vignette 1: My class in world religions was on its annual visit to a synagogue. We were listening spellbound as a young woman named Tina told of her spiritual pilgrimage and her decision to convert to Reform Judaism. She had grown up in a Christian church. As a child, she had made a profession of faith. When she became a teenager, she started to raise questions about what she believed. Is Christ really God? Does the Trinity make sense? What can we as modern people believe to be true? Her pastor had told her that she should not ask such questions. He said that it is wrong to doubt and she should simply believe what she had been taught to believe. Now she was abandoning Christianity for good.

The Only Doubter?

Vignette 2: I was sitting in my office grading papers. The student scheduled for my two o'clock appointment was already ten minutes late. Eventually Bill showed up. "I was hung up in my computer class." So we conversed about computers, schedules, course loads, anything but what we were supposed to talk about. I could tell that he did not feel very comfortable yet. Finally Bill got to the point: "I just can't believe any longer the way I did back in high school. Back then I could accept anything on faith. Now I'm not even sure all the time that God exists." After we had talked a little while he said, "You know what's the worst part for me. As far as I can tell, I'm the only person at this Christian college who's going through these doubts." My conversation with Bill was the third of this type I had had that week.

Doubting Thomas

Vignette 3: When I was a young school boy in Germany, one item on the weekly schedule was Wednesday morning worship service. Protestants and Catholics each went to their respective services. As a Baptist, I was assigned to attend the service in the Lutheran church. There we would sit, pinching each other, whispering, making faces, and trying to sing interminable hymns that were too high even for our screechy voices. Needless to say, I do not remember much of what I heard in those sermons, but one of them sticks in my mind. It was the senior pastor's turn to preach. He was a kind man with white hair and a red face that had obviously seen and conquered many a roast pork with potatoes. When he emphasized a point in his preaching, he would lean forward in the pulpit, rest himself on his forearms and hands, and push himself up and down, looking rather like a friendly seal doing push-ups. This Wednesday morning he spoke on Jesus' appearance to doubting Thomas. "Leave my Thomas alone!" The pastor admonished us, looking more than ever like a seal with a mission. "Thomas wanted to find out for himself what was true. He was not content with hear-say testimony."

But Is It True?

"But is it true?" This is the guiding question of this book. As paradoxical as it may sound, many people believe in the truth of Christianity without ever contemplating this question. They will assert all of the right statements and beliefs; they have all of the correct answers; and the truth of what they believe is self-evident to them. The only answer to the question of whether Christianity is true or not is that it obviously is. In fact, many people even claim that any other attitude constitutes doubt, which must be understood as an inherently rebellious act against God and treated as a sin. This book is not written for those people.

Many of us do struggle with questions of the truth of Christianity. We are not fighting God, the church, or our upbringing; we just want to know the truth. Is Christianity believable? Can one with a clear head accept that Christ is God or that the Bible is the inspired Word of God? There are issues here that demand an answer, and they are suppressed at a potentially great cost.

Unbelievers Need to Know

The issue of truth appears in two particular arenas. First, there is the context of evangelism. To invite a person to receive Jesus Christ as Savior, two things are imperative. A person has to understand the gospel. If people do not understand the need for salvation and Christ's provision for us, it makes no sense to ask them to commit themselves to Christ. A person also has to accept the message of the gospel as true. I have seen non-Christians state clear reasons why they cannot believe in the truth of Christianity, and Christians respond by challenging them to ignore their questions and accept Christ anyway. Surely we do not want people to commit their lives to what they honestly feel is not the truth. Rather we should be able to show people why Christianity is true.

Of course there is a difference between questioning that is based on a search for truth with integrity and the kind of questioning that unbelievers sometimes hide behind. All too frequently we encounter the person who asks, "So where did Cain get his wife?" and if we do not have a satisfactory answer handy, he preens himself triumphantly, thinking that he has disproven the Bible, the church, and all of Christian dogma. This attitude needs to be treated by elevating the conversation to the level of personal need and commitment. Yet sometimes we are also guilty of treating an honest questioner's concerns with the cold shoulder or even contempt. If we are to meet persons' needs in the name of Christ, surely that ministry includes responding honestly to their intellectual questions. By the way, an honest "I don't know" is always better than making up an answer we do not really believe ourselves or simply ignoring someone's question.

Of course we are also not saying that a person would become a Christian on the basis of rational arguments alone. Salvation depends on our faith; no one is going to be in heaven simply because he or she tried to disprove God's existence but could not. However, clearing away the rational issues can very well be what makes it possible for people to place their faith in Christ. I have also seen this happen.

When Believers Have Questions

Second, the question of truth appears in our personal growth as Christians. There comes a time when we need to ask ourselves whether we really can subscribe to the truth of what we have said we believe. Many of us spent most of our lives in fairly restricted Christian environments. Growing up in Christian homes, we have been nurtured in church and Sunday School, some even in Christian schools. If we went to public schools, Bible clubs and youth ministries were available to us. Thus we have grown up with many beliefs as part of our heritage without examining alternatives or reasons why they should be true.

There is nothing inherently pernicious about this fact. If no one were ever to believe anything unless he or she had a solid core of arguments accumulated, most of us would have to go through life as skeptics. An eighteenth- and nineteenth-century rationalist attitude proclaimed that, somehow, unless you were able to support all of your beliefs with airtight arguments (at the so-called bar of reason) you were not entitled to hold them. That attitude is obviously neither realistic nor tenable. However, that fact does not give us the luxury of escaping into unreason whenever our faith is challenged or we are coping with personal doubts. We need to be honest with ourselves and ask ourselves why we do claim truth for what we say we believe. At that point, not confronting the issues of evidence will not firm up our faith.

We even need to go one step farther. There should come a period in our lives, as we mature in our faith, when we need to confront our inherited belief system and ask ourselves whether it has really become ours. The developmental psychologist James W. Fowler sees a personal re-examination of beliefs as necessary for full maturity.[1] Through most of our adolescent years we are very peer-oriented in all of our life's decisions. We respond to groups and easily pick up the group's beliefs as our own. This is why evangelism on the high school level needs to be socially oriented. Many times during this period we recommit ourselves to our family's

---

[1]James W. Fowler, *Stages of Faith* (New York: Harper & Row, 1981). See especially page 179.

values. However, in late adolescence or early young adulthood, we ought to escape from the peer-oriented mode; we need to decide whether we can really claim ownership in everything we have taken on as beliefs. In most cases, this process involves raising questions about the truth of these beliefs.

This re-examination does not mean tearing down everything so that it can be rebuilt. It may simply be a matter of making sure all of the nails are holding and applying a little more glue here and there. Unless a person is willing to go through such a process, his or her faith may always be suffering from a lack of conviction.

It is very difficult, if not impossible, to maintain an effective Christian life if we are nagged by doubts. The Bible demands that we dedicate our lives to the cause of Christ, but it hardly makes sense to have any kind of commitment if we are not sure that the cause of Christ is based on reality. It certainly is possible to ignore our questions and try to bury them in endless successions of activity. People will put pressure on us to do exactly that. Yet such an escape can also be a ticking time bomb (cf. vignette 1). In any event, we do not need to do that to ourselves. We are free to ask questions and search for answers.

Toward that end we need to become clearer on the relationship between faith and reason, and that clarification will have some implications on the nature of truth.

Faith and Reason

We use the term *faith* in three ways in the context of Christian theology: saving faith, growing faith, and knowing faith.

Saving Faith

In terms of the Christian gospel, saving faith may be the most crucial. In Acts 16:31 are Paul's instructions to the Philippian jailer: "Believe on the Lord Jesus Christ, and you will be saved" (NKJV). In Galatians 2:16, we read that we are saved by faith, not by works of the law. Ephesians 2:8-9 reiterates that we are saved by grace through faith. What is this faith that saves us?

A good synonym for saving faith may be "trust" or "reliance." When people have this kind of faith, they are expressing to Christ that they are lost without Him, that they cannot possibly redeem themselves, and that they are relying on Christ and His work alone for His gift of salvation. This kind of faith is an act of abandonment to God; it is not some kind of work. Instead it is the renunciation of all works and reliance on His work alone.

Saving faith is an all-or-nothing phenomenon. As Paul points out to the Galatians, it is not possible to supplement this faith with works of the law without undercutting the work of Christ (Gal. 5:2-4). Reliance that also looks elsewhere for support really is not reliance at all; trust that is not willing to accept what someone says is not trust at all. In the same way, trust in Christ that also tries to look elsewhere for help for salvation really is not trust in Christ at all. Thus this kind of faith by its very nature excludes works.

A word of clarification needs to be added. This kind of faith, if it is genuine, will manifest itself in good works as evidence. Though the works are not a precondition for faith, they are a definite consequence of true faith. This is also the teaching of Paul, for example, in Galatians 5 or in Titus 2 and 3, just as it is found in James as he proclaims that faith without works is dead (2:26). See our further discussion of this issue in chapter 12.

Growing Faith

I am calling the second kind of faith "growing faith." Jesus encouraged us to have this kind of faith when He told us not to worry about tomorrow but to rely on the provisions of our heavenly Father. Growing faith is different in some ways from saving faith. First of all, it has no implications for our salvation. It comes under the heading of living the Christian life once we are born again. Thus it presupposes that we are already in a relationship with Christ. A second point of contrast to saving faith is that in growing faith we can speak of degrees of faith. I can indeed grow in faith in terms of my daily trust in God. Over a lifetime of living in Christ, hopefully I come to trust Him more and more.

But growing faith also has something important in common with saving faith—both rely on God. Once again, the point is to learn not to occupy ourselves with our concerns, worries, and efforts but to turn them all over to Christ.

Many people, in their zeal for these first two kinds of faith, draw a wrong conclusion. They say that, because faith in both of these senses means to abandon ourselves to God, this faith is blind. Such a statement implies that we ought not to use our minds in any questioning or reasoning way; trust in God implies lack of critical thinking about God.

A little reflection on this attitude shows it to be unacceptable. We cannot trust someone or something we know nothing about. We need to know that the object of our trust is trustworthy. This concern does not mean that we want to compromise the nature of faith, but faith needs to be real, and this involves basing it on a reality, not a fantasy. In the Book of Hebrews, we read that those who want to come to God, must first of all believe that He exists and that He rewards those who seek Him (Heb. 11:6). In short, before we can come to have faith in Christ, we need to know that faith in Christ is meaningful.

Knowing Faith

Thus we come to the third type of faith, which I am calling "knowing faith," often called "belief," because it has to do with accepting certain statements as true. This faith refers to the way in which we may come to accept certain intellectual truths without which a trusting faith would be impossible. It is not possible to respond to the gospel without knowing the gospel; it is not possible to trust in Christ without knowing what Christ is all about. Thus even though we can only be redeemed through "saving faith," such saving faith presupposes some essential items of knowledge.[2] James tells

---

[2] I recall seemingly interminable youth group discussions on the topic of how much one really has to know in order to become a Christian. I fear that much of that discussion was based on a complete misunderstanding. Of course we are not saved by knowing anything. The real question should be: How much "head

us that the devils believe that God is one, but tremble, for they cannot be saved by such knowledge (Jas. 2:19). Neither are we saved by knowledge, but genuine trusting faith presupposes some knowledge.

There are several different ways we may aquire the knowledge on which we can base a decision. Let us lump them together into two categories: faith and reason, where "faith" stands for the "knowing faith" under consideration. The medieval scholar Thomas Aquinas has provided us with a helpful analysis of faith and reason in this context, and the following discussion will rely to a certain extent on his description.[3]

People usually learn about the facts of their faith from some form of authority. These sources might include parents, clergy, teachers, or the Bible. Because we are taught to respect these authorities, we accept what they teach us about God. No one can be expected to examine all of his or her beliefs before committing to them as true. Many people do not have the capacity, time, or interest to undertake a thorough evaluation of a doctrine and its alternatives. For that matter, if the world had to wait for the "experts"— theologians and philosophers—to come to agreement on beliefs before accepting any of them, nobody could believe anything. So God has seen to it that some people are commissioned to represent His truth as He has revealed it in His Word, the Bible. Such is the obligation of all parents to their children and all others who occupy a teaching or preaching capacity in the church. We see then that it is both possible and proper for all articles of belief to be accepted on the basis of faith, that is, out of respect to the authority that teaches them.

However, the path of knowing faith does not preclude a second path based on reason. When I was a child, my father told me that water consisted of oxygen and hydrogen. I

_____

knowledge" is needed to make an intelligent decision for Jesus Christ? I do not think it would be all that hard to agree on most of the basics, for example, that there is a God, that we are sinners unable to save ourselves, that Christ is the Son of God, who died as God's only provision for our sins, that Christ is alive, that we receive salvation as we trust in Christ, and that there is a heaven.

[3]Thomas Aquinas, *Summa contra Gentiles*, I, 3-10.

believed him, for I respected his authority. However, that
faith in him did not prevent me from taking a course in
chemistry in college in which I carried out an experiment of
producing water by combining oxygen and hydrogen. I still
accept the same belief as true, but on different grounds—I
first knew it by faith, now I know it by reason. The same
logic may apply to our knowledge about God.

Many truths are accessible to us only on the basis of faith
in God's revelation, including the facts concerning the plan
of salvation. Nevertheless, there are also truths that we can
know on the basis of reason as well as by faith. These truths
might include such items as the existence and unity of God.
There is nothing in the nature of knowing faith to preclude
our accepting some truths on the basis of reason.

When we talk about finding a grounding for our faith, we
mean that we ground some beliefs on reason—beliefs we had
earlier accepted on the basis of knowing faith. Does this
sound insidious to you? If it does, it might be because you
still are missing the distinctions on faith I made above.
Reason can never replace saving faith or growing faith. It
cannot simply supplant knowing faith, but it can provide a
second avenue towards the same items of belief that are
usually accepted on the basis of authority alone.

The Unity of Truth

We should never fear investigating truth. If we have to
run from truth, maybe it is because we have something to
hide. Could it be that we are afraid that, if we look too hard,
we might discover that what we have accepted to be true by
faith turns out to be false? I am convinced that faith and
reason, if used properly, will arrive at the identical truth.[4]
This conviction is in turn premised on the fact—with which

[4]Francis Schaeffer has done us a great service by contrasting the truth of divine
revelation with the faltering search for truth in humanistic endeavors. See his
Escape from Reason (Downers Grove: InterVarsity Press, 1968). Unfortunately in the
heat of his battle at times he inadvertently fired at his closest allies. Probably no one
came closer to Schaeffer's ideals on knowledge than Aquinas. Sadly, Schaeffer laid
the blame for the "divided field of knowledge," which no one eschewed more than
Aquinas, at Thomas' doorstep (see 9-12). Francis Schaeffer should have focused on
Aquinas' contemporary—and intellectual foe—Siger of Brabant, who indeed taught

Aquinas also began his discussion on this subject—that all truth originates with God and points us to Him.

Consequently we do not need to be gingerly in our investigations of truth. If a belief cannot withstand hard questioning, it may not be worth holding. If Christianity is true, it should be able to withstand the hardest questions we can bring to it. If Christianity is not true, we should reject it.

That last statement sounds daring, but it is actually a fairly gratuitous thing to assert. Should we ever believe something that has been shown to be false? Of course not! I can make that kind of statement because I am convinced that Christianity is true and that it will hold up under the severest scrutiny. It must be kept in mind that it is not as easy to show Christianity to be false, even hypothetically, as some people think.

A key to this discussion lies in the integrity of the questioning. We are concerned with honest questioning. However, many religious arguments consist of someone's merely trying to score points. The critic tries one approach after another, hoping the Christian cannot answer his latest volley, while the Christian piles up a mountain of arguments in the expectation that sooner or later the critic will throw in the towel. Questioning with integrity does not mean finding defenses for or against a pre-established point of view but wrestling with those real doubts that never stop pricking us.

We can conclude this opening chapter with an invitation. You are invited to ask some hard questions. Let us see whether we can show Christianity to be true. You must learn to understand the questions as well as to master the answers. You must learn to question with integrity. In the final analysis, the answer will require a personal response of faith commitment from you. When you start asking for truth, the stakes are high. Now we can apply some of these insights to our opening vignettes:

_____

a theory of double truth—what is true by faith may not be true by reason, and vice versa. Thomas repudiated all forms of dualism, including that between nature and grace.

Response to Vignette 1: We should not feel like we need to take all of the blame whenever someone who seemingly was a Christian departs from the faith. Many factors are at work, including the decision-making ability with which God has endowed us.[5] However, from our finite perspective I cannot get away from the feeling that the pastor's judgmental attitude contributed to this tragedy. People who have genuine heartfelt questions are not helped by making them feel guilty for their "doubts." I do not know if the pastor could have answered Tina's questions or helped her find the answers. Not everyone is required to be able to answer everyone else's questions. However, I am quite sure that by telling Tina her questioning was illegitimate he did contribute to her searching for a different religion. After all, that is what she said herself.

Response to Vignette 2: Most people go through periods of serious questioning. As I stated above, it may even be beneficial for further maturing in the faith. There is nothing wrong with someone who is reevaluating his or her beliefs. The best thing to do in such a case is to find someone who can carefully and respectfully work through the issues with the questioner on an individual basis. Sharing pressing doubts in a group setting will most likely set off undesirable dynamics, such as superficial answers or a condemnatory atmosphere. If you are going through a period of questioning right now, be assured: you are normal; you are not alone; there are answers.

Response to Vignette 3: "Leave my Thomas alone!" I too want to echo that statement. Christianity is something that cannot be had second-hand; you must know for yourself. Jesus did not condemn Thomas; that prerogative was left to the church. Jesus gently invited Thomas to check out His scars. He praises Thomas for believing on the basis of what he has seen and then praises even more those who believe without having seen —and that is us! We can never see what the first disciples saw, but we can believe. There is nothing that mandates that this faith be an irrational leap into unknowing. Just as Thomas did not want to commit

---

[5]Many evangelical churches teach that a person who has truly accepted Christ as Savior will remain saved to the end. Frequently this doctrine leads to the qualification that a person who does leave Christianity thereby gives evidence of never having been saved to begin with. This seems to be the point of what the apostle John teaches in 1 John 2:19. If those who are walking out of the Christian fellowship truly had been saved, they would not have walked out but would have remained. Thus in this case, one theological interpretation would be to say that Tina had never actually made a genuine commitment to Christ. Let us remember, though, that only God can see what the inside of our heart looks like.

himself on the basis of secondhand testimony, we too may believe on the basis of firm personal knowledge.

For Growth and Study

Mastering the Material

When you have studied this chapter, you should be able to:
1. Tell why it can at times be a good and helpful thing to question some of your beliefs.
2. Distinguish between three types of faith.
3. Show in what way knowledge on the basis of reason does not undermine knowledge on the basis of faith.
4. Make a case for the unity of all truth.
5. Identify the following names with the contributions to which we alluded in this chapter: James W. Fowler, Thomas Aquinas.

Thinking About the Ideas

1. In this chapter we have said that doubt can sometimes be a good thing. When can doubt be bad?
2. Can you think of an experience in your life when questioning something brought you closer to the truth?
3. To what extent are the three different types of faith interrelated? Why do people tend to confuse them with each other?
4. What are some truths that can be known only on the basis of biblical authority? Are there any truths that can be known on the basis of reason alone?
5. What are some areas in which faith and reason overlap? What are some areas in which reason seems to challenge faith?
6. What are some attitudes that keep people from searching for truth with integrity? How can you make sure that you are not just playing games with the truth?

For Futher Explorations

Gary R. Habermas, *Dealing with Doubt* (Chicago: Moody Press, 1990).

Paul Little, *Know Why You Believe* (Wheaton, IL: Scripture Press, 1967).

Clark H. Pinnock, *Set Forth Your Case* (Nutley, NJ: Craig Press, 1968).

2

Truth, Knowledge, and Relativism

Buddhist Logic

Vignette 1: After a small evangelistic rally on the University of Maryland mall, a fellow student and I were talking about Christianity. We were sitting in the grass, enjoying the sunshine and playing with blades of grass and little sticks, while I was trying to share the gospel with him. The conversation was proceeding without the heat and excitement that characterizes so many of these discussions. I was a senior now and had read enough to answer his objections and give him clear evidence why Christianity is true. Finally he said that just because Christianity is true, other religions aren't false. I tried to show him why that approach does not work.

"Jesus Christ claimed to be the only way to God. To say that He is the only way and that there are other ways would be illogical."

He replied: "But there are other logics. In Buddhist logic, what is contradictory to us, is not contradictory at all."

What's True for Linda

Vignette 2: Our college and career group had adopted the habit of getting together after Sunday night service in a restaurant. There, over onion rings, hot fudge sundaes, and soft drinks, we would make plans, talk about the day's events, or just enjoy being together. One week the conversation turned to evangelism. Some of us shared how we had attempted to present others with the gospel and the usual mix of success or lack thereof. Linda had been quiet up to now, apparently more absorbed in her strawberry ice cream cake than in the conversation. In a moment of silence she broke in, "I don't witness with words; I try to share my testimony through my life. I know that Christianity is true for me, but that doesn't mean that it has to be true for everyone else."

Pontius Pilate—What Is Truth?

Vignette 3: Jesus had been convicted by the Sanhedrin and turned over to the Roman procurator, Pontius Pilate. The charge brought against Him was claiming to be king of the Jews. As Pilate began to cross-examine Jesus in private, they bandied back and forth what Jesus' kingship was all about.

"My kingdom is not of this world," Jesus told him.

"So You are a king?" Pilate thought he was onto something. But instead of answering directly, Jesus said: "I have come into the world, to bear witness to the truth. Everyone who is of the truth hears My voice."

Pilate looked puzzled at Jesus for a moment. Then he shrugged his shoulders, made a face, and said, "What is truth?" He went out to consult Jesus' accusers (see John 18:33-38, NASB).

Relativism

In this chapter we will examine contemporary relativism and why it creates an obstacle for trying to present a rational defense for Christianity. Then we will respond to it and show how, despite some legitimate concerns, we can still have a valid concept of objective truth and knowledge.

Definition of Relativism

"But is it true?" This question assumes that truth is different from falsehood and that it makes a difference whether a belief is true or not. If in the final analysis all beliefs, even those that are mutually contradictory, are true, it matters little whether one particular system can be shown to be true.

All human thought is based on three principles: identity, contradiction, and excluded middle. The principle of identity states that a thing or a statement is identical with itself. In other words, this tree is this tree.[1] The principle of contradiction states that if something is true, its contradiction

---

[1]Do not try to read anything "deep" into this statement. Every once in a while some students get really frustrated with a statement like the above because they think that they cannot find its full meaning. They are looking for something that is not there. The principle means only what it says.

cannot also be true. If it is true that this is a tree, then it must be false that it is not a tree. The principle of excluded middle states that it must be one or the other. Either it is a tree or a non-tree; there is no middle ground between the two.

It has become fashionable of late to question the universality of the law of excluded middle, but, I think, on erroneous grounds. For example, some people are saying that we cannot always tell whether something is a tree or not. Or, on some drizzly day, it is hard to say whether it is really raining or not. Thus it seems that the law of excluded middle, which makes us choose between absolute alternatives, does not hold. These concerns are simply reflecting the limits of our knowledge. It is certainly true that we cannot always pinpoint what something is, but the law of excluded middle is not intended to claim universal knowledge for us. It simply says that, whatever a thing may be, it must be either that or not that—even if we cannot ever decide which is the case.

What we are calling *relativism* addresses the law of contradiction. Relativism calls into question whether we have the right to label as false something that does not fit into our understanding of truth. In more popular settings, we usually hear of relativism within the context of morality. What you believe to be right and what I believe to be right can both be right. This is true even if our beliefs are contradictory, just as long as we are sincere about our personal standards. This is also the nature of relativism when it comes to knowledge. Two mutually opposed systems of beliefs may both be right.

Thus the force of relativism lies in the fact that it attempts to rob all of our arguments for Christianity of any significance. If relativism is true, we are wasting our time with rational arguments. An unbeliever can accept all of them and still be unaffected by them, for in this case even beliefs that totally contradict Christianity might be true. It leaves us in the position of a person who goes on a long, arduous journey only to discover after many months that he has not moved one inch from home.

Thus relativism poses one of the severest obstacles to our project. It leaves the word "truth" vacuous and makes the defense of supposed truth meaningless. It appears that relativism is more at home in our age than at any other time. Where did it come from?

Roots of Relativism

There are a number of reasons why our contemporary culture has allowed relativism to come in and make itself at home. We will list six, though no doubt more are possible.

1. The knowledge explosion. Next time you are in the library, look up *Chemical Abstracts* or any other index volume that lists all of the articles published in major scholarly journals. Acquaint yourself with *Dissertation Abstracts* and get a feel for how many Ph.D.'s are granted every year and the dissertations on which they are based. Even if your school has a relatively small library, pay a visit to the acquisitions room and notice how many new books are coming in and how many more works are advertised as "indispensable for any good library." After doing this, you will begin to get a small feel for the so-called knowledge explosion.

Every day more information is brought to the attention of the world. Much of it is junk; but much of it is not, and that is where the problem lies. Much of this information is based on careful research and documentation and there is too much of it. No one person can keep up with it. Even experts can no longer know everything in what they thought was their area of expertise.

As a consequence, it would appear that the wise person is aware of these limitations and does not speak in absolute terms of truth and falsehood. Since nobody can know everything pertaining to a particular subject, it would seem foolhardy to speak too rashly on any subject. What looks absolutely true from my limited vantage point may be just one side of a much larger picture.

The Jains, adherents of a minority religion of India, illustrate this point with the story of five blind men who encounter an elephant. Each one of them touches a different part of the elephant and thinks that he knows the whole elephant. One of them embraces a leg and says that the elephant is like a column. The second man grabs the tail and states that the elephant is like a rope. The third one fondles the ear and says that the elephant is like a fan. The fourth one holds on to the trunk and exclaims that the elephant is like a snake. The fifth one runs his hand along the side and concludes that the elephant is like a wall. They are each right, but, seen from a broader vantage point, they are both right and wrong. Each of us seems to be such a blind man, grappling with a limited piece of information; how dare we pronounce on the whole elephant?

2. *Totalitarianism and intolerance.* The twentieth century has seen persecution and genocide on an unprecedented scale. Nazi Germany and the Stalinist Soviet Union lead the long list for systematic exterminations based on ideologies, but there are many other instances. Frequently such persecution occurs in the name of religion. For example, in some Islamic countries the populace has been stirred to war by declaring a certain cause a *jihad,* or "holy war." In 1989 some Muslim leaders called for the death of Salman Rushdie for allegedly slandering the prophet Muhammad in his book, *Satanic Verses.*[2]

There is blood in the history of Christianity as well. We can point to the crusades, for example—and even if we do not, the rest of the world does. Eastern and Western churches are guilty of sponsoring large-scale actions against Jews in the name of Christ.

For that matter, there is intolerance even in our own backyard. Again and again we read in the newspapers of Christian groups trying to enforce their views on the rest of the country through legal action. Do we really want to send people to jail because they hold different beliefs from ours? Would we use more force if it were available to us?

The upshot is that there seems to be a correlation between holding to one's views and intolerance. So it would appear that it is best to accept one's own beliefs without necessarily saying that everyone else's are wrong.

3. *The sincerity of believers in other religions.* There was a time when we did not know much about people who hold to other beliefs. Thus it was always possible to fantasize about

---

[2]Actually Rushdie did no such thing. He committed the far more volatile "crime" of satirizing the Islamic establishment—along with all other establishments. Salman Rushdie, *Satanic Verses* (New York: Viking, 1988).

them and to exaggerate the differences, usually much to their detriment. We could imagine the "heathens" as brutal and as inhumane as our own arrogance would allow.

However, as the cliché goes, the world has grown smaller. We encounter people from different cultures and religions every night on television. It is now possible to travel all around the globe with very little effort. Travel broadens and it can also undermine our prejudices. One of the lessons we have to learn is that people of different persuasions are just as sincere in their beliefs as we are in ours.

I have discovered that, as I have taken students on trips into other countries, some of them are genuinely surprised at the obvious commitment of believers in other religions. Somehow they had the idea that since these people were not Christians they must be either hypocrites or searching. Of course the truth is very different. The shoe can even be on the other foot. A few months ago I walked into a Hindu temple and asked a Brahmin priest to give me a few explanations. He immediately assumed that I was "searching" and was only too delighted to try to lead me into the truth as he understood it.

Rightly or wrongly, we tend to judge the truth of beliefs by how strongly we hold them. When we realize how much other people hold differing beliefs just as strongly as we do ours, we feel that we can no longer claim ours with the same absolute conviction. Thus it seems best to decide that they have their truth and we have ours.

4. *The influence of Eastern thought.* On a fairly popular level, the notion has spread that in certain Eastern world-views one is not tied to the law of contradiction. For example, my fellow student in vignette 1 seemed to be of the opinion that, when pushed into a corner on a logical point, he could simply invoke "Buddhist logic" and be immediately lifted out of the dilemma.

The very fact that there seems to be more than one way of correct thinking can lead one to question the universality of our so-called "Aristotelian" logic. Without immediately resorting to some other form of logic, it still appears best to treat our way of thinking as only one way out of many. That way, an inference derived from our logic is not necessarily universally valid. Even though it may yield truth, it does not necessarily yield truth for everyone.

5. *Individualism.* An important ingredient of current thought is the individual's right to decide for himself or herself. This idea has given way to the notion that you are your own authority. If that notion is accepted as true, it is easy to understand how it will quickly lead into relativism. With no greater court of appeals than oneself, it would seem outrageous to make any universal pronouncements on truth and falsehood. I can speak of what seems true to me; you can tell me what seems true to you. If we disagree, each of us can go our particular way without being able to settle the issue.

6. *The virtue of humility.* Partially arising out of the previous five points, but perhaps not exclusively so, relativism also comes from a new emphasis on humility. There seems to be something inherently arrogant about the idea that on some important point I could be right and everybody else wrong. Even though such a scenario is certainly a theoretical possibility, what are the chances of its actually being so every time that I find myself holding a position that differs from that of others? The very idea somehow puts me into a privileged position. I must be someone special to be able to pronounce right and wrong in absolute terms to the rest of the world.

An attitude of true humility seems to be the best response to this temptation. I do not want to put myself on a pedestal ahead of everyone else, so I will speak softly, I will not deny that I have the truth, but I will also not deny that you might have truth as well, even though we apparently disagree with each other.

A Careful Response to Relativism's Roots

These are potent forces directing us to embrace relativism. They cannot be dealt with effectively simply by saying that we have absolute knowledge. Further, invoking divine revelation at this point would miss the point, for the very existence of an authoritative divine revelation is at issue. To confront contemporary relativism by quoting Bible verses does not help us resolve the intellectual challenge.

We will respond to relativism in two stages. First we will address each of the above six points sympathetically, but critically. Then we will attempt to reconstruct what we can say about truth and knowledge in a positive way.

1. *Partial knowledge is still knowledge.* The point about the vast increases in knowledge is valid, but its relativistic conclusion is overstated. It is true that, because of the incredible accumulation of knowledge in our day, it is impossible to speak authoritatively on many subjects. There simply is too much to know, and nobody can keep up with a great amount of it. Consequently the wise person will always keep his or her limitations in mind and refrain from unwarranted generalized pronouncements.

Nevertheless, it is a logical fallacy[3] to conclude from this caution that we cannot have any genuine knowledge. If one blind man tells us that the part of the elephant he is touching is like a snake, while another one informs us that, as far as he has come to know the elephant, it resembles a wall, then they are stating truth. The remedy is not to deny the things that we know, but to qualify our standpoint.

Can we ever know that we have delimited our knowledge claims sufficiently to speak without running into danger of having made a mistake? In one sense we cannot. It is always logically conceivable that we have made an error somewhere, that we have mistaken the part for the whole. As we will argue later in this chapter, in another sense that question is not as forceful as it sounds. When we construct a positive concept of knowledge below, it will become apparent that at times it may be possible to reach a point at which it becomes arbitrary to make a presumption of error. Theoretical possibilities aside, it makes no sense from a practical standpoint to try to find a way in which I might be mistaken. (Before we reach that part in the chapter, can you think of some times when that would be true?)

2. *Intolerance does not have to be the result of knowledge.* First of all, let us stop making excuses for intolerant behavior.

---

[3] The fallacy of composition and division. (For example, the human race is a countless multitude; I am a member of the human race; therefore I am a countless multitude.)

People (and that includes Christians) do act intolerantly toward each other, frequently with no more excuse than that they have the truth and do not want others to hold or believe anything less. Even as I am writing this paragraph there are evangelical Christians in the United States who are looking for ways to make it illegal to not teach their views or to teach ideas different from their own. Having truth (or thinking you do) often does lead to intolerance. This does not have to be a necessary connection. There is nothing compulsory about hating those with whom we disagree. To the contrary, the Bible sets a different example.

Second, we have to hold our ground on one important point: it is not intolerant for me to label someone's views as false. That act can unfortunately lead to intolerance, but it becomes so only if I engage in some effort to try to keep others from holding and spreading their "errors" with the same freedom with which I would like to be able to hold and spread my "truths." Thomas Jefferson, when asked how he felt about people who did not believe what he believed, is supposed to have said: "It neither picks my pocket nor breaks my leg."[4] In other words, it does no harm, so we can tolerate pluralism. That attitude in no way entails having to mitigate our claim for what we consider to be true or false.

3. *We cannot use sincerity as a guide to truth.* Even though we are often convinced of our own beliefs because we somehow feel them strongly, those feelings can hardly be a reliable guide for truth. People who think that perhaps Hinduism or Buddhism are also true in their own way because their adherents are so sincere, would find a similar argument repugnant if it were made for Nazis or Satanists. The sincerity of people who hold a set of beliefs cannot be used as a test for the truth of those beliefs. Truth has to be assessed some other way.

Observing the sincerity of others lets us see the full humanity in all people. The Hindu who holds to his religion with the same fervor as I do mine is just as much a human being as I am and needs to be treated in the same way I expect to be treated. Our dialogues and debates must

---

[4]Martin E. Marty, *Protestantism in the United States: Righteous Empire*, 2nd ed. (New York: Scribner's, 1986), 45-46.

consequently begin at the point of sympathy and compassion. The apostle Paul said with reference to his fellow Jews that he would gladly forfeit his own salvation if it would bring them to Christ. We recognize with tears and concern that some of our fellow human beings are in error, but the truth cannot be altered by our feelings.

4. *Eastern logic is inappropriate.* People who make reference to Buddhist logic are twice mistaken. First of all, there is no legitimate reason why someone caught in an argument should all of a sudden be allowed to say the magic words, "Buddhist logic," and thus immediately get off the hook. To be able to invoke the words "Buddhist logic," you have to know what you are saying, and you cannot actually make use of Buddhist logic unless you are a Buddhist.

Second, Buddhist logic does not give us license to dispense with the principle of contradiction at will. What it states is that any statement can be seen from two perspectives. There is the everyday life perspective in which a tree is a tree and not a non-tree. Buddhism maintains that ultimate truth is beyond the world that we experience in day-to-day life. From the absolute perspective, everyday reality (*maya*) is only an illusion that in the final analysis, is pure nothingness (*sunyata*). Thus the tree is actually a non-tree. Putting the two together, one can say that the tree is both a tree and a non-tree—but only in two different senses.

It would be true from the *maya* perspective to say that it is a tree and false that it is not. It would be false from the *sunyata* perspective to say that it is a tree and true that it is not. In other words, the law of contradiction is not put aside—it is upheld by making sure that it is not violated. It would be contradictory to say that what is true from one perspective is true from another, and so Buddhist logic has us qualify our observations to make sure we do not overstep the boundaries of any given perspective—so that we do not contradict ourselves! The law of contradiction reigns unimpeached in each given level. Thus the statement that Buddhist logic does away with the law of contradiction is mistaken. Buddhist logic enhances the law of contradiction.

5. *We are not our final reference points for truth.* Events occur beyond our conceptualizations. The philosopher Paul Weiss makes the point that reality often treats us "defiantly." When we think that we have everything figured out, suddenly we are "opposed" by the facts. There is nothing like a miscalculation or two to remind us that reality is bigger than our imaginations.[5]

Like it or not, what is true or false is often defined for us by reality. The person who denies the law of gravity will still die if he or she jumps off a skyscraper. That does not mean that we should not try to figure out what is true by ourselves (see the last chapter), but it does mean that what you figured out and what I figured out cannot be equally true if we contradict each other. Reality, not our preferences, needs to be the ultimate source and authority of truth.

6. *Humility does not mean denying you know what you know.* Humility refers to an attitude. We already made reference to that attitude in the discussion on tolerance. Humility does not mean that I can change reality.

Let us imagine that you and I are both learning to play the guitar and I have just mastered the D-chord while you have not. Humility means that I am grateful for my accomplishment, give credit to everyone who has helped me, and feel badly for anyone who has not had the opportunity to learn this chord yet. Yet it would be fatuous if I said that I did not know how to play this chord, or if I said that you did, even though it is obvious that you do not. That is not humility.

Another point needs to be made here. Sometimes a false sense of humility can be an excuse not to live up to the implications of knowing a certain truth. Truth can imply responsibility. For example, having acquired a certain life-saving technique may bring with it an obligation to share it with others. What if Louis Pasteur had said that the germ theory was true for him, but that it need not be true for everyone else? If Heimlich had been too humble to share his innovative technique with others, a lot more lives would

---

[5]Paul Weiss, *First Considerations* (Carbondale: Southern Illinois University Press, 1977), 7-12.

have been lost. Without overgeneralizing this insight, the following statement needs to be made: sometimes apparent humility can become a cloak behind which people hide their apathy. Truth, as we said in the previous chapter, demands commitment.

A Double Critique of Relativism

Even though many people profess a relativistic view, relativism is untenable so long as one wants to maintain some form of rationality.

1. *Relativism leads to the impossible attitude of skepticism.* In the most theoretical sense, relativism and skepticism are two different things. Relativism says that everything, including contradictory statements, can be true. Skepticism says that we cannot know anything to be true. Theoretically one can be a relativist without being a skeptic.

In the real world, however, things are otherwise. Let us say that a person looks at two mutually exclusive world-views and is asked to adopt one for himself or herself. The person is not going to say that either one is true and therefore it does not matter which one he or she chooses. The person is going to say that since you can make a case for either one, we cannot know which one is really true. Contemporary people, despite all of their relativistic claims, still have a rudimentary sense of true and false (see the second critique). Thus, when they are told that anything and everything could be defended as true, their most likely reaction is going to simply be to suspend judgment. So we see that relativism, the claim that contradictory things can both be true, leads to skepticism, the claim that you cannot really know anything to be true.

It turns out that skepticism is a position that nobody can hold. Note that I did not say that one *ought not* to hold it; I said that one *cannot* hold it. Skepticism states that one cannot know anything. Does the person who makes that statement know it or not? If the skeptic thinks that skepticism is true, then it is false. The skeptic argues that we can know at least one thing, namely, that skepticism is true. If the skeptic does not claim that skepticism is true, he or she is not saying anything meaningful.

We must distinguish here between what can be said and what can be affirmed meaningfully. Anything can be said, yet that does not mean that we are affirming anything meaningful in the process. I can say, "A married bachelor drew a square circle in the sand that was also non-sand," but that proposition is gibberish. It has no more meaning than the random sounds produced by a six-month-old baby. Skepticism is unaffirmable in the same way. You can say that you cannot know anything, but you cannot affirm it meaningfully. You cannot even think it: as soon as you think that it is true, it must also be false. The true skeptic, if there were one, would have to suspend all thoughts, including any thoughts about skepticism, and play the role of a brainless plant. Insofar as relativism leads to skepticism, that unfortunate state must also be the fate of relativism.

2. *Relativism cannot be lived out.* Relativism plays the role of Zorro in the world of knowledge. It stays in concealment for long periods of time only to suddenly appear at crucial moments, conquer the day, and go back into hiding.

An individual will live his or her life almost entirely on a nonrelativistic true-false basis. Either I missed the bus, or I didn't miss the bus. Either this is Friday, or it is not Friday. Either I have eaten lunch, or I have not eaten lunch.

This is the context of Eastern cultures as well. The Buddhist monk tells me that I may enter his temple. He does not say, "You may both enter and non-enter the temple that is also a non-temple." He forbids me to take a picture of a certain image or of himself. He does not say (or mean), "You may not and may take a picture here." He makes certain statements and expects me to respect their truth, and he does not intend for these statements to be both true and false; their truth excludes their falsehood. (As we saw above, this point is perfectly compatible with Buddhist logic.)

Relativism only seems to pop up at certain crucial moments, usually in the sphere of morality or religion. I am referring not only to the lame debating technique of trotting out relativism as a last resort to pull logical chestnuts out of the fire. By and large one only hears relativistic statements when one talks about God, right and wrong, and salvation. One never hears the idea that mutually exclusive statements could be true when it comes to the stock market, the sports page, or the kitchen. The person may say that Christianity is true, but that a religion which is incompatible with Christianity is also true. That same person, however, will not invoke the same relativism when it comes to distinguishing between milk and cyanide.

Why? Because one simply cannot live out relativism. All of life consists of one true-false judgment after another. One cannot even live out relativism in the areas in which it is invoked, religion and morality. Sooner or later one has to commit oneself to something as true and its opposite as false. If relativism is true, then non-relativism must be false. If you deny that fact, then you have become a skeptic. If you accept it, then relativism is false because there are some absolute true-false distinctions after all. In any case, a commitment to relativism can only lead to a muddle and, consequently, cannot be lived out.

Of course the best critique against a position like relativism may be to show that there are better alternatives than to suspend judgment. Thus we can now turn to the positive side of the issue and show that it is not necessary to try to live out relativism because truth can in fact be known.

Truth and Knowledge

Truth

"What is truth?" was Pilate's question. He probably asked without any intent of really finding an answer. Nevertheless, what is truth? Many answers could be (and have been) given to this question, some with specific content in mind, others on a purely theoretical basis. For our purposes at this point all we need is a minimal definition that will allow us to show that, contrary to relativism, truth is an objective category.

What do we have in mind when we ask whether something is true? Take the sentence "My car is in the parking lot." When is this sentence true? When my car really is in the parking lot. When is the formula "the square of the hypotenuse equals the sum of the squares of the two sides of a right triangle" true? When the geometric relationship in a right triangle really works out that way. When is the statement "God exists" true? When God really exists.

In each of these cases, what we understand by the statement's being true is something along the following line: there is some kind of reality that is constituted independently of what we say about it. In other words, either my car is in the parking lot or not; either the geometry of right triangles follows the Pythagorean theorem or not; either God exists or He does not. This reality is a given. Our statements are true if they correspond to the reality in question; they are false if they do not correspond. We call this the *correspondence theory of truth,*[6] which we can express in briefer form:

truth = what corresponds to reality.

For purposes of this theory of truth, it makes no difference how we view the nature of reality. Most of us think of reality as a rather complex combination of physical, spiritual, and mental phenomena. In that case statements which accurately represent any of those aspects of reality can be true. In short, the correspondence theory of truth claims that a statement is true if it corresponds to reality—whatever reality might be.

The actual nature of reality must then be discovered by investigating it. Thereby we bring up the sequel to our first question, "If there is truth, can we know it?" Can we ever actually figure out if a statement does correspond to reality?

Knowledge

This last question seems to launch us into a never-ending morass of deep metaphysical questions that can only be answered through intense meditation, but appearances are deceiving. Actually, if we limit ourselves to modest examples, it is easy to answer this question.

What do we commonly mean when we ask if we can know that something is true? Let us go back to the example

---

[6]Later on we will learn and use a second theory of truth, the "coherence theory." For our present purposes the correspondence theory will suffice. In any event, a good argument can be made that a coherence theory must in some way presuppose a correspondence theory. Cf. Bertrand Russell, *Problems of Philosophy* (New York: Oxford University Press, 1959), 119-130.

of my car in the parking lot. How can I know if my statement corresponds to reality? How can I know that it is true? Obviously the answer is that I can go out and look. If I see it, the statement must be true. Yet how can I be sure? I can take some friends with me; I can check out the serial number of the car; I can ask the FBI to establish the identity of the vehicle's owner. After all the appropriate tests have been passed, and there is no other appropriate way of checking whether it is so, I can be sure that my car is indeed in the parking lot. Then I can say that I know that my car is in the parking lot.

We can then follow an old tradition and define knowledge as "justified belief."[7] This is to say that if a belief passes all of the appropriate tests, it is "justified." We have only two options: either we consider it genuine knowledge or we must resign ourselves to skepticism. Many beliefs are not so justified, and we must be careful to distinguish between opinions, guesses, possible truths, and genuine knowledge. To deny the possibility of any knowledge, given all of the right tests and right results, however, is not to be cautious, but to be skeptical. As we saw earlier, skepticism is an untenable position. Thus,

knowledge = justified belief.

Some Qualifications

This discussion is not meant to imply some form of human infallibility. It is based on the realistic possibility that, for a number of areas of human beliefs, it is possible to array the appropriate tests and to establish the beliefs to be true to the limits of our capabilities. Any further demands by way of justification would then have no meaning; but certainly there is plenty of room for error. We may not have all of the tests, or some of them may not be appropriate. We may not draw the proper conclusions from the tests. Those are real possibilities, but they are not reasons to change the definition

---

[7]Again we call brief attention to the fact that this particular description of knowledge is not the only one found in philosophical literature. For example, there has been a lot of interest of late in the question of when a person is justified in holding a belief, as opposed to our present concern with the belief itself. It seems to me that this other question cannot be addressed adequately unless we are sure that the belief itself has integrity. Could a person be justified in holding a false belief?

of knowledge; they merely show that as human beings we sometimes do not approach the ideal of knowledge. At the risk of belaboring the point, to say categorically that we can never have that kind of knowledge will only land us in the self-destruction of skepticism.

Another crucial point we have to keep in mind is that there are many different tests for truth, depending on the particular belief in question. For the belief that my car is in the parking lot, the most obvious test is to go and look. You could not test the truth of a geometric theorem that way— your geometry professor would never accept anything but a deduction as the valid test for a geometric truth. At the same time, if I tried to deduce the fact that my car is in the parking lot along the lines of a geometric proof, I would be doing something odd and probably unsuccessful.

Much non-productive discussion in the history of philosophy has resulted from the fact that people thought that there should be only one way of testing truth. Much worse, when that test then turned out not to be universally applicable, people decided that no tests for knowledge are possible.

How can we know whether we have exhausted all appropriate tests for a particular belief? The answer can only be vague since it obviously depends on the belief at issue. We have probably availed ourselves of all appropriate tests when the objections to a belief carry more problems than the belief in question, or when the objector claims that we must test against a position no normal human being would ever hold.

Let me illustrate this point with a silly example. Let us come back again to the belief that my car is in the parking lot. I have checked things out as thoroughly as I could with the help of my friends and the FBI, and I am convinced that there is a vehicle which is located in the parking lot and which is mine. Now some beginning philosophy student may suggest that perhaps that car on the lot is actually a hologram projected into this space and time by Martians hovering over the earth in a flying saucer. How do I respond to that objection?

The answer is that I have no good response, and I do not need one either. The person who comes up with this notion would be able to develop it to the point that any test against

Martians that I could come up with would immediately be ruled out. To demand that I handle such an objection is not reasonable. I would not claim to be able to defend my belief about the location of my car against *any imaginable doubt*. All I need to do is to be able to defend it against *any reasonable doubt*. The person who came up with the objection most likely does not believe it either and is just advancing this silliness as ammunition against my belief.

In fact, we can turn the table on the person making such demands on us and point out that the demand is not even legitimate. It implies the thesis that in order to be true a belief must be able to withstand any conceivable doubt. No belief can withstand that requirement—including the belief that in order to be true a belief must be able to withstand any conceivable doubt. What is at issue is not all of the objections and alternative views a person can conjure up as debating ammunition, but the reasonable objections and demands of rational people. Those are hard enough to respond to. If there were a group of people who genuinely on (at least to them) reasonable grounds thought that my car was a Martian hologram projection, I would feel a lot more pressure to be able to handle that objection.

We have defined relativism and explored its origin in various facets of our lives. We tried to show why those factors need not lead to relativism. Then we went on the attack and showed that relativism and its evil twin brother, skepticism, are not tenable positions. Finally, we tried to show how it is possible to talk about knowing truth without lapsing into mere dogmatism, by defining truth as correspondence to reality and knowledge as justified belief. How it is that we can even attempt to justify religious beliefs, and to what extent such an effort can be successful, are questions that we have not prejudiced at this point and need to take up in the next chapter. For now let us take another look at the opening vignettes.

Response to Vignette 1: I do not remember what I said to the student in this conversation. What I *should* have said is something along the line of the critiques of relativism found in this chapter. I should have shown him that he was not living by relativistic standards at any other time and that this particular avowal was a mere escape hatch because I had him verbally cornered. I should have made the point that, unless he bought into the Buddhist worldview, he had no business invoking Buddhist logic, though even that would not get him out of the pickle. Hopefully I would have done so in a sympathetic and friendly manner. I should not have let the conversation end without making sure that he understood the offer of God's free grace, which to me was the real issue, not the nature of logic. Finally, I should have made arrangements to talk to him again sometime. Relativists appreciated non-relativistic friendship even in the age that coined the phrase, "Do your own thing."

Response to Vignette 2: I have always been puzzled by folks like Linda who say these things (and she is not alone). For one thing, I do not know how many people lead such obviously Christian lives that everyone else can unequivocally see Jesus in them. That does not mean that our lives ought not to be clear witnesses for Christ (they should), or that we ought to turn every conversation into a religious argument (we should not), but I am amazed at the refusal of some people to give even minimal verbal witness to Christ. First Peter 3:15 exhorts us always to be ready to give an account (a defense) of the hope that is within us. This is a far cry from the relativistic, "It's true for me, but maybe not for you." The problem with Linda's relativism is that apparently Christianity is not really true for her either, for at the heart of Christianity is God's one and only plan of salvation. "For God so loved"—not merely the ones who were comfortable with the idea, but—"the world."

Response to Vignette 3: I picture Pontius Pilate as a pretty cynical man for whom truth is a matter of expedience. His question seems to make him a man born two thousand years before his time, but Pilate's relativism illustrates another important side to this issue. Truth is about reality, and by turning the matter of truth into a debating point, we may miss reality. For Pilate it was a matter of sliding by the one who said that He was the truth. Let us not forget that, when we talk about truth, the reality of Jesus is the focus of the intellectual issue, not the other way around.

For Growth and Study

Mastering the Material

When you have finished studying this chapter you should be able to:
1. Define relativism.
2. Explain six reasons why relativism has become a popular form of thinking.

3. Show why the above six reasons are not compelling for a case for relativism.
4. Give two head-on critiques of relativism (based on the ideas of skepticism and not being able to live out relativism).
5. Explain the idea of truth as correspondence to reality.
6. Explain the idea of knowledge as justified belief.
7. Show how a basic understanding of knowledge need not be dogmatic in order to avoid skepticism.
8. Be able to identify the following name with the contribution to which we alluded in this chapter: Paul Weiss.

Thinking About the Ideas

1. Find examples of relativism in newspapers, magazines, TV shows, etc. What subjects are involved?
2. Looking at individual people, not an entire culture, why can relativism be an attractive position?
3. Can you pinpoint any reasons beyond the six in this chapter why our culture has cottoned to relativism so much lately?
4. We have critiqued relativism for being a position that cannot be lived out consistently. To what extent is this a fair standard to apply to other positions as well? In what way would this standard have to be clarified?
5. We have defined truth as "correspondence to reality." How might one respond to the argument that, since different people have different ideas of reality, there must be different truths as well?
6. We have defined knowledge as "justified belief." Do I have to be aware of whether a belief has been justified or not before I can claim to know it?
7. To return to the question raised early in the chapter and responded to in the last part, at what point does it become unnecessary to respond to theoretical objections raised against a particular belief? Can you think of any situations in which one might want to make use of this idea?

For Further Explorations

Allan Bloom, *The Closing of the American Mind* (New York: Simon & Schuster, 1987).

Richard J. Mouw, *Distorted Truth* (San Francisco: Harper & Row, 1989).

Lesslie Newbigin, *The Gospel in a Pluralist Society* (Grand Rapids: Eerdmans, 1989).

Francis A. Schaeffer, *The God Who Is There* (Downers Grove, IL: InterVarsity Press, 1968).

3

Knowledge:
Some Important Components

No Proof Needed

Vignette 1: About halfway through my course in apologetics I usually lecture on the cosmological argument for God's existence (see chapter 6). I ask the students to put on their "skeptical faces" and to challenge each premise as I present it and try to defend it. One year a student about six rows back raised his hand and announced, "As far as I'm concerned, all this junk about trying to prove God's existence is a total waste of time." How do I handle that one? He didn't even put it into the form of a question. So I asked a question back, "Well, Frank, why do you believe that there is a God?" "I just know," Frank replied, "I have fellowship with Him; He is real to me. I have a personal relationship with God. So I cannot doubt His existence, and you don't need to prove it to me."

Beyond the Shadow of a Doubt

Vignette 2: It was another Saturday night at The Natural High, the evangelistic coffeehouse I managed. I was carrying out my usual duties of coordinating entertainment, making sure there was enough staff around the tables, and troubleshooting as needed. The one thing I did not have to pay attention to was the popcorn; everyone loved to head into the kitchen and do evangelism by salting the corn, if not the earth. Suddenly a staff worker called me over to a table to help out with the conversation. Two college-aged men were defending a humanistic position, and the staff worker was not sure what to say. I slowly attempted to guide the conversation to my favorite theme: How do we know which worldview is true? After a few minutes one of the two young men leaned back in his chair, actually folded his arms, and said, "Prove to me beyond the shadow of a doubt that there is a God."

The Scientific Method

Vignette 3: As a sophomore I was sitting in the large lecture hall waiting for the day's installment of Introduction to Psychology. I was half listening to the conversation in the row behind me.

A student was complaining about the course. "It's too scientific for me," she said. "You can't study human beings in the same way as atoms and chemicals."

The guy sitting next to her took the affirmative in this mini-debate. "You want to have truth, don't you? The scientific method is the only way we have of getting to the truth of anything."

Life-Changing Truth

Vignette 4: A member of a local professional football team was addressing our youth group. He told of the problems he had faced in his life and how Jesus Christ had raised him from the depths. After the talk someone raised his hand and asked him how he could be sure that Christianity was true. What made him think he was not wasting his life on an illusion? The athlete responded, "How can you even question if Christianity is true after what I have experienced? I know it is true because it has changed my life. And if you let Christ change your life, you too can know that He is real."

In the previous chapter we defined truth as "what corresponds to reality." We said that we have knowledge when a belief has passed all relevant tests for its truth. Then we can say that it has been justified. Finally we made the point that there is no one test for all types of belief. Which test is relevant depends on the belief in question.

We will now move ahead and start thinking in terms of testing the truth of Christianity. By way of example, one particular aspect of Christianity, namely the existence of God, will play an important role in our discussion. For the moment the goal is not so much to test either God or Christianity, but to discover a method of testing it. Thus this chapter still occupies itself with preliminary, but crucial, matters.

Some people might wonder why we want to spend so much time and effort on this question of truth and knowledge. It would indeed be nice if we could just assume these matters and move on to more concrete issues. As we discussed in the last chapter, however, the very possibility of knowing truth is a major objection raised against the case for Christianity. Only a very careful documentation of how knowledge really works can ultimately win what otherwise has to remain a battle of overgeneralizations.

Any method of investigating truth and knowledge is called an "epistemology." Let us describe four important components of knowledge.[1] Almost all of our efforts at justifying beliefs include one or more of them. The catch to this discussion is this: at various times people have attempted to use one or the other as the sole reason for justifying Christian truth. Unfortunately, each of these attempts has fallen short. We shall see in the next chapter how knowledge needs to be treated more holistically in terms of systems and worldview views. For now we will concentrate on the four components. They are:

- self-evidence;
- rationality;
- sensory information;
- workability.

For each of these four components we will show:
- its importance in knowledge in general;
- how it has been used as an exclusive attempt to justify religious belief; and
- in what ways these attempts by themselves have been inadequate.

Self-Evidence

We accept a large number of beliefs as self-evidently true. By this I mean that it would not even make sense to us to attempt to provide a justification for them. Simply to understand them is to know that they are true. These beliefs

---

[1]The outline of types of knowledge used here and in the next chapter is based closely on the work of David L. Wolfe. See his book, *Epistemology: The Justification of Belief* (Downers Grove, IL: InterVarsity Press, 1982).

include analytic statements, basic beliefs, and knowledge derived from immediate sensory awareness.

Analytic statements. These are statements that are true simply due to the meaning of the words being used. For example "a circle is round," or "a bachelor is unmarried." If you understand what "circle," "round," "bachelor," and "unmarried" mean, then it will be obvious to you that both of these sentences would have to be true. They are self-evident as long as you know the language.

The same is true of *basic beliefs.* I cannot honestly claim to be able to give you a cogent proof of the fact that I exist, that there was a significant past (namely, the world did not come into existence—complete with memory—one second ago), or that life is worthwhile. I accept them all wholeheartedly as true. I would also say that anyone who would seriously question them has a problem beyond intellectual curiosity. To be sure, they are not analytic statements; to deny them does not involve us in some unthinkable logical contradiction. Yet it makes no sense to deny them. They are an integral part of every rational person's beliefs. They are basic; they are self-evident.

We also derive much of our knowledge from *immediate sensory awareness.* I am writing these words on a transatlantic flight to Europe, and I am experiencing the typical dull headache I always get about an hour into a flight. Suppose my neighbor asked me to prove to him that I have a headache. I would not know what to say. I have it; I feel it; I am sure of it. Yet I cannot provide anyone with proof of the fact that I have this headache. What is true for headaches is probably also true for other sensations we experience, though we need to be careful of not overstating ourselves since most of the time our minds are quick to package our sensations into beliefs, concepts, and attitudes. Yet there seem to be certain sensations, such as seeing a color, feeling hungry or happy, which are undeniable to us when they are present. Someone might doubt our reasons for thinking we have these feelings, but if we do have such an awareness, it is impossible for us to doubt it. It is self-evident.

Thus we see that self-evidence is an essential ingredient in human knowledge. *The question now is whether self-evidence is sufficient to account for religious belief.* Some people think so. We can mention two categories.

The first is *mysticism,* or direct personal experience. A religious person might claim that, just as a direct sensory awareness cannot be doubted, neither can the direct awareness of God. Sometimes it is appropriate to label a direct, unmediated experience of God as "mystical." In a mystical experience, the person feels that he or she has direct personal communion with God. In that circumstance it would make no more sense to require proof of God's existence, let alone attempt to provide it, than it would be for me to occupy myself with proof for a headache I am feeling. For the mystics who have experienced God, His existence is self-evident.

The second is *belief in God as basic.* The contemporary philosopher Alvin Plantinga has recently popularized the idea that for the Christian, belief in God is as basic as the other beliefs mentioned earlier; for example; "I exist."[2] For the Christian, the fact of God's existence is at the very core of all knowledge. It makes no sense to the Christian to question God's existence; nor is the Christian under some ethical obligation to possess proof for God prior to believing in God. The nonexistence of God has become an impossibility, not in the sense of something illogical (such as a square circle), but as something unthinkable (such as my nonexistence). In short, God's existence must be self-evident.

It is hard to find fault with the idea that beliefs should be self-evidently true. A faith-commitment that rests on self-evident truth certainly brings with it an unsurpassable amount of certainty. However we need to remind ourselves of the agenda set out in the first chapter. *As a tool to confirm the truth of Christianity, the appeal to self-evidence can only be circular.*

The whole point of this exercise is to deal with the occasions when the truth of Christianity is not self-evident. To tell someone that it is self-evident would then simply be begging the question. To say that it *ought* to be self-evident is

---

[2]Alvin Plantinga, "The Reformed Objection to Natural Theology" *Christian Scholars Review* 11 (1982): 187-98.

incoherent; self-evidence can hardly be commanded. In sum, *although self-evidence is a significant ingredient in the complex make-up of all that we call knowledge, it is insufficient by itself as a meaningful test for the truth of Christianity.* For it can only ever be accepted by those who are already committed to the truth in question.

Rationality

In response to the above difficulties with relying on self-evidence, we need some method of knowing that is truly universal. What could be more universal than basic human rationality? The second component of knowledge for us to consider then is logic and the deductions that it makes possible.

Logical Deduction

Logic, as alluded to in the previous chapter, is an essential ingredient of knowledge. In fact, it is hard to imagine what we could even mean by the idea of human thought if it were not for logic. With it we can link up our thoughts and create meaningful new ones.

Take a simple argument, such as:

If Paris is in France, then it is in Europe.

Paris is in France.

Therefore Paris is in Europe.

We call the first two sentences the premises, and the third one the conclusion. Note that when we conclude that Paris is in Europe we are not simply calculating probabilities. If the premises are definitely true, then we are not just saying that perhaps there is good reason to suppose that Paris is in Europe. Paris is definitely in Europe. The principle involved is that anytime an argument has true premises and valid logical form, it is sound, and the conclusion must be just as true as the premises. If that were not the case, human thought would be nothing more than a random collection of incoherent words.

Logical deduction finds one of its purest examples in geometry. If you have taken a course in geometry, you may remember the procedure. Certain pieces of information were "given." They could include postulates, axioms, and theorems, as well as other items which were not to be questioned. Then your task was to prove a particular conclusion using only the given information and certain basic rational laws. Any resort to outside information would invalidate the proof.

We can use geometry as a model for a rational epistemology in its own right. In that case we could apply this method to other beliefs in order to justify them. We would then need a certain "given" starting point, something on which all people could agree; then we should be able to deduce the belief in question from the given information by means of logic alone. Geometry shows that it can be done; maybe it works in other areas as well. We can call this epistemology *rationalism*. *In rationalism a belief is considered justified if it is logically deduced from an undisputed "given" starting point.*

The Ontological Argument

Can we apply rationalism to religious beliefs? Again, some people have argued that it could be done and have attempted to show us how. Among this group of thinkers are the medieval theologian Anselm and the seventeenth-century philosopher René Descartes; these thinkers invented and renewed the so-called ontological argument for God's existence.[3] Because it is simpler than Anselm's version, we shall look at the argument the way Descartes presented it.[4]

Descartes begins by reminding us that certain ideas are always logically connected with each other. For example, you cannot have a mountain without a valley; a triangle is always a geometric object whose three angles add up to 180 degrees. Philosophers express this connectedness by saying that certain concepts (e.g., mountains) entail other concepts (e.g., valleys). Descartes stipulates as a given that the idea of God is always connected to the idea of having all perfections.

---

[3]The name was coined much later by Immanuel Kant. "Ontological" means "of the order of being." It is probably wisest not to read any particular significance into this name, which has now become the traditional label for this argument. Neither Anselm nor Descartes would have called it "ontological."

[4]René Descartes, *Meditations on First Philosophy*, trans. Donald A. Cress (Indianapolis: Hackett, 1979), 40-45.

The word *perfection* carries a different meaning in this context than the way we usually use it. We can define it technically as a positive property that is intrinsically better to have than not to have, or, not so technically, it is what always makes something good. I can have some perfections in this sense, even though I am certainly far from perfect in the usual sense; but I have some qualities that presumably contribute to whatever goodness I might have. We would then say that what makes the concept of God different is that God would have to have all of these perfections and possess them in an unlimited way.

Descartes singles out "existence" as one such perfection. He makes the assumption that it is intrinsically better to exist than not to exist. Thus "existence" must be included among the perfections that we ascribe to God. Now we have enough information for two strong premises and a conclusion:

God, by definition, has all perfections.

Existence is a perfection.

Therefore, God exists.

This argument rarely (if ever) wins over any fans on first reading. Most people have an instinctive reaction against the possibility of proving God's existence in three quick steps. So do I; but let us establish a perspective before consigning the argument to oblivion.

The argument, as stated above, is formally valid. There is no fallacy being committed, and it does not beg the question.

This argument has appeared in many different versions. Anselm provided two versions that had slightly different ways of expressing the same approach. There are a number of contemporary philosophers who advocate complex versions of the ontological argument. Among them is Alvin Plantinga, who at first criticized all available versions, but later came up with a version of his own.[5]

No obvious reason exists why we should not be able to prove God's existence in three quick steps (though again I confess to being quite leery of it). We must resist the temptation to dismiss a rational argument just because it works.

----

[5]Alvin Plantinga, *God, Freedom, and Evil* (Grand Rapids: Eerdmans, 1974), 85-112.

Evaluation of the Ontological Argument

Since we are only using this argument as an example, we need not go into a lengthy discussion of all of its merits and defects.[6] At this point we will simply show that it is inadequate if considered along the line of pure rationalism. Let us raise two questions.

First, is there a universally given starting point? In the context of this argument this question means, do all people accept the idea that God by definition has all perfections? The answer is that many people clearly do not; it is a matter of controversy, sometimes even for people who do believe in God. Thus it is not a true given as required by the epistemology. It is true that we can perhaps make a pretty good case that the idea of an all-perfect being is an acceptable possibility. However, then it is the conclusion of an argument, no longer a given. One already has to buy into a particular concept in order to get this argument off the ground.

Second, does the argument proceed purely by means of logical deduction? Again the answer is no. What sticks out is the highly dubious assertion that existence is a perfection. Many philosophers would agree that it is; but many others would follow Immanuel Kant and say that existence is not a perfection since it is not even a property. Instead, existence means that the properties are real; it does not add any properties. In any event, regardless of which side is right, it becomes obvious that this is a controversial metaphysical issue, not merely a logical uncovering of a given starting point. So we see again how the argument already presupposes certain convictions in order to be acceptable.

Here we encounter the fate of rationalism as applied to religious truth. Even though it holds a lot of promise for objectivity and universality, rationalism winds up suffering from the same drawback as self-evidence: it is limited to the initiates. No pure given can be identified, so the argument will inevitably have to feed on further information than mere

---

[6]For a lengthier discussion of the argument in its various ramifications, see Norman L. Geisler and Winfried Corduan, *Philosophy of Religion,* 2nd ed. (Grand Rapids: Baker Book House, 1988), 123-49.

logical deductions. Thus, even though rationality is an indispensable component of knowledge, it has no power to serve as a test for truth when it comes to such large-scale matters as the existence of God.

Sensory Information

Our third component seems best to address the issue of universality. What if we bring in the fact that much of our knowledge is rooted in sensory experience? Many philosophers including Aristotle have argued that all meaningful knowledge begins with our senses.

Empiricism

Traditionally we speak of five senses—vision, smell, hearing, taste, and touch. We can begin by making the very simple statement that much knowledge includes information directly gleaned through these senses. It would be absurd to question this statement since you would have come across it through your senses, either by reading it or by having it read to you. The fact that knowledge includes a sensory component is beyond dispute.

Thus we can already begin to address the possibility of turning this component into a test for truth. We now need to make a sensory observation and then draw inferences from it, but we must be careful to distinguish between the limited cases of direct sensory awareness that we mentioned in the context of self-evidence and this more complex method. Then we talked of such things as feeling headaches, which may be as close as we ever actually come to raw sensory data. Here we are concerned with information that may be less directly derived from the senses. In some way the data has been processed. Thus we talk about observations, not just sensory impressions; and we do not really have knowledge until we draw inferences from these observations. We call this way of testing truth *empiricism*. We can then say that *in empiricism a belief is justified if it is a sound inference from a sensory observation.*

Of course this way of knowing is at the heart and soul of natural science (as well as in certain phases of the social sciences). Whether you are speaking of biology, chemistry, physics, or any other discipline, the scientific inquiry centers around observations. There is something special about these observations: they must be in principle repeatable. Look at the layout of some articles in a professional scientific journal sometime. You will find that most of the space is given over to the methods the scientist used and the results he or she observed; remarks on the significance and the larger conclusions of the experiment—the kind of information the popular press picks up—are usually limited.

In theory any person should be able to repeat any experiment and get the same results. In principle, given the background and resources, we must be able to confirm a scientist's results in order for the experiment to be considered valid. In 1989 there was a big controversy in the scientific world over two researchers associated with the University of Utah who claimed to have discovered commercially valuable cold fusion. Unfortunately their research turned out to be nonrepeatable, and thus scientifically useless.

All of which is not to say that professional scientists always follow the "scientific method" as you may have had to memorize it in an eighth-grade science course.[7] Usually a far greater degree of flexibility exists in scientific research than any rigid series of steps moving from hypothesis to theory to law. Experiments and field observations tend to have very definite expected results from the start, but the point is that, regardless of how one might want to describe the method, *observation is always at the core.* Science surely fits our pattern for empiricism: a set of inferences derived from observation.

The Teleological Argument

Is it possible to use an empirical epistemology on behalf of religious belief? Let us look at one attempt to do so, again involving the question of the existence of God. This time we

---

[7]Usually the description is that the scientist makes an observation, forms a hypothesis, and tests the hypothesis in the lab. Appropriate results confirm the hypothesis, which then becomes a theory. A universally confirmed theory is acclaimed as law. It is questionable whether a scientist even *could* work in such a totally regimented way.

focus on William Paley who in the nineteenth century advocated an argument we call the "teleological argument."[8]

Paley's argument does begin with the observation that in many ways the universe resembles a watch. The inference is that, by an analogy, various things that are true of the watch must also be true of the world—particularly the property of having a maker.

To be more specific, Paley invites us to take a walk with him through the forest. Let us say that we find a watch by the side of the path. We would immediately recognize it as a piece of smooth-functioning machinery, something that did not simply grow there in the forest, but must have been made by an intelligent designer. Now Paley directs our attention to the universe and asks us to observe how much more it is a complex, well-running machine. Everything that can be said of the watch in this respect can be said all the more of the universe. If the watch needs a maker for these reasons, then the universe must need a maker all the more, and the world maker is the one to whom we refer as God.

This is a highly plausible argument. It has been used by many different people in various versions. All of them appeal to the inherent improbability of something as complex as the universe simply having happened. Try the following experiment. Take an atheist friend of yours to a planetarium. Treat him or her to the show, and enjoy their amazement at the wonderful display. Then, when it is over, inform your friend that the planetarium and the show simply came up by chance. He or she will probably dispute the very idea. Then point out how much more the universe needs a creator. Whatever else you may have done, you would have made use of a teleological argument similar to Paley's.

---

[8]Once again it is wisest not to get too serious about the original name of the argument. It is derived from the Greek word *telos*, which means "goal" and is used to indicate that, according to this argument, the universe evidences divine purpose. William Paley, *A View of the Evidences of Christianity*, the teleological argument is excerpted in Donald R. Burrill, ed., *The Cosmological Arguments* (Garden City, NY: Doubleday Anchor Books, 1967), 165-70.

Evaluation of the Teleological Argument

This argument also has some weaknesses, which will shed light on the more general weaknesses of empiricism. David Hume, the eighteenth-century skeptic, pointed out some problems with an argument of this type.[9] He did not actually destroy the argument with an effective counterargument, but he showed that the argument had not completely closed off all options other than the existence of God. We can summarize Hume's reservations with the following statements:

First, the only reason we know that watches need watchmakers is because we have seen watches being made. We have no such experience for universes since we have never seen them being created.

Second, Hume argued, we know of things other than mechanical contrivances that are complex and functioning, namely living beings such as plants and animals. They come into existence through reproduction and grow organically. Maybe in this respect the world is more like a plant than like a watch. Then it would not need a maker.

Third, he continued, many things are made by several individuals working together. There seems to be no good reason why the universe could not have been created by a committee of gods.

Fourth, there seems to be no good reason why the maker of the universe needs to be a great, all-perfect God. Another alternative would be that the universe was made by a baby god just learning how to create worlds.

Fifth, Hume concluded, even granting a lot of force to the argument, it still has not decisively ruled out that maybe on balance a better explanation for how everything came about is by chance.

Hume's five criticisms are far from devastating, but they show that the argument is not so conclusive as we might like

---

[9]David Hume, *Dialogues Concerning Natural Religion,* excerpted in Burrill, ed., *The Cosmological Arguments,* 185-98.

to think. They open up a hole in the method of the teleological argument. Paley looked at the universe and saw a watch needing a watchmaker. Hume looked at the same universe and (at least facetiously) saw a plant that just happened to sprout. The very observation is already subject to interpretation. What one sees is at least partially determined by what one expects to see.

One does not have to be a relativist to realize that perceptions are selective and often highly subjective. Stop reading for a moment and take stock of how many different background noises your mind has filtered out over the last few minutes—people, machines, cars, air conditioning, heating, breathing, sounds of nature. At any given moment our observations are very selective and focused. Now that you are reading again, you have come to realize how our minds are quite effective in governing our observations.

Thus we have to back away from the idea that we can point to observations as neutral starting elements that all people can use to glean the same information. Our observations are already a function of how we are geared to see something. After all, that limitation applies to science as well. The nonscientist walking into a lab does not make the same observations as a scientist. The scientist's observations are very much a matter of his or her training. A chemist, for example, will bring to the lab not only test tubes, Bunsen burners, and various substances, but also the periodic table and many years of training and experience.

Of course our point is not to debunk empiricism completely. After all, one can hardly argue with the success of science in the modern world. The reservations that we have brought up render the empirical method by itself insufficient, especially when applied to religious questions. In this arena the fact that our predispositions tend to color our perceptions becomes paramount because, when it comes to religious questions, our predispositions increase in strength and variety. After all, our basic commitments to how we look at the world are what is at issue. Thus we can conclude that, even though empiricism is an important ingredient in human knowledge, by itself it is not enough for our quest.

Workability

A fourth component of knowledge has been identified as especially typical for American thinking. This is the emphasis on the notion that any true belief must have practical applications. Conversely, if a belief does not have practical consequences, it must not be true. A European might tell you that if this sounds like common sense to you, that fact is true partially due to your American cultural conditioning.

Pragmatism

It would not seem sensible to want to get along without any kind of workability criterion for truth whatever. If I sell you a wonderpill on the claim that it will cure all of your physical ills and the pill gives you a headache, you have good reason to believe that my claim is false. On the other hand, let us say that I cannot get my car started. Someone comes along and tells me, "You flooded your carburetor. Let it sit for an hour and try again. Then it will start." I wait an hour, try to start my car, and it fires right up. I am inclined to believe that the person was right—I had flooded my carburetor. Perhaps that does not make that theory true, but at that moment the practical consequence was probably a sufficient test for its truth. This particular component of knowledge has also been allowed to become a test for truth in its own right. In this case it is known as *pragmatism.* It has been advocated by the American philosophers C. S. Peirce, William James, and John Dewey. These three thinkers were interested in different matters, but they shared the notion that the truth of a belief is measured by whether it makes a practical difference in the world. *In pragmatism a belief is justified if the belief has practical consequences that are consistent with it.*

Pragmatism and Religious Truth

Pragmatism has also offered itself as an exclusive test for religious truth. The example I want to cite comes from the area of Latin American liberation theology. The theologian Juan Luis Segundo[10] looks at the intolerable social situation

---

[10]Juan Luis Segundo, *Our Idea of God,* trans. John Drury (Maryknoll, NY: Orbis Books, 1974).

in Latin America and claims that what it needs is an ideology that enhances human personhood, justice, and community. He finds these points in the traditional beliefs about God as Trinity: three Persons who are equally the one God. Supposedly, only someone who is clear about God and personhood within God can be correct about human persons in relation to each other. Thus Segundo holds that belief in the Christian God is true, not on independent grounds but because it provides the necessary beliefs to bring about the social changes Segundo desires. Thus the practical outworkings of these beliefs become the hallmark of their truth.

Evaluation of the Pragmatic Approach to Religious Truth

The best way to critique the pragmatic approach to truth is to read the pragmatists themselves. For what is the desirable result for one person is not necessarily a desirable result for someone else. William James addressed this phenomenon and decided that, since different beliefs work for different people, different mutually exclusive beliefs could be true;[11] once again we embrace relativism. On the other hand, John Dewey took a look at what our society needs and made a case for a purely secularized, atheistic "faith."[12] The point is that, given the pragmatic test for truth, almost anything can be defended as truth, as long as it is expedient.

Furthermore, the pragmatic test does not set well with what we intuitively think of as truth. Imagine someone who lives carelessly and as a consequence has not amounted to much in life. Let us say that this person has come into a few hundred dollars that are then stolen from him through no fault of his own. Yet he does not know that; he thinks he misplaced the money through his slovenliness. He says to himself, "This is the last straw. I lost my money through my own carelessness. From now on I'm going to live a careful, well-ordered life so that this kind of thing won't happen to me again." He keeps his word, and ten years later he is president of a corporation. The belief that he lost his money

---

[11]William James, *Essays in Pragmatism* (New York: Hafner, 1955), 159-76.
[12]See John Dewey, *A Common Faith* (New Haven: Yale University Press, 1934).

through his carelessness worked for him. This belief occasioned significant positive changes in his life, but it still was not true. The truth is that the money was stolen from him, even if he never realized it. The truth is unchangeable regardless of this man's beliefs about what happened and how those beliefs worked out in practical consequences. Thus we see that we have a basic understanding of truth to which pragmatism cannot do justice.

For the fourth time we make a similar observation. That a belief should fit into the arena of practical life is an important aspect of knowledge, but pragmatism as a test by itself is not sufficient.

In this chapter we looked at four epistemologies, found some worth in each, then discarded each in turn. We showed that each epistemology was insufficient by itself as a test for religious truth. Each of them plays a role in the rather complex task of testing for the truth of religious beliefs, just not an exclusive one.

What this chapter leads to is the observation that we need to think of knowledge as a large system with many components. A belief never occurs in isolation but always together with other beliefs and predispositions. In the light of this conclusion we can look again at this chapter's vignettes.

Response to Vignette 1: I am happy for Frank that he has no problems with God's existence at this point in his life, but many other people do. The fact that God's existence is self-evident for him unfortunately does not make it so for anyone else. The fact that Frank does not require proof does not mean that no such proof is available or that it would be illegitimate to use it. My verbal response to Frank is to encourage him to pay attention anyway because sooner or later he may run into another person who still needs to be convinced that there is a God. It may even be himself.

Response to Vignette 2: I have learned an important lesson over the years when it comes to people demanding proof. After innumerable fruitless debates, it has become apparent to me that I need to start by asking back, "What would you accept as evidence?" Frequently it turns out that what my questioner wants is totally different from what I would have given him or her. If the person is troubled by suffering in the world, there is no purpose in presenting the cosmological argument. If the difficulty centers around the possibility of miracles, there would be no point in talking about how the Resurrection verifies Christ's deity. Frequently the answer to my question reveals that the person is making a demand that no human being can fulfill, such as a purely deductive proof along rationalistic lines that would automatically convert even the most hardened skeptic. When such a demand comes out we need to talk about why Christianity is not like geometry. In fact, the only part of life that is like geometry is geometry. I wish I had been that smart that night in the coffeehouse. As I recall, I must have summarized my entire master's thesis to those people before I realized that they were only interested in debate for debate's sake.

Response to Vignette 3: I am in no position to pronounce definitively on whether the scientific method is always the right approach in psychology, though it seems to me that it ought to be. However, to make this method the one and only method for secure knowledge in all areas of life is clearly to overstep the bounds. I wonder, however, if the fellow whose voice I heard really meant rigid scientific procedure. Maybe he had in mind a looser notion of knowledge based on evidence and rational investigation. In that case we could be much more sympathetic toward his statement.

Response to Vignette 4: When called upon to share our faith it is always a good idea to tell what Christ has done for us. There is nothing wrong with telling others that Christ can do great things in their lives as well. Still we need to be on guard against basing the truth of Christianity on our experience. Christianity works because it is true, not the other way around. Adherents of many different faiths sell their beliefs on the basis of their experience as well. From the Christian's perspective, their experiences must be based on falsehoods. That issue must then be settled on other grounds, not simply experience.

For Growth and Study

Mastering the Material

When you have studied this chapter you should be able to:
1. Describe how self-evidence works as a test for truth and give three types of examples for it.

2. Show how self-evidence has been used to support religious belief, and why that attempt may not be helpful.
3. Describe how rationalism works as a test for truth.
4. Supply a simple version of the ontological argument, point out its weaknesses, and show how those weaknesses are typical for rationalism.
5. Describe how empiricism works as a test for truth.
6. Supply a simple version of the teleological argument, point out its weaknesses, and show how those weaknesses are typical for empiricism.
7. Describe how pragmatism works as a test for truth.
8. Show what happens when one tries to use pragmatism as a test for truth for religious beliefs.
9. Identify the following names with the contribution to which we have alluded in this chapter: Alvin Plantinga, Anselm, René Descartes, William Paley, David Hume, Juan Luis Segundo, William James, John Dewey, and C. S. Peirce.

Thinking About the Ideas

1. Can you think of examples of self-evident beliefs not mentioned in this chapter? Are any of them beliefs that are indispensable for human life?
2. A follower of Hare Krishna once told me that it was self-evident to him that Krishna was God and that we ought to obey his commandments. Devise a response to him.
3. Find examples outside of geometry where a pure form of rational deduction is used to discover truth.
4. In this chapter we criticized the ontological argument primarily because it does not measure up to the standards of a rationalistic epistemology. Yet maybe it is valid if understood in some other way. Support or defend the argument in its own right.
5. Find examples outside of natural science in which a rigorous form of empiricism is used to discover truth.
6. In this chapter we criticized the teleological argument primarily because it does not measure up to the standards of an empirical epistemology. Yet maybe it is valid if understood in some other way. Support or defend the argument in its own right.
7. One issue in a pragmatic approach to truth is whether one can consistently live out a set of beliefs. To what extent is this a valid demand on any belief system? How does Christianity fare in that case?

For Further Exploration

A. J. Ayer, *The Problem of Knowledge* (Baltimore: Penguin Books, 1956).

Roderick Chisholm, *Theory of Knowledge*, 2nd ed. (Englewood Cliffs, NJ: Prentice-Hall, 1977).

Alvin Plantinga, ed., *The Ontological Argument* (Garden City, NY: Doubleday, 1965).

William James, *Essays in Pragmatism* (New York: Hafner, 1955).

David L. Wolfe, *Epistemology: The Justification of Belief* (Downers Grove, IL: InterVarsity Press, 1982).

4

Knowledge: Testing Worldviews

Blind Unbelief

Vignette 1: My undergraduate major was in zoology. I did not take my first philosophy course in college until I had already read a few books on Christian apologetics. When I took Introduction to Philosophy, I encountered the typical array of arguments against God and Christianity with very little positive said about what I believed. So I took the matter up in conversations with Jerry, the graduate student in charge of my discussion section. We met several times and debated back and forth. One morning we spent an hour talking outside on a bench next to the chapel building, and he allowed me to present the whole case for the deity of Christ as best as I could muster my arguments (see chapter 10). When I had finished he said, "I must confess that you have me snowed. I don't know how to refute your arguments. Still I can't accept them; there must be something wrong. I just don't know what it is yet."

Stan Gets the Picture

Vignette 2: I was chatting with Stan, a Christian friend, about our differing backgrounds. I grew up in a solidly Christian home, and I have always lived within a Christian worldview. Stan had only been a Christian for two years. I asked him what his worldview was like before his conversion.

"I thought of the world as a machine," he replied. "Everything and every event somehow fit into this vast cosmic apparatus. But nothing had meaning other than just being a cog in the machine."

"What led you to consider Christianity?" I asked.

"It wasn't any one argument," my friend reflected. "Somehow my whole picture of the world no longer made sense. It denied all meaning, and yet I clung to the notion that my life had to be meaningful. When Christianity, based on a personal and loving God, came along, I knew I had found what I was looking for."

In the last chapter we looked at some tests for truth that turned out to be too limited for our purposes. When it comes to religious truth, knowledge is an extremely complex thing involving many considerations, not the least of which is the fact that our predispositions play a large role. Perhaps our discussion of empiricism made it the clearest: what we observe is to a large extent dependent on what we are prepared to observe. We seem to have a filter in our minds through which all of our information is channeled before it reaches our consciousness. This much can hardly be disputed. Some people have taken this idea to an extreme. We will first present this extreme version and then offer a more palatable application.

Conventionalism

Philosophers have used many different terms to refer to this filter through which we process knowledge:
- system,
- worldview,
- interpretive scheme,
- conceptual framework,
- any combination of the above and others.

The philosopher W. V. O. Quine[1] argues that our understanding of truth is like a web of beliefs: each of us carries around in our heads an interconnected system of all that we believe. Tied together more or less coherently in this web are all of the beliefs we hold as true. These include the basic beliefs (such as "I exist" and "life is worthwhile") and the more trivial ones (such as "I hope we won't have liver again"). No belief exists in isolation; each belief is connected with all others in one big network.

[1] W. V. O. Quine, *From a Logical Point of View* (New York: Harper & Row, 1961); Quine and J. S. Ullian, *The Web of Belief*, 2nd ed. (New York: Random House, 1978).

Where did this network come from? Quine and others who hold this view say it came to us along with our culture. We were educated into it, for the most part, when we were children. Just as we learned how to behave at the table and how to be polite to others, we were brought to accept numerous beliefs as true. We never tested them; we never gave their opposites a chance. We only believed them because our parents told us that they were true. So they became a part of our systems. Because under this description knowledge is merely a convention, such as which side of the street to drive on, it is called conventionalism.

To what extent can one test for truth under conventionalism? Systems as a whole cannot be tested. Since all beliefs are a part of systems, there is no neutral ground one could appeal to in order to decide between systems. Since all beliefs in all systems can only be a part of the integrated whole, there can be no common ground between any two systems. No neutrality; no common ground. Consequently, one appears to be trapped in a particular system.

Think of it as though each belief were a football player on a particular team. Each player has to be on one team. There are no players who do not belong to a team. The placekicker cannot say one Sunday afternoon, "I think I will not take sides today." He must play for his team, and his team only. The other team does not have the option of saying, "We forgot to bring our placekicker today. Could we please use yours?" The player is exclusive property of one team. In the same way, a belief is integrated into a system. It functions within that system, and it cannot be integrated into another system without being significantly altered. No neutrality; no common ground.

This description explains why so many debates wind up going nowhere. Has it not happened to you that you bring out your best arguments, and your conversation partner does not even seem to understand them, let alone be convinced by them? A conventionalist could use this kind of experience as evidence for his or her view. You cannot argue persons out of their worldview because worldviews are not the product of argumentation.

Under conventionalism you could still test individual beliefs. Of course conventionalism does not think of truth as corresponding to reality, since it is impossible to have any idea of reality apart from the worldview. So here a belief can be considered to be true if it fits into a person's worldview. Whether a belief fits or not could be evaluated by such matters as whether it is relevant to the worldview or whether it is logically consistent.

Take two silly examples. Let us say I try to tell you about a visit I received from an extraterrestrial creature. Chances are you will not believe my story even before you ask for any evidence or other way of testing the truth of my claim. Aliens do not fit into your worldview; they are irrelevant, and so you rightly reject my story as false. Or, consider your reaction if I tell you that there is no such thing as the sun. This would be a highly relevant claim, but you would reject it immediately because it is logically inconsistent with all of your other beliefs. Thus you test the truth of beliefs by checking whether they fit into your system or not. If they do not, you will often give them no further thought. A conventionalist would say that this is precisely what is supposed to happen. In this epistemology a *coherence theory* of truth has replaced the correspondence theory.

Critique of Conventionalism

The problems with conventionalism are evident. First, it becomes impossible to do apologetics. One would not be able to defend the truth of Christianity. Some people have bitten this bullet and have indeed denied any possibility of apologetics. Karl Barth, a well-known Swiss theologian, is a case in point. He argued that there could be no rational point of contact between the Christian system, which is based on the God who revealed Himself, and any others. Consequently no attempt to build an argument based on human reason can lead from the non-Christian's system to God.[2] In a moment we will address the question of whether

---

[2]Karl Barth, *Church Dogmatics*, vol. 1, trans. G. T. Thomson (Edinburgh: T. & T. Clark, 1936), 141-283.

this description represents a realistic assessment of the possibilities.

Second, conventionalism also plays havoc with our understanding of truth. Mutually exclusive beliefs fit into differing systems. For example, the belief that Jesus is the only way to God is integral to Christianity; its denial is a part of Hinduism. Thus once again we are confronted with relativism, which seems to allow for dual truths but in the process denies truth altogether. The point is this: people want to know which is really true, whether Jesus is the only way to God or not. Pointing out that this belief is compatible with one system and not with another is not helpful in settling the concern. After all, a system might conceivably be consistent with a falsehood. If the conventionalist says that there is no way of checking it out, then we are back in the disaster of relativism. The natural way of understanding truth is that the idea of a reality behind our worldview views makes sense and becomes the backdrop against which we check truth. Then conventionalism violates a natural understanding of truth.

Third, conventionalism has to explain away the fact that people do change beliefs and even whole systems for reasons of rational evidence. Quine argues that such a shift would be purely pragmatic. In other words, I might change my mind if it makes my life work more smoothly. For example, put someone who has grown up within one denomination into the context of another denomination, and he or she may eventually switch allegiance, not because the person became rationally convinced of the new doctrines, but because it made life easier.

This approach reveals a cynical view of the value of human thought and reason. I have a hunch that, when Quine wrote those ideas, he expected people to be persuaded by them, and many have been. In fact, people give testimony to having changed their minds, on both large and small scales, on the basis of rational evidence. I can certainly attest to several occasions when I changed my mind about a belief on the basis of evidence. Sometimes such a shift flies in the face of a simple pragmatism; life gets much more complicated, not more convenient.

Take the case of a Muslim responding to the preaching of the gospel. I know such a person; she had to give up her family, culture, security, even to the point of risking her life. She found answers in Christianity that she could not find in Islam. I cannot bring myself to interpret this experience along pragmatic lines. She was persuaded to accept the truth of another system; she did not make her life easier. Furthermore, to psychologize the whole event and claim that there were subconscious pragmatic reasons is simply a case of the fallacy of appeal to ignorance. You cannot explain something with evidence you do not have.

Thus *conventionalism suffers from the disease of overstatement.* It recognizes that our thinking does occur within worldviews, but it pushes this undeniable truth too far by locking us into our worldviews views as a life sentence in prison. The facts run otherwise. We know intuitively that our quest for truth cannot be scuttled in this manner, and our practical experience bears out this fact. We can and do evaluate beliefs and systems rationally.

Hypothesis Testing

After the above discussion, it should occasion no surprise that many people, who at first announce a conventionalist approach to knowledge, violate their own precepts. One might say that this is a case of fortunate inconsistency.

A good example in point is the work of the Reformed apologist Cornelius Van Til.[3] Like Barth, Van Til denies that the Christian and non-Christian systems can have anything in common. The Christian worldview is based on the sovereign God who created the world and has revealed Himself in Scripture and in Jesus Christ. On the other hand, the non-Christian view is ostensibly based on the human being's autonomy; but since the human being is only finite and a mere part of the world, ultimately the view has to be based on chance as the fundamental principle. There cannot be anything more ultimate. Clearly the Christian and non-Christian views cannot have anything in common. A system

---

[3]Cornelius Van Til, *The Defense of the Faith* (Philadelphia: Presbyterian and Reformed, 1955).

that begins with God can contain objective values of goodness, truth, and beauty. Where chance is ultimate, such values are possible only as accidental conventions. Van Til claims that even the basic understanding of what it means to know something does not transfer across systems. In the Christian view, knowledge of some object means that one comes into contact with God's creation; the chance-based knowledge of the non-Christian view can only be a guess. In short, the watchwords, "no neutrality; no common ground," seem to be at home here.

Nevertheless, in contrast to Barth, Van Til claims that an apologetic is still possible. As the Christian and the non-Christian are talking, the Christian can, *for the sake of the argument alone*, step into the non-Christian's system and show him or her the disastrous consequences of a system based on chance and human autonomy. None of the values by which the non-Christian tries to live, not even knowledge, are actually feasible in that system. Then the Christian can invite the non-Christian to step into the Christian system, again only *for the sake of the argument*. The goal is to show the non-Christian that only a system that presupposes the sovereign God of the Bible makes the knowledge and values that the non-Christian desires possible. The Christian can then appeal to the non-Christian to shift from an impossible system to a possible one.

It does not take a Ph.D. in philosophy to see that even this kind of dialogue is only possible if there is some common ground between Christians and non-Christians. Even though Van Til is sometimes ambiguous on the point, he appears to leave room for a rudimentary common ground involving the following ideas: *common grace,* that is, God's revelation to all people involving a basic consciousness of His existence, right and wrong, and of our sinfulness as covenant breakers; the fact that the non-Christian may have *borrowed concepts* from the Christian's worldview, even though these may be inconsistent with his or her non-Christian presuppositions; a very limited *elementary rationality,* such as the laws of logic (though at times Van Til makes it sound as if even those are not legitimate property for the non-Christian). To put it very simply, Van Til does not carry out his announced agenda of denying all neutrality and common ground in order to leave room for the possibility of dialogue between Christian and non-Christian.

Let us not consider this criticism as too negative. I think that Van Til, by his inconsistency, has done us a service. He has introduced us to a workable approach to truth within worldviews views. Van Til showed us that one can recognize that all of our beliefs are integrated into worldviews views without shutting the door on the possibility of testing the worldviews views as a whole. We see that what we can do is to assume the systems or beliefs in question as hypotheses which are then tested for suitability.

Actually we already approached this method when we first dealt with the question of testing the truth of beliefs. At the time we said that a belief is considered to be justified if it passes all relevant tests. The addition now is that we want to include whole systems of beliefs as well.

Let us call this method *hypothesis testing. Hypothesis testing: a belief system is to be considered true if it proves to be superior to all other reasonable systems in all relevant reasonable tests.* This formulation sounds more tentative than it is. Just think of an example. Say a murder has been committed. The following are the facts surrounding the case: the murderer was in the castle at seven o'clock, had a key to the study, spoke Transylvanian fluently, and was named in the will; the butler meets all of these qualifications; there are no other suspects that meet all of the qualifications. The hypothesis that the butler did it may be considered to be true. Once again we may dispense with unreasonable hypotheses, such as Martians disguised as butlers. This same pattern of accepting as true a hypothesis that shows itself to do justice to all the relevant concerns is the basis for this epistemology.

We can go no farther until we answer two crucial questions. Where do we find common ground between worldviews views? What are the criteria we can use to test worldviews views as hypotheses?

Common Ground

Where do we find common ground? Wherever it happens to appear. Behind this flippant-sounding assertion lies a weighty point. There is no need to try to identify one universal set of beliefs common to all worldviews views.

In fact, I do not believe that there are any universally accepted significant content beliefs. Even a proposition as basic as "I exist" is not universally accepted; it is denied in Theravada Buddhism. Now it is all very well to say that to deny your own existence is crazy; all people ought to subscribe to this proposition. Yet some people do not, and so we cannot appeal to it as universal common ground.

Still universal common ground is not necessary. It suffices that between any two systems there be enough overlap to allow for dialogue. For example, I have a good friend, Phil, with whom I share an interest in sprint car racing. Whenever we get together, sooner or later that topic of conversation comes up. With another friend, Paul, the persistent topic is Old Testament literary criticism. Thus I have something in common with both friends, but it is a different interest. Neither one knows much (if anything) about the other person's topic. If they tried to talk to each other, they would have to find something else to talk about. In the same way, two worldviews views will overlap somewhere, but it will not always be in the same place. The concern is whether two systems have some overlap. Whether the same overlap exists for a third system or not is not relevant.

To borrow a concept from the philosopher Ludwig Wittgenstein, we can say that there is "family resemblance" among human worldviews views. Not all family members look alike, nor is there often one feature that all family members share. Still some typical features are sprinkled over the family members, so that any two of them resemble each other in some features. In the same way, our belief systems manifest family resemblance.

How can one verify this assertion? Ultimately one would have to list all human worldviews views and show where any two of them overlap. That task sounds impossible; even if someone could bring it off, nobody would want to read it. Thus we will settle for the following claim: I have never encountered a worldview that does not share some significant content belief with mine. For example, even though a Theravada Buddhist and I would disagree on whether I exist, we would agree that excessive attachment to the material goods of this world is counterproductive to spiritual life—not a bad starting point for further conversation.

The situation is better than it sounds. For our purposes here I need not compare and contrast Marxism-Leninism with Australian aboriginal thought. One system is given: evangelical Christianity. Other systems need not be so disparate. It is impossible in a book of this type to do everything, but let us assume that some basic beliefs are generally accepted in our day. If our arguments do not carry any weight in respect to a worldview that I have ignored, that does not mean that no good argument is possible. It simply means that none has been given so far—and that one should be given sometime.

Criteria

How do we evaluate competing worldviews views? We need criteria that most people would not question. It appears that such criteria are available. They are relevancy, consistency, and viability.

Relevancy

A worldview must be *relevant* to the concerns at hand. Whatever the common ground between the systems is, it raises certain concerns. If one system does not address the issue, it fails the test. For example, if Buddhism and Christianity both raise the question of how to make this a better world, but then it turns out that Buddhism only directs us away from the world towards non-existence, Buddhism might not pass the test of relevance.

Consistency

The worldview must be internally *consistent*. It will be helpful here to clarify exactly what that means since the issue of consistency will come up several times. Can two statements both be true at the same time and in the same sense? If it is conceivable that two statements can both be true, then they are consistent. If they cannot both be true, then they are either inconsistent or contradictory.

Let us look at two statements:

1. Some fire engines are red.
2. Some fire engines are green.

These statements are consistent. They can both be true—as indeed they are.

The following statements are inconsistent:

3. All fire engines are red.
4. No fire engines are red.

They cannot both be true. They could both be false, and this time they are. Even if one or the other happened to be true, they could never both be true (at the same time, in the same sense). Thus a pair of statements is inconsistent if they cannot be both true (though they could both be false).

We call a set of sentences contradictory if they follow the pattern of these two sentences.

3. All fire engines are red.
5. Some fire engines are not red.

You will notice that once again they cannot both be true. A little thought will make it evident that they also cannot both be false (at the same time, in the same sense). One must be true; one must be false. All sentences of this type are contradictory. If we put them together we have a simple contradiction which must always be false.

The intent of this criterion in evaluating worldviews views is to show that a system containing inconsistent or contradictory statements at its core must be false. Of particular interest to us is the category of inconsistency. For, in contrast to contradictions, with an inconsistency we do not have to choose which of the two sentences is true. Imagine two statements that could be considered to be at the heart of a Marxist worldview:

6. There is no higher value than the personal happiness of the worker.
7. All people (including workers) must subordinate their personal happiness to the good of the state.

These two statements are inconsistent. If they are at the heart of a Marxist worldview, then this fact gives us good reason to question the Marxist system. What is particularly helpful here, though, is the fact that, in contrast to what would be true if it were a contradiction, both statements, not just one or the other, could be (and are) false.

Now it is important that, when we apply this criterion, we direct ourselves to statements of beliefs that are at the core of the system. Most of us, if not all of us, carry some inconsistencies around in our heads, and that does not usually cause great harm. For example, I know a pacifist who enjoys reading Robert Ludlum's violence-packed novels. This idiosyncracy does not invalidate his pacifism; but if there were a basic inconsistency at the heart of his pacifistic worldview, if he thought violence was legitimate if it suited him, then his view would be highly suspect.

Viability

It must be possible to live out a worldview. We are reviving the criterion of *viability*, which we brought up against skepticism. An idea or a system that cannot be lived out is worthless. We saw that pragmatism went too far in making workability the sole criterion of truth. At this point it is best to think more in terms of a negative criterion: if one cannot live according to the precepts of a worldview, it fails an important test.

It is important to distinguish between "do not" and "cannot." If a worldview could be falsified because some people who claim to accept it do not live according to it, possibly no worldview could be true, certainly not Christianity. Even so, the fact that people do not live by their professed beliefs may not at all be the fault of the worldview. So it is not thereby falsified. If a system is of such a nature that it is intrinsically impossible to live by it, it must be false.

For example, every now and then a person I talk with informs me (frequently as though it were the discovery of the century) that there are no objective values. Invariably a short conversation establishes (a) that this person certainly lives by an objective set of values and (b) that he or she cannot do otherwise, though the person rarely concedes that point. What is at stake here is that a totally valueless worldview cannot be lived out and is consequently false.

In addition to relevancy, consistency, and viability, two other criteria have at times been suggested: comprehensiveness and aesthetic quality. According to the criteria of comprehensiveness, a worldview ought to pull all of life together, not just part of it. Those concerned with aesthetic quality argue that a worldview ought to constitute a pleasing whole that addresses our feelings positively. It appears though that these two criteria do not carry the same weight as the previous three and may themselves become the subject of debate rather than facilitating the debate between worldviews.

We are now at a point where we can conclude our discussion of truth and knowledge. To sum up, when we talk about religious truth (if not all other types) we must consider total systems. These systems typically include the components discussed in the previous chapter: self-evidence, rationality, sensory input, and workability.

Within these systems, the truth of beliefs is tested on the basis of how well they fit into the system by using the aforementioned components. We do not totally reevaluate all of our presuppositions and accepted beliefs each time we confront a new belief.

The systems themselves are subject to testing. To bring this task about, we need to discover common ground between whatever systems are competing and then apply significant shared criteria, such as relevancy, consistency, and viability.

So far we have only supplied random examples of how this procedure might work. The major example for this epistemology of hypothesis testing will be all that follows in this book. Thus a judgment on whether or not it gets the job done must wait for the last page.

Now we can turn to the vignettes for this chapter.

Response to Vignette 1: This sad occurrence shows why many philosophers adopt a conventionalist view of truth. People do not change their entire systems of thought on the basis of one or two good arguments to the contrary. Even though we do not like this fact when we try to persuade someone of our beliefs, the shoe certainly also fits the other foot. We should not be inclined to abdicate Christianity just because someone brought up an argument against it for which we do not have an immediate answer. What a mess our brains would be if we allowed all of the little arguments that come our way daily to seriously affect us! The conventionalist makes the mistake of saying that rational persuasion has no value whatsoever. This is clearly an exaggeration. As a case in point, it would appear that Jerry was promoting a point of view towards which he had been persuaded by his professors and his reading.

Response to Vignette 2: Here we see how rational persuasion usually works. It came down to total world pictures. Dan found that his whole way of looking at life was crumbling. In contrast he perceived that Christianity provided answers at exactly the points where he had questions. His struggles were intellectual as well as personal and spiritual. When the change came, he did not work up slowly to a Christian system piece by piece, but he underwent a complete turn-around. When Christ came into his life, his whole way of thinking changed as well.

For Growth and Study

Mastering the Material

When you have studied this chapter you should be able to:
1. Describe conventionalism and tell why people hold to it.
2. Tell why conventionalism does not provide an adequate understanding of knowledge.
3. Describe how hypothesis testing works as a test for worldviews.
4. Explain how "family resemblance" helps us identify sufficient common ground to do hypothesis testing of worldviews.
5. Clarify the three criteria used in hypothesis testing of worldviews: relevancy, consistency, viability.
6. Identify the following names with the contribution to which we have alluded in this chapter: W. V. O. Quine, Karl Barth, Cornelius Van Til.

Thinking About the Ideas

1. A major point of this chapter was that all of our thinking occurs within systems of beliefs. Can you think of some areas of life in which this insight becomes important?

2. Defend a position on whether or not we can find common ground between a Christian and a non-Christian worldview. If yes, where can we find it? If no, how can we talk to each other?
3. Evaluate the total contribution that rational evidence plays in a person's change of worldviews.
4. Do research on some likely areas of common ground between a Christian worldview and various non-Christian philosophies or religions.
5. Assess your own spiritual pilgrimage and present beliefs in the light of relevancy, consistency, and viability.

For Further Exploration

Edward John Carnell, *An Introduction to Apologetics*, 5th ed. (Grand Rapids: Eerdmans, 1956).

William C. Placher, *Unapologetic Theology* (Louisville: Westminster, 1989).

Cornelius Van Til, *A Christian Theory of Knowledge* (Philadelphia: Presbyterian and Reformed, 1969).

5

Worldviews in Trouble

Why Can't I Be a Revelation?

Vignette 1: It was another routine night in a coffeehouse, this time at "Rahab's" in Chicago. I spent most of the night in earnest conversation with Gus, an out-of-work postal worker in his forties—and an amateur philosopher. I managed to share the gospel with him and show him the many evidences for Jesus as the way to God. Surprisingly, Gus was not inclined to dispute what I was telling him. But he kept on saying, "That's good, Win. But why can't I be a revelation too?"

I responded, "Gus, can you really look at yourself in the mirror and say, 'I'm a revelation from God'?"

Then he showed me that I had missed the point. "I'm not saying that I am a revelation, but why *can't* I be one?"

Is It Rational to Hope?

Vignette 2: I attended a conference on science, technology, and the humanities. At this interdisciplinary gathering we listened to a number of speakers address critical issues and how various academic areas ought to respond to them—not an entirely encouraging meeting. The last full session turned out to be the most depressing. The speaker gave a detailed account of most of the pressing environmental problems from the ozone layer to nuclear waste disposal. He confessed to not having any answer for them. He then closed with the following remarks, "Sometimes I want to despair. Then I remember that as long as there is humanity, there is hope. So I go on hoping."

In the ensuing question period someone asked, "Since we have no answers, is it rational to hope?"

The questioner was shouted down. The assembled scholars were offended and let the questioner know that they thought he was out of line even to raise the point. Needless to say, he never received an answer.

Absolutes in Morality

Vignette 3: Another conference, another topic. This time the discussion was on pornography. The first speaker asserted that, even though there are no absolutes in sexual morality, some things, such as pornography, are wrong. Her reason: "Sex is about relationships." The second speaker disagreed. "Sex does not have to involve a relationship," she asserted. Yet she too was opposed to pornography. She said it offended her. As the two speakers continued to discuss the topic, it became obvious that neither one had a good reason, other than what they felt emotionally, to believe that pornography was wrong.

In the last chapter we showed that it is possible to test the truth of religious worldviews. By means of hypothesis testing, which involves all of the components of knowledge, we can show which one of the competing systems can legitimately lay claim to being true.

In this chapter we begin to apply these insights by starting to work toward a defense of the worldview of theism, the belief in God. We will first show that various competing worldviews are internally deficient in some way. In the next two chapters we will mount a defense of theism (via the cosmological argument) and clear ourselves of charges that theism is inconsistent (the problem of evil) respectively.

Definition of Theism

Theism is the worldview based on belief in God, but not just any idea of God. The word "God" is used in many different ways; when we speak of "theism" we have some specific ideas in mind. At this stage in our discussion the point is not that this is the only legitimate concept of God— that remains to be seen—but that this is the concept of God we are interested in defending. Let us list the following characteristics of theism:

1. There is only one God.
2. This God is unlimited (or infinite) and possesses His attributes in an unlimited way. Thus He is:
   - eternal
   - unchangeable (immutable),
   - omnipresent,
   - omnipotent,
   - omniscient,
   - omnibenevolent (all-good and all-loving), etc.
3. God is personal.
4. God created the world; therefore, the world is dependent on Him, but He is not dependent on it.
5. God is transcendent, that is, He is over and beyond the world.
6. God is immanent, that is, He is actively present within the world.
7. The God of theism is the source of the standard for right and wrong. He is holy and good, completely untainted by any evil. He commands His creatures to live by the standards of morality He has established. To accept belief in this God implies accepting this code of behavior as well. Consequently theism is sometimes referred to as "ethical monotheism."

The understanding of God described by the above seven points is not unique to Christianity. It is also at the core of Judaism, Islam, Zoroastrianism, and African indigenous religion, among others. Of course significant differences would show up among the ideas of God in these various religions if we were to focus on greater detail. For now we want to defend this broad conception of God. The third part of this book will focus on the defense of Christianity in particular.

In this chapter we will attempt to show serious problems within each of the following worldviews that compete with theism:

- Atheism, the denial that there is any God.
- Agnosticism, the dogmatic assertion that we cannot know if there is a God.
- Deism, the belief that God created the world, but is no longer involved with it.

- Pantheism, the view that God and the world are identical.
- Panentheism, the belief in a finite, changing God, who is dependent on the world.

Atheism

Let us define atheism as the denial of any God whatsoever, not just the denial of the God of theism as we defined Him above. According to an atheist, there is no supreme being. The world is all there is.

One example of an atheist is the French existentialist philosopher Jean-Paul Sartre.[1] He describes his philosophy as the consistent outworking of the basic premise that there is no God. Consequently, according to Sartre, we are on our own and have to decide what to do with our lives apart from some external authority presenting us with a ready-made pattern to which we must conform our lives.

Atheism suffers from three serious problems: it is unprovable; it is contrary to human nature; and it lives on borrowed capital. We must now describe these three problems.

Atheism Is Unprovable

It is virtually impossible to prove a negative. For example, how could I prove that there are no unicorns? Two options are available to me. Either I would have to be able to show that I have exhaustively explored all possibilities for finding a unicorn and each one yielded unequivocal negative results. Or, I could try to show that unicorns are inherently impossible. If I cannot do one or the other, I am not entitled to state dogmatically that there are no unicorns.

Similar things would be true of any attempt to disprove the existence of God. The atheist would have to show that he or she has control over all potential avenues of knowing that God exists and that all of them come up empty. No

---

[1] For a good self-description, see his essay, "Existentialism Is a Humanism" in Walter Kaufmann, ed., *Existentialism from Dostoevsky to Sartre* (New York: World, 1956), 287-311.

human being could make that claim, for our knowledge is always finite.

Alternatively, the atheist would have to prove that the idea of God is intrinsically impossible, as it might be if it were logically self-contradictory. Some atheists have in fact attempted to do just that, but without success. In each case they had to begin with a highly questionable premise that they invented for the single purpose of dispensing with the idea of God.

For example, Kai Nielsen[2] argues the following:
1. God is supposed to be a nonmaterial (spiritual) being. He does not have a body.
2. God is supposed to be a being who performs certain actions.
3. The only intelligible notion of actions that we have is associated with material (embodied) beings.
4. The idea of a nonmaterial being performing actions is incoherent.
5. Therefore, the idea of God is incoherent.
6. Therefore, there cannot be a God.

Why should we accept premise 3? Believers in God would say that they find the idea of spiritual actions performed by God perfectly intelligible. The only motivation one could possibly have for accepting premise 3 as true is if one intended to use it to disprove God. Yet that would be a blatant case of begging the question. If there is a God, then spiritual action must be coherent. Other attempts to demonstrate the impossibility of God are equally unconvincing.

Thus atheism cannot be proven. It cannot be anything but an unverified assertion. That is all it is in Sartre's writings. Now, a belief is not false simply because it has not yet been proven to be true; but these considerations surely take the wind out of the sails of anyone believing that in the twentieth century it has been shown that one can no longer believe in God. Nothing of the kind has transpired.

---

[2]Kai Nielsen, *An Introduction to the Philosophy of Religion* (New York: St. Martin's Press, 1982), 17-42.

Atheism Is Contrary to Human Nature

Usually when Sartre spoke of his atheism, he referred to the human need to be weaned off a natural inclination to believe in God. He admitted that he himself experienced the need for God. Sartre is not alone. Many atheistic writings give testimony to a basic need for something transcendent.

Of course one cannot prove the existence of God through sheer appeal to the numbers of those who claim to believe in Him. Our point is not to prove God's existence but to throw aspersions on the denial of His existence. The argument is as follows: there is good evidence that there is a universal human need for God. A real need demands an objective reality to fulfill it. Then the burden of proof that the reality does not exist lies with the atheist, who even in his or her own life demonstrates the need for this reality. Such a proof, as we just saw, cannot be provided.

A word needs to be said here about the so-called projection theory of belief in God. This is the idea that belief in God is the result of human beings inventing a higher being on which to cast all of their idealized conceptions of themselves. The nineteenth-century philosopher Ludwig Feuerbach created this doctrine; it was popularized by Sigmund Freud. The essence of this argument is that since belief in God *can be understood* as a human invention, we can conclude that this God *is* nothing more than a fantasy. Therefore God is not real.

Even a quick reflection on the projection argument reveals that it does not work. It pivots on the assumption that because the idea of God *can be* a projection of human aspirations, it *is* nothing more than the projection. This does not follow. Human beings may very well project their ideas on something that does exist. Of course, again, that refutation does not show that there is a God, but it does show that the contrary argument does not work.

Atheism Lives on Borrowed Capital—and Cannot Pay Its Bills

Traditionally, people have justified their values on the basis of religious beliefs. This is a part of theism: all values originate with God; in God we find truth, beauty, and moral standards.

A too hasty judgment concludes that if you do not believe in God, you cannot have any values whatsoever. Ivan, in *The Brothers Karamazov*, declares that since there is no God, anything is permissible. Still there is no particular reason why this should be true. Atheists can have values, and they can justify them on various grounds.

The real question is how plausible such a justification of values by an atheist can be. An atheist may say, "I justify my values on the basis of human nature"; or, "I justify my values on the basis of evolutionary progress." He or she can then tell us how this understanding of human nature or evolution leads him or her to justify the values. Is there something inherent in human nature that demands that we ought to act in one particular way?

The atheist's problem shows up on two levels of thought. First, given this worldview, the values by which an atheist lives can only be arbitrary. If there is no God whatsoever, then this material universe can only be the product of the interaction of time and chance. So-called laws can only be statistical generalizations of how the universe usually operates without a guarantee that it must always do so. This fate besets the atheist as he or she attempts to find meaning and values in the world as well. Cornelius Van Til has an apt illustration of this point:

> Suppose we think of a man made of water in an infinitely extended and bottomless ocean of water. Desiring to get out of water, he makes a ladder of water. He sets this ladder upon the water and against the water and then attempts to climb out of the water. So hopeless and senseless a picture must be drawn . . . upon the assumption that time or chance is ultimate.[3]

If the universe is governed by chance, chance occurrences are all we can expect.

The atheist's problem with values persists to a deeper level. Let us assume, for the sake of argument, that the atheist had a reliable set of laws about the universe; he or she could announce accurately exactly how things are. There would still be no reason why things *should* be the way they

---

[3]Cornelius Van Til, *The Defense of the Faith* (Philadelphia: Presbyterian and Reformed, 1955), 102.

are. Talk about values implies that some things are preferable to others, and values tell us what things should be like, not just what they are like. If things are going one way, our values tell us that perhaps they ought to go a different way. For example, most parents teach their children that just because everybody else does something, that does not make it right. If we discovered that part of the evolutionary process were an overwhelming desire to torture cats, we could not conclude that all people ought to torture cats. Thus we see that certain sets of facts do not necessarily imply moral obligation.

Philosophers have expressed this idea by saying that you cannot get an "ought" from an "is." Statements of moral obligation are "ought" statements. They inform us of a duty or command we are under. A description of what "is" does not necessarily entail what we "ought" to do unless we smuggle in another "ought" premise. For example, a description of the world hunger situation does not by itself tell us that we ought to do something about it; we need to be told that this is the kind of thing that demands our help.

The atheist is committing the fallacy of trying to get an "ought" from an "is." He or she is trying to justify *prescriptive* moral laws on the basis of *descriptive* data. The atheist is after an obligatory moral code without anything that makes it obligatory. To have commandments, they must be commanded in some way, but the atheist's system does not allow for such a possibility.

Of course atheists, like all human beings, live according to certain fixed values, but then they are plying their existence on the basis of borrowed capital—borrowed from the theist whose system can spawn such values. For the atheist any affirmation of objective values can be no more than an irrational escape. Francis Schaeffer described the atheist's problem in the following way.[4] On the level of rational thought, atheists are stuck with the inescapable conclusions of their philosophy. These conclusions can only lead to meaninglessness, and, consequently, despair. Thus they escape their predicament by an irrational leap into asserting

[4]Francis A. Schaeffer, *The God Who Is There* (Downers Grove, IL: InterVarsity Press, 1968). The diagram in question is on p. 61.

values to which they are not entitled. The following diagram illustrates the point:

**Upper Story—Truth, Meaning, and Values
Grasped for Irrationally**

**Lower Story—Logical Conclusions of the Atheistic
Worldview: No Truth, No Meaning, No Values**

In short, the atheist as a human being is compelled to live by truth, meaning, and values. Yet the worldview of atheism cannot provide compelling truth, meaning, or values; atheists can have these things only from outside of the worldview. Thus atheism is intrinsically inviable. It cannot be lived out.

Agnosticism

For the reasons mentioned above many people have refrained from espousing atheism and have identified themselves as agnostics. *Agnosticism* is the view that we cannot know if there is a God or not. The term was coined by T. H. Huxley, the celebrated defender of Darwin's theories. Huxley referred to an ancient belief system called "gnosticism," from the Greek word *gnosis*, which means "knowledge." Its adherents prided themselves on their great spiritual knowledge. Huxley added the negative prefix "a" making "agnosticism." He intended thereby to show that he did not know.

We need to distinguish between benign and malignant agnosticism. At a certain point in our lives we say honestly that we do not know if there is a God. All of us feel that way at certain times, and there is nothing to be gained by denying it (see chapter 1). This is *benign agnosticism*. What concerns us here, however, is agnosticism as a dogmatic worldview based on the premise that we cannot know if there is a God. This version is *malignant agnosticism*.

Agnosticism as a dogmatic worldview suffers from similar ailments as atheism. In fact, it is tantamount to saying that we cannot prove atheism to be true, but that we will assume that it is true. The agnostic's agenda invariably is this: to argue that since we cannot know if there is a God, we cannot make reference to God. Agnostics never argue as follows: since we cannot know whether there is a God, let us just assume that there might be. Thus agnosticism becomes atheism in the guise of epistemological humility.

Yet agnosticism turns out to be just as indefensible as atheism. We still cannot prove a negative. The statement "It is impossible to know if there is a God" becomes just as impossible to demonstrate as the statement "There is no God." Again one or the other of the same two conditions would have to apply. One would either have to be an expert on all potential ways in which one could come to know if there is a God, but this is not in the realm of finite human minds. Or one would have to be able to show that the concept of knowing of God's existence is logically impossible, but this is clearly not the case.[5]

In the final analysis a consistently voiced agnosticism leads to skepticism, for it obligates its advocates to say that they have knowledge on a subject for which they claim knowledge is impossible. On the one hand, the agnostic claims that it is impossible to know anything about God whatsoever, not even that He exists. On the other hand, such an assertion presumes quite a bit of knowledge about God and His nature. How can an agnostic know even that much if he or she cannot know anything about God? Thus agnosticism pivots on a contradiction by having to maintain that at one and the same time it is both possible and impossible to know something about God. As we have seen several times already, such contradictions lead to skepticism, which is an impossible position. Thus dogmatic agnosticism self-destructs.

---

[5]In order to avoid confusion we need to keep in mind here the important distinction between *knowing that* God exists and *having direct personal knowledge of God*. A lot of legitimate philosophical dialogue centers around this latter concept. Many philosophers argue that since God is infinite and we are finite, it is never possible for us to have direct knowledge of God. I disagree with them, but my point here is that this is a different issue altogether. The issue on the table with agnosticism is the simpler factual question of whether we can know that such an infinite Being exists in the first place.

Deism

The best way out of the dilemmas posed by atheism and agnosticism would appear to be the following: let us say that there is a God. This God created the world. He issued to the world a moral law, a code of behavior that all of His creatures are supposed to follow. God will someday judge His creatures on how well they obeyed His commandments. In the meantime He does not interfere with His creation. He made it the way He wanted it to be, and He will not contradict His own will. For the moment, we worship God and try to live by His law, but we must not expect Him to do supernatural things for us.

This worldview is called "deism." Sometimes it is described with the analogy that God created a watch, wound it up, and is now letting it run on its own. This analogy captures part of what is involved in the worldview, but it misses the moral element. God is not just a disinterested spectator, but He is deeply interested in the moral progress His creatures are making. In addition to having disclosed His expectations through special human beings, such as Jesus, He also made His will known through nature. However, we ought not to expect special help from God in trying to live by His law.

A good example of how deism works is provided by Thomas Jefferson. He believed that no one religion had a monopoly on the way to God, though he found its clearest expression in the teachings of Jesus. To that end he set out to publish an edition of the Gospels containing only Christ's moral teachings but omitting anything requiring faith or belief in the supernatural. Jefferson's edition of the life of Jesus, which has come to be known as the *Jefferson Bible*[6] includes nothing supernatural about Christ's birth—Jesus did no miracles, drove out no demons, did not claim to be God. In fact Jesus did not claim to be different from other human beings, and when He was dead He stayed dead. The *Jefferson Bible* ends with the words, "There they laid Jesus, and rolled a great stone to the door of the sepulchre, and departed."[7] There is no resurrection.

---

[6]*The Jefferson Bible: With the Annotated Commentaries on Religion of Thomas Jefferson* (New York: Clarkson N. Potter, 1964).

[7]Ibid., 137.

Deism has the clear advantage of acknowledging that there is a God. Thus there is no problem with the question of where the world came from or why there should be moral obligations. At the same time deism attempts to maximize the benefits of atheism or agnosticism by saying that at this point God is not directly involved in our lives.

Is deism a rational worldview? Even though it prides itself on its rationality, we find that it has some serious flaws. More than anything else, it seems to be the product of wishful thinking. Deism can probably best be understood as one form of the irrational escape to which an atheist might resort in order to salvage the values by which he or she must live, for the deistic worldview is arbitrary and inconsistent.

To understand the problem with deism, one has to appreciate the strength of the deist's aversion to miracles. It would be a perfectly plausible position, compatible with theism, to say that God has chosen not to do any miracles at this point in time. Then God could do miracles; He just won't. That is not what deism says. According to deism, it is contrary to God's nature to do miracles. God is a rational God; He has instilled rational laws in His universe, and it would be absurd to think that He would break His own laws. In deism God and the supernatural are considered to be incompatible.

Now we can see that deism is actually irrational. The worldview begins with a stupendous supernatural event— the creation of the world out of nothing. Deists would agree that it is a fundamental law that "nothing comes from nothing." It is precisely for this reason that they believe the world needed a Creator. Yet if it took a miracle to give the world existence, then the objection to God's doing miracles loses all credibility. If God can perform the miracle of creation, there is no good reason why He cannot do other miracles.

Thus deism has an inconsistency at its core. Two affirmations are at the heart of deism:
- God performed the miracle of creation; and
- God does not perform miracles.

If you are a deist, you must believe both of them, and yet these affirmations cannot both be true. Therefore deism is

not a believable worldview. It founders on the criterion of
consistency.

Pantheism

Some people hold a belief diametrically opposed to deism.
Rather than thinking that God is "out there," they say that
He is "in here." Theologians would say that the God of
deism is only *transcendent*, or beyond the world. The
alternative we want to consider now has God as being only
immanent, or in the world; God and the world are so closely
intertwined that you cannot tell them apart.

In this worldview, God and the world are identical, not
just in the sense of identical twins, who merely resemble each
other strongly, but in the sense of being one and the same
thing. The words "world" and "God" are then used as two
different descriptions for one thing. We might use the
expressions "the former outfielder of the Atlanta Braves" and
"the man who holds the record for the most home runs ever"
to refer to the same person, Hank Aaron. With each
expression we are calling attention to a particular aspect of
the person, but it is the same person of whom the expressions
are true. In the same way, "world" and "God" describe a
single reality in two different ways without ever becoming
two separate things. This worldview is called "pantheism."
Pantheists believe that all is God and God is all.

Now it is crucial to realize that even though pantheism
sounds like a theory about the cosmos, it is almost always
intended to be about you, the individual human being. Since
you are part of the universe that is God, you share the divine
nature of the universe. You are God. This is the teaching of
many Eastern religions, such as Hinduism; it is also
represented by the seventeenth-century philosopher
Benedict Spinoza and the contemporary New Age
movement. "I am God!" shouts Shirley MacLaine, standing
on the beach with her hands raised in the air.[8]

On the surface pantheism appears to have a lot to offer.
Rather than being burdened with looking for answers
outside of ourselves, we are free to look within ourselves for
all that we need. We are our own source of truth. We can

---

[8]Shirley MacLaine, *Out on a Limb* (New York: Bantam Books, 1983).

decide for ourselves what is right and wrong. All the power that we need to cope with life lies within the untapped reservoir of human potential. Since we are God, sin or redemption are unnecessary, only a state of forgetfulness and reawakening to this glorious truth is possible. What rational person would turn his or her back on this message?

Pantheism, however, cannot be true. I am not just writing this harsh judgment because it does not agree with my Christian dogma. Pantheism is built around a contradiction, and a contradiction can never be true. No matter how spiritual or profound or enticing a message may appear it must be false if it contradicts itself.

The primary contradiction of pantheism is that the two descriptions "world" and "God" are irreconcilably mutually exclusive. It is as though we described Hank Aaron as "the man who holds the record for the most home runs ever" and as "a man who has never played baseball in his life." The two descriptions cannot possibly both be true. Let us begin a careful documentation of this contradiction.

Who (or what) is God? Pantheists agree that God is infinite, which includes that He is eternal, omnipotent, unchanging, and so forth. This understanding of God as infinite is at the heart of pantheism. In the next section we will discuss the idea of a finite God, but this has nothing to do with pantheism. In pantheism God is infinite. For example, Alan Watts describes God as infinite and then explains this term to mean that God is timeless (eternal), spaceless (omnipresent), and all-knowing (omniscient).[9]

What is the world? The world is finite. It is temporal, limited, and changeable. Yet pantheism tells us that this description of reality as finite world and the description of reality as infinite God are both true. Can this be? Can something be both finite and infinite? The answer is clearly no.[10]

---

[9]Alan Watts, *The Supreme Identity* (New York: Random House, 1972), 53-56. See Baruch Spinoza, *The Ethics and Selected Letters* (Indianapolis: Hackett, 1982), 31-47.

[10]Some people might see a difficulty with this assertion. After all, does not Christian theology teach that Jesus Christ is both God and a human being, therefore both infinite and finite? The answer is no, not in the sense in which one and the same reality is both infinite and finite. The accurate version of the doctrine of Christ is that He has *two natures*, one infinite, one finite. The contradiction would only exist if one said that Christ had only one nature which was both finite and infinite. Cf. my discussion of this issue in *Handmaid to Theology* (Grand Rapids: Baker Book House, 1981), 149-57.

Of course the pantheist, being as intelligent as the next person, would not usually fall into a contradiction that simple. All forms of pantheism have some sort of answer to this puzzle. Usually they involve the idea that the finite world is illusory. Like a magician's sleight-of-hand the apparent reality of the finite world misdirects us away from the true reality of the infinite. In other words, the apparent finitude of the world is not real, whereas the infinity of God is. Again we ask, can this be?

Let us consider Shirley MacLaine as she stands on the beach proclaiming, "I am God!" We would like to know, specifically, who is God? It cannot be the Ms. MacLaine who is a part of the finite world of appearance, for we just learned that this Ms. MacLaine can only be an illusion. So it must be the infinite God who is now announcing to the world something she has just come to realize, namely that she is God. This is absurd. The infinite cannot forget something and then learn it. It must have always been God and always known it. In short, for the finite Shirley MacLaine to claim that she is God is impossible; for infinite God to become Shirley MacLaine and learn that she is God is incoherent. It just does not make sense.

The point here is not to ridicule but to show that the pantheists' attempts to identify God and the world with each other cannot work. It is not just too hard, it is impossible. There is a categorical distinction between God and world. Thus we are back to our original point: to say that one and the same reality can be both infinite God and finite world is a contradiction; it must be false.

One other thing needs to be said: I have never been able to persuade a pantheist of the above point and see little hope of ever doing so. The inevitable response becomes that my insistence that a contradiction cannot be true, no matter how gently expressed, is arbitrary, dogmatic, and intolerant. Who am I to say that a contradiction cannot be true? Maybe the truth of pantheism lies beyond our logical categories.

I am not just being pig-headed; I am right. Alleged insight beyond rationality can never be expressed coherently. Let us consider two sentences:

"This statement is beyond logic."

"This statement is false."
Both of these sentences suffer from the same disease. If it is, then it is not. But if it is not, then it is, and so forth. It takes logic to deny logic. Such a mess cannot even be thought, and saying that it conveys a deep spiritual insight does not change anything. The following pantheistic dictum is in the same position:

"God and the world are identical."
Anyone attempting to sell this is advertising goods that cannot possibly be delivered.

Panentheism

One option (besides theism) remains. The problem with pantheism, as I have presented it, lies with the irreconcilability of an infinite God and a finite world; but does God have to be infinite? A very popular worldview these days is that God is in fact finite. This worldview is sometimes called "pan-en-theism," which means that God is in the world; thus He is neither beyond the world nor simply one with it.

Now we must be clear on what we are trying to say if we want to assert that God is finite. God must still somehow be God. For God simply to be one item in the world among many others obviously will not do. He still has to be more exalted and in a different category from all of the other things that constitute the world. God must still be recognizable as God.

Now it would appear to be very easy to deny one or the other of God's attributes. One could, for instance, say that God is not omnipotent (all-powerful). Then He would not be infinite. Once we have denied that God is infinite, we do not have any reason to think that He should be any of those other wonderful things we say He is. Then He lacks a rationale for His being all-knowing, all-loving, eternal, and the other attributes that are based on His infinity. Take away the infinity, and you take away the justification for believing any of the standard attributes of God. Thus the arbitrary denial of any one attribute does not yield a finite God but yields nothing at all.

What would be needed is a coherent system in which there is a rationale for whatever is supposed to constitute a finite God. Such a model has been supplied by the school of *process philosophy* founded by Alfred North Whitehead earlier in the twentieth century.[11] In Whitehead's system a finite and changing God plays the role of superintendent to the world in its continual process of change.

To understand the nature of God in Whitehead's system, we must come to terms with how Whitehead wanted us to think of the world. He came up with a different way of understanding reality, partially motivated by the insights of modern physics. Put briefly, rather than thinking of things that change, we ought to think of *changes that take on the forms of things*. Take the following example. Let us say we are watching a football game. We see players, referees, cheerleaders, and spectators. They are running, kicking, whistling, clapping, and shouting. Whitehead would want us to reverse the picture and think of the actions first with the people second. We observe running, kicking, whistling, clapping, and shouting which has taken on the form of players, referees, cheerleaders, and spectators. The action is of first order. In fact, it would be correct to say that we are observing the "football game event." This is strange language intended to make the point that nothing is as fundamental to the world as change. Whitehead even wanted us to think of the whole universe as one big event.

What is change? Suppose we bake a cake. We mix together the ingredients and create a batter. Then we put the batter into the oven and out comes a cake. We changed the batter into a cake. The batter had the potential to become a cake, but it was only after the change took place that it actually was a cake. The potential cake became an actual cake; in other words, the potential of the batter to become a cake was actualized. All change can be understood in this way. When something changes, a potential has been actualized.

So when Whitehead says that the world is one big event, we need to picture it in terms of constant change. Thus the

---

[11]Alfred North Whitehead, *Process and Reality* (London: Macmillan, 1933).

world must consist of two parts—or poles—an actual pole and a potential pole. The actual pole is everything that is true of the world at a given moment. The potential pole is the vast reservoir of everything that the world is not but could *become*. As the world is changing, potential is constantly being actualized. Picture an arrow in perpetual motion flowing from the potential side to the actual side.

In this picture created by Whitehead, God watches over this process. Keep in mind that this God is supposed to be finite: He too changes. We must think of God in the same terms as the world: He has a potential pole and an actual pole (though Whitehead calls them God's "primordial" and "consequent" natures). Every moment some new potential in God is actualized; He changes in response to changes in the world.

Like the God of deism, the process God does not intervene in the world. He is strictly finite. In the football game of reality, He is the cheerleader. He presents the world with ideals to aim for; He entices the world to follow His plans; He grieves if the world strays; but He cannot make the world do anything. As the world changes, He changes, too, in order to coax the world along. Whatever He wants done needs to be accomplished by the world apart from His direct help.

Note the advantages of this worldview. It provides a lot of help where some other systems fall short. Like the God of deism, the process God is the author of moral commandments who gives us complete freedom to obey or not to obey. Yet this picture of God does not engender the difficulties of deism. God is not seen as omnipotent Creator; so there is no inconsistency between a supernatural creation and the denial of the possibility of miracles. This view solves the problems of pantheism by maintaining a distinction between God and world.

Even so, panentheism is impossible. It leaves out a crucial element in change, namely causality. It is true that every change is the actualization of some potential, but that does not happen by itself. Try actualizing a bowl of batter's potential to become a cake without putting it into an oven. A coffee cup has the potential to be filled with coffee, so let us see if it will fill itself. Of course it won't. Cakes cannot bake themselves; coffee cups cannot fill themselves; *potentials cannot actualize themselves.* Where a change occurs, there must be a cause to bring about that change.

People who believe in a finite God live by this principle as much as all other human beings. This fact is obscured by the popular myth according to which modern science has somehow shown that we can dispense with the principle of causality. Nothing could be further from the truth. Take away causality, and you have taken away any meaning to science, modern or not-so-modern.

Two considerations have given some the impression that the principle of causality is no longer valid. First, on the subatomic level, it is not possible for us to specify mathematically the exact position of a particle without simultaneously distorting it (the Heisenberg uncertainty principle). All we can do is estimate areas of probability where the particle may be located. Second, Stephen Hawking has shown that it is possible mathematically to balance certain equations related to the Big Bang without bringing in a cause of the universe.[12]

These two considerations demonstrate that at times causes are mathematically either unspecifiable or not required. Yet we are concerned with reality beyond mathematical descriptions. These scientific conclusions do not provide one shred of evidence that there has ever been any change observed in reality that did not require a cause. In fact, 100 percent of the evidence goes the other way. It is an indispensable principle that all change requires causes, whether those causes show up in mathematical equations or not.

Panentheism attempts to circumvent the principle of causality. In its picture of God and the world there is constant change. Potentials are actualized, but the cause is missing. This is a particularly embarrassing deficiency when it comes to its understanding of God. The panentheist is faced with a Hobson's choice on how to understand God. Either his or her God is the metaphysical impossibility of a potential that actualizes itself (akin to the coffee cup that fills itself) or there has to be a cause outside of God (a God behind God) that

---

[12]Stephen Hawking, *A Brief History of Time* (New York: Bantam, 1988).

actualizes His potential. This would mean that God is no longer God in any recognizable sense. Either an impossible God or a God who is not really God; this is the panentheist's dilemma. It boils down to practical atheism.

This last assertion sounds inflammatory only to someone not familiar with the writings of panentheists themselves. Process theologians start with the premise of secularism: the idea that humankind can pretty well manage its own affairs apart from a God. The process God is then brought in primarily to undergird our human aspirations. This God is certainly optional.[13] As we have shown, as such He is also impossible.

Let us summarize what we have learned in this chapter from looking at nontheistic worldviews. We need a system in which
- God and the world are distinct;
- God is infinite, and the world is finite;
- God is both transcendent and immanent;
- God is the author of moral obligations.

In short, we need theism.

We have not yet shown that theism is true. All we have demonstrated is that nontheistic systems are beset with serious difficulties that allow us to question their truthfulness. Whether there is good reason to believe that theism is true remains to be seen in the next chapter.

Meanwhile, let me address this chapter's vignettes.

Response to Vignette 1: I remember what I said to Gus. I challenged him to see if he could *really* think of himself as a revelation. My point was that we have a basic consciousness of our finitude that no coating of pantheistic philosophy can obscure. We would like to be our own revelation; in fact we would like to be our own God. Yet, in our more honest moments, we do not have to be told that the idea of our being infinite beings is contradictory to everything we know about ourselves. The point I am adding here to the previous discussion about pantheism is this: when I say that pantheism is contradictory, I am not just

---

[13]See, for example, John B. Cobb, Jr., *God and the World* (Philadelphia: Westminster, 1969).

addressing a logical concern. I find the idea that I should be infinite God contradictory to my experience of myself as well.

Response to Vignette 2: The assembled scholars who broke academic decorum by shouting down the man who raised a pertinent question were right in one respect: hope is an essential ingredient in what it means to be human. There are two kinds of hope: rational hope and irrational hope. Rational hope is based on realities with reasonable expectations. Irrational hope is wishful thinking without basis. Of course, there is no law against wishful thinking, but I would not want to stake my destiny on it. In any worldview in which God is not in charge and human beings are left in control, hope cannot be more than wishful thinking. Looking at the history of the twentieth century, human beings have shown that they are better at fouling up things than at fixing them. Nontheistic worldviews beware! You can only offer people irrational hope.

Response to Vignette 3: It is difficult to go through a day with your eyes open without encountering the paradox illustrated with this episode. People not only hold values, they even lecture on them and attempt to impose them on others without having a basis for them. We emphasize tolerance, but only within the limits of our personal self-interest and preference. Humanistic ethics need not be binding on anyone who does not choose to play by those particular rules. Thus these values are arbitrary. What people need is not half so much a better code of ethics as a basis for ethics in theism.

For Growth and Study

Mastering the Material

When you have studied this chapter you should be able to:
1. Define and describe theism.
2. Define atheism and give three reasons why it is not an acceptable worldview.
3. Define agnosticism and show why it is self-defeating.
4. Define deism and point out its central inconsistency.
5. Define pantheism and describe why it is contradictory.
6. Define panentheism and illustrate why it is an impossible worldview.
7. Identify the following names with the contribution to which we have alluded in this chapter: Jean-Paul Sartre, Kai Nielsen,

Cornelius Van Til, Francis Schaeffer, T. H. Huxley, Thomas Jefferson, Shirley MacLaine, Alfred North Whitehead.

Thinking About the Ideas

1. Is it possible to combine some of the worldviews mentioned in this chapter? Why or why not?
2. Find contemporary illustrations for one or more of the worldviews.
3. Study the writings of a person committed to one of the worldviews criticized in this chapter. Can you find illustrations of the problem mentioned here?
4. Different worldviews have become dominant in particular periods of time. Make a list associating the popularity of various worldviews with specific historical eras. To what do you attribute this fact?
5. Do you find that your understanding of God and the world has been influenced by some of these nontheistic worldviews? To what extent can you correct it?

For Further Exploration

David K. Clark and Norman L. Geisler, *Apologetics in the New Age* (Grand Rapids: Baker, 1990).

Norman L. Geisler and William D. Watkins, *Worlds Apart*, 2nd ed. (Grand Rapids: Baker, 1989).

Royce Gordon Gruenler, *The Inexhaustible God* (Grand Rapids: Baker, 1983).

6

The Existence of God

Impossible Proof

Vignette 1: I was sitting in the lobby of Neues Leben Seminary in Germany writing an earlier chapter of this book. Helmut, a student at the seminary, was on duty straightening chairs and answering the phone at the desk. After a while he came up to me and started to ask me questions about being a professor in America and how it compares to teaching in Germany. Then he wanted to know what I was writing, and I told him.

"Apologetics?" was his response. "I'm not sure how much that helps. I mean, of course, you can't prove the existence of God."

No Evidence for God

Vignette 2: During my sophomore year in college, my "hang-out" on campus was the student union cafeteria. There were a number of us commuters who would sit around the tables between classes, drink coffee, make a pretense of studying, and talk as though the problems of the world were mere annoyances, given our superior powers to solve them. Pretty soon I had acquired a reputation in this circle as the guy who thought that Jesus was the answer to a lot of our troubles. Frequently that led to a fair amount of good-natured ribbing, though every once in a while the conversation would get more serious.

I remember talking with Donald.

"With all that God has to offer you," I pled, "why don't you want to turn your life over to Him?"

"That's simple," Donald shot back. "I do not believe that there is a God, and there is no evidence to say there is."

What Caused God?

Vignette 3: I was talking with a fellow student at the Christian book table we had set up in the student union. I was there to share the gospel; he had stopped by for some quick entertainment between classes.

"Why do you think I should believe in God?" he asked—undoubtedly not really wanting to know.

"Because God is real," was my answer. "You want to believe in reality, don't you?"

"But how can I know that God is real?" The conversation was going according to script.

"Because without God, there couldn't be any world. He caused everything that exists."

"OK. So you say everything needs a cause, and that cause is God. But if everything needs a cause, what caused God? Got you there!"

He left, brilliantly victorious in his own eyes.

Does God exist? Surely there cannot be any more crucial question. Yet many people do not think that it is legitimate to raise it. We ought simply to accept an answer without getting involved in "proof" or "argumentation."

Nevertheless, in this chapter we will look at the evidence. The big issue is this: there are two mutually exclusive hypotheses:

- God, as described in theism, exists;
- God, as described in theism, does not exist.

In the last chapter we tried to show that there is good reason not to accept the second option. Now we will attempt to demonstrate that there is good reason to accept the first one.

Can You Prove God's Existence?

"You cannot prove God's existence." How many times have we heard this assertion! I hear it a lot from people who have never really thought about the issue. They repeat it because they have heard it so many times from other people. Sometimes it comes up as a defensive statement to protect them from intellectual challenges. Rarely does their defense go beyond a further generalization, such as "God would no longer be God if we could prove Him!" Why not?

Sometimes the objections to proofs for God's existence run a little deeper. Here are some of the better ones.

"The Bible does not try to prove the existence of God."

Even if true, this statement does not carry any weight. To be sure, Genesis 1:1 does not begin with the ontological argument, and I am just as happy that it does not. Still that truth does not make it illegitimate to ask whether it is reasonable to believe that the God of Genesis 1:1 is real.

As a matter of fact the Bible does give some strong pointers in the direction that belief in God is reasonable. "The fool has said in his heart, 'There is no God' " (Ps. 14:1, NKJV). In several places we read that we learn about God from nature: "The heavens are telling of the glory of God; and their expanse is declaring the work of His hands" (Ps. 19:1, NASB). "For since the creation of the world His invisible attributes, His eternal power and divine nature, have been clearly seen, being understood through what has been made, so that they are without excuse" (Rom. 1:20, NASB). We do not see any direct attempt at proof here, but the door to proof is definitely left open.

"God exists whether we can prove His existence or not."

I would not even want to bring up this objection if it were not for the fact that I run across it in all seriousness every once in a while. Of course God's existence or nonexistence boils down to objective fact. No argument in the world can change that fact. The idea of God's existence depending on our arguments is nothing if not ludicrous. He would not need our arguments if He existed, and our arguments could not help Him if He did not exist. Furthermore, if He does exist, I doubt that it is a major issue with Him whether our arguments come out in favor of Him.

All of this is irrelevant to the issue. The point is not to make God exist with an argument but to come to a decision on the supposed fact of His existence or nonexistence. We simply want to know if that alleged fact is true.

"Finite beings cannot prove an infinite God."

This objection can be taken in two senses: they cannot or they should not. Let us look at each in turn.

First objection: *Finite beings cannot prove God's existence.* This objection might be taken to mean that an infinite God is by nature too high above us to ever become the subject of our tests of Him. Since our minds are finite, any proof of Him can only consist of finite information. How can you possibly put together all of those finite things and come up with an infinite God? You cannot treat God like an object in a lab.

This is a good objection, depending on what one tries to accomplish with an argument. The objection would be on target if what we tried to do was actually to comprehend the essence of God. That cannot be done, of course. A finite being cannot possibly understand an infinite being. However that is not the object of the argument. We can know *that* something exists without necessarily comprehending it.

Consider the following example. I once talked to someone who happened to mention that he did not understand Maxwell's equation on electromagnetism, a point that I did not hold against him. He had taken physics twice, in high school and in college, and each time he had had a hard time when it came to solving this equation. In short, he did not comprehend it. This deficiency did not preclude his knowing that there is such a thing as Maxwell's equation or what in general it is intended to show. In the same way, we can possibly demonstrate that God exists along with some truths about Him without necessarily comprehending Him exhaustively.

Second, *finite beings should not try to prove the existence of God.* Somehow the very attempt is seen as compromising God's greatness. "You can't isolate God in a test tube," a popular book stated.[1] Surely not, but again one wonders who ever seriously thought you could. To show that God exists is not to reduce Him to an object among many. It is simply to show that God is real.

On more than one occasion I have heard people declaim, "A God whose existence can be proven is not worthy of worship." Why not? That statement is not only arbitrary and unfounded, it is also dangerous. It promotes the idea

---

[1]Barbara Jurgensen, *Quit Bugging Me* (Grand Rapids: Zondervan, 1968).

that only an irrational faith is worth having. Then why not simply plunge into Hinduism and be done with it?

"An argument for God's existence can never compel someone to believe in God."

Here we have a specific example of a problem that afflicts all rational argumentation. In chapter 4 we saw how complex human reasoning actually is. An argument, in order to be considered sound, must have true premises and valid logic. Because we think within the context of world-views, someone may not be convinced by a perfectly sound argument. This is an everyday occurrence in all human reasoning and attempts at persuasion. That is no fault of the argument. Nor can we thereby rule out the possibility that someone else at some other place or time might be persuaded by the argument. The point here is this: if we stopped engaging in rational argumentation each time we discovered that someone is going to be predisposed against our argument, then we would have to stop reasoning with each other altogether. Thus we also need not stop trying to prove God's existence before we ever get started. As a matter of fact, some people do find various arguments for God's existence to be persuasive.

"Human reason cannot prove the existence of God."

This objection, which appears to be very similar to the third one, has a slightly different twist to it. The third objection focused on the difference between finite and infinite beings; this one looks at the inherent capacities of human reason *per se*. It claims that human reason inherently cannot do such a thing as prove God's existence. Sometimes this objection is put into the context of human sinfulness: our fallen minds are incapable of proving God's existence.

The easiest way of dealing with this objection is to let the argument speak for itself. If it does not work, this objection may or may not be true. One thing is clear: if it works, then the objection is false. If we come up with a sound argument (true premises, valid logic), then obviously human reason is capable of such a thing. It makes no sense to say that reason cannot do what it just did.

What Proof Can Do

The other day I went out to collect the first spring strawberries in our little patch next to the four tomato plants and twelve radish plants. I found one large dark strawberry. As I picked it up exuberantly, I was in for a sad shock. A big hole had been eaten into the fruit, almost to the point of hollowing it out. Then I noticed a trail of silvery slime around the area where the strawberry had been. A slug had eaten what could have been my prize strawberry.

I never saw the slug, but I am sure it was there. I did not deduce the existence of the slug from unquestioned premises. I inferred the existence of the slug from its effects. If pressed to express the matter in formal reasoning, I would have to say something like the following: unless there had been a slug, there would not have been the hole eaten into the strawberry or the slime trail.

Similarly, a detective may figure out that the butler committed the murder without having seen the butler do it but on the basis of the evidence the culprit left behind. A chemist detects the presence of a chemical in a solution by the effects the solution has on another chemical. My students know that I am on campus when they see my car in the parking lot.

This is the general pattern of argumentation we want to employ concerning the existence of God. We cannot make some kind of direct check to "see" if He is here. Nor can we deduce His existence from universally accepted premises. Yet we can see if His effects are there. In other words, we can look at the world and see if the world is constructed in such a way that it is reasonable to believe that there must be a God. Thus our first question must be: What is the world like? If the world bears the marks of God, then it is reasonable to infer that God must exist.

This pattern already showed up in the teleological argument discussed in chapter 3. The effects pointed to at that time were the orderliness and harmoniousness of nature. Then the argument inferred from this apparent design in the world to a designer. Now let us remember that the problem with this argument was not with its logical structure. The problem was with the tenuous epistemological foundation: whether or not there is this evidence of design in the world was too arbitrary a judgment. Still the methodology of accounting for what we see in the world by invoking a creator is healthy and may continue to stand.

The "Unless" Argument

The fact that we have chosen hypothesis testing as our methodology allows us a certain flexibility in another respect. We are not confined to the rigors of pure deductive or pure inductive argumentation. We may not violate the laws of logic, but we do not need to follow the formal rules of argumentation, just as we do not do so in everyday life.

Take for example the following very simple inference: "Rick Mears must really know how to drive because he has won the Indianapolis 500." If someone were to challenge such a statement, what could we say in response? We would point out that being able to drive a car well is a necessary condition for winning the Indy 500. Strictly speaking, we would offer neither an inductive nor a deductive argument. We would appeal to what hopefully counts for common sense and experience to make our case: "Unless Rick Mears knew how to drive a car well, he would not have been able to win the Indy 500."

This kind of reasoning has been called transcendental logic. *Transcendental logic is the type of reasoning process whereby we uncover necessary conditions without which certain phenomena could not be true.*

Transcendental logic is a way of thinking we employ all of the time. If I meet a Taylor University alumnus, I can know immediately that he or she has passed certain Bible courses because that is a necessary condition to graduate from Taylor. When you name any U.S. president, you can be sure that you are naming a person over thirty-five years old, because the U.S. constitution makes this a necessary condition.

The reasons why something is a necessary condition may vary widely. They can be purely logical, empirical, scientific, consensus-based, and many more. In all such cases the conclusion follows because in some way it represents the necessary prerequisite for whatever item is under discussion.

Overall, this is the methodology of our argument. We will try to show that God is the necessary condition for the world. Or, to put it more simply, "Unless there were a God, there could not be any world."

The Cosmological Argument

The argument about to be presented is a form of the cosmological argument for God's existence. The name of the argument is derived from the word *cosmos* meaning "world." The idea is that we infer the existence of God from what we see in the world. The version I am presenting here is an adaptation of the cosmological argument of Thomas Aquinas.[2]

Here is a quick summary of the argument. Afterwards we will slowly walk through each step and defend each premise. Look for whatever terms are unknown to you now to be defined at that point.

1. Something exists.
2. Each thing that exists is either necessary or contingent.
3. A necessary being would have to be God.
4. The world cannot be a necessary being.
5. There can be only one necessary being.
6. Unless there is a necessary being there cannot be any contingent beings.
7. A necessary being exists.
8. Therefore, God exists.
9. Therefore, only one God exists.
10. The God of theism exists.

1. Something exists. Anything will do. I exist. You exist. The universe exists. A flower exists. My pen exists. It does not even have to be a material object. If you doubt this statement, your doubting exists, and that is good enough. In short, if you find anything controversial in the statement that something exists, you are reading something into it; and that

---

[2]Thomas Aquinas, *Summa Theologica*, I, question 2, article 3.

"something" would have to exist, and you would have to exist in order to read it into the statement. No rational person ought to doubt that statement.

Let me add two comments. First, I am aware that some rational people do doubt this statement (for example Theravada Buddhists). My point is that they should not, because insofar as they do so they are being irrational. Nevertheless, since their dispute over this statement is a matter of record, I cannot put it forward as an undisputed starting point in the way in which rationalism would require of me. I am advancing it as a statement that I can expect the overwhelming majority of my readers to accept. If there should exist any Theravada Buddhists who would not accept it in my readership, their very existence makes my point. Theravada Buddhists exist.

Second, I want to emphasize that this statement is very different from René Descartes' famous argument, "I think, therefore I am."[3] We met Descartes in chapter 3 as a proponent of the ontological argument. In the argument to which I am referring now Descartes begins by doubting that he can know anything. Then he reasons that since he is doubting, he must be thinking; and since he is thinking, he must exist in order to think. Philosophers have taken sides with regard to this argument. More could be said about it, but my purpose in stating my premise is not as ambitious as Descartes'. I am not out to prove the existence of any one thing with my statement. I am just asserting a reasonable truth, namely that something exists. We can stop with "my doubting exists" if we really care to. Let us agree that something exists.

2. *Each thing that exists is either contingent or necessary.* *Contingent* means "dependent on something else"; *necessary* means "totally independent of anything else." If you think about it, you realize that these two properties are mutually exclusive. If you are one, you cannot be the other.

Here is a fact of logic. Give me a pair of genuinely contradictory properties. For example, keep in mind that regardless of what you thought in kindergarten, the opposite

---

[3]René Descartes, *Meditations on First Philosophy*, trans. Donald A. Cress (Indianapolis: Hackett, 1979), 17.

of "dog" is not "cat," but "non-dog." It is a fact that each thing that exists in the world must have one or the other property of the pair. So each thing in the world is either a dog or a non-dog. Each thing in the world is or is not a major-league baseball player, is or is not blue, is or is not a carnivorous predator, and so forth.

Of course when we say such things we are not making any specific judgment on any particular thing as to which side it fits on (we may not be able to tell whether an animal in the zoo belongs to the dog family or not) or on the total distribution of members of one option or the other in the universe (we do not know the total number of dogs in the world). For any given pair it is always possible that either all or none or numbers in between partake of the option. In other words, we still know nothing of how many things are dogs versus non-dogs, how many things are blue versus non-blue, etc. The only thing we can know for sure is that each thing must be one or the other.

I am saying that the contingent/necessary dichotomy represents one such pair of options. As will become more apparent, these are mutually exclusive, contradictory notions. Consequently one or the other must be true of each thing in the universe.

Here is more specifically what I mean by a contingent being:[4] a contingent being is a dependent being. It exists because of the influence of other beings on it. Among such influences we would have to include three:

A contingent being is caused. Let us recall the actuality/potentiality distinction which we mentioned at the end of the last chapter. A contingent being is one that had its potential to exist actualized. That actualization would have required a cause. The cause would have been another separate being since nothing can cause its own existence. Remember: coffee cups do not fill themselves, and potentials cannot actualize themselves. For example, my existence was caused, at least to a large extent, by my parents.

---

[4]The word "being" can be ambiguous in English. What I mean by this term is something that exists, a thing, an entity, something that is. It could be either personal or impersonal.

A contingent being is sustained. It would also not continue to exist were it not for certain sustaining causes. For example, my continuing existence is made possible, among other factors, by food I have eaten, medicines I have taken, and the laws of the universe of which I am a part.

A contingent being is determined. Contingent beings not only get their raw existence, but also the specification of what they exist as, from external causes. I did not choose to be many things that I am (a German-born white male of various abilities and dispositions); these were forced onto me by my causes and sustaining factors.

We can leave as homework the question as to whether it is possible for a contingent being to fit into one or two of these categories without having to fit into all three (I am inclined to think not). For our purposes here we can settle on a minimal answer and simply decide that we are going to consider any being that fits at least one of those categories (if it is caused, sustained, or determined) as contingent.

By definition then, we shall call a "necessary being" something that fits into none of those categories. At this point we do not need to commit ourselves to the idea that a necessary being really exists. We are simply saying that if there were one, then by this definition it would have to have the following qualities: it would have to be uncaused, unsustained by anything outside of itself, and undetermined by outside factors. It would exist totally independently of all other beings.

Can a being be contingent in some respects and necessary in others? Our definition would not permit it. As soon as it fits into the criteria for a contingent being in one respect, it drops out of the category of necessary being. A partially necessary being is an impossibility.

I am admittedly providing a very stringent definition for a necessary being. Can such a thing possibly exist? The answer to this question needs to wait for the completion of the argument. In the meantime our logical disjunction stands: each thing that exists must be either contingent or necessary. Either it is dependent on other beings in some way, no matter how slight (in which case it is contingent) or it is completely uncaused and independent (in which case it is necessary).

3. A necessary being would have to be God. At this stage of the argument we still do not know if there is a necessary being. We can analyze the properties in such a way that we can say that, should one exist, it would be the kind of being that is properly referred to as "God."

By our definition, a necessary being is uncaused, unsustained, and undetermined. It exists completely apart from any external factors or influences. This idea would not foreclose that it could freely choose to respond to other beings, but it would neither need them nor be compelled by them. Thus the necessary being would be:

- Independent;
- Unlimited;
- Infinite—really a synonym for "unlimited";
- Eternal—unrestricted by time;
- Omnipresent—unrestricted by space;
- Immutable—unchangeable;
- Pure actuality—it would have no potentiality;
- In possession of all of its properties in an equally unlimited way.

Thus if we can demonstrate that it has power, knowledge, and goodness, it would have to be omnipotent, omniscient, and omnibenevolent.

What all of this boils down to is that the necessary being has all of the properties normally associated with God. You and I, when presented with an uncaused, independent, infinite, eternal, omnipresent, immutable being, would immediately recognize it as God.

Sometimes people object to this line of argumentation and question our right to call the necessary being "God." Just because it has all the attributes commonly associated with God does not mean that it is God, according to their objection. There is some logical validity to the objection, but it evaporates in the face of ordinary language usage. What else would you possibly call an uncaused, independent, infinite, eternal, omnipresent, immutable being but "God." If these attributes do not suffice, what could? Language is not so static that we can arbitrarily withhold a word if on all available grounds it is the only appropriate one.

A different question altogether is whether the necessary being is the true God. Is it the God whom we worship in church, who revealed Himself in Scripture, and who sent His Son to die for our sins on the cross? We cannot now assume that identity for the necessary being. This will have to wait for further argumentation.

At this point we cannot say that a necessary being exists. We have shown that, hypothetically, if one did exist, it would be God.

4. *The world cannot be a necessary being.* A number of people have attempted to halt the forward march of the cosmological argument by granting that a necessary being exists but insisting that the world is this necessary being. Given all that we have shown until now, it becomes clear that this thought is not a viable option. To say that the world is the necessary being is tantamount to saying that the world is God. This is pantheism, and pantheism is impossible because, as we argued in chapter 5, it is contradictory.

Of course people who say that the world is the necessary being do not usually mean to assert pantheism and would resent the allegation that they do. The reason is that in our era few people occupy themselves too deeply with metaphysics. Few have thought through the implications of what they are saying, but that fact does not mean that they should get away with it. If you say that the world is a necessary being, you are hitching your wagon to the metaphysically impossible star of pantheism, whether you are conscious that you are doing so or not.

5. *There can be only one necessary being.* We are still not in a position to say that there is a necessary being. With this premise we want to prove that if there is one, that is the limit. There cannot be more than one.

If two things are supposed to be different from each other, they must differ in some respect. If they do not differ, they must be one and the same thing. The seventeenth-century philosopher Gottfried Wilhelm Leibniz called this the *principle of the identity of indiscernibles.* Let me illustrate it.

Suppose you and a friend are talking about people you know at another college. You tell her that you know a guy there who is named Aaron Huxtable. He is a business major, drives a red Ferrari, is dating a girl named Imogene, and has a mole on his right cheek. Now your friend says that she too knows an Aaron Huxtable at that same college. He also is a business major, drives a red Ferrari, dates an Imogene, and has a mole in the same location. Would the two of you sit and marvel at the fact that two such totally similar people should exist at one college? Of course not! You would decide that you are talking about the same individual. You would be using the principle of the identity of indiscernibles. Since the two descriptions agree in every respect, the two things referred to must be identical.

Of course this principle is airtight only in an ideal situation in which there really are no differences between the two alleged objects. As soon as one of them has a property that the other one does not have, they cannot be identical. So-called identical twins are not identical in this sense. Even if they should be uncannily indistinguishable—as twins at times are—they have to differ in one important respect: they consist of different portions of matter which occupy different spatial coordinates. If they did not, we would indeed have to recognize them as one single individual.

Given this principle, could it be possible for there to be two necessary beings? Let us see why that cannot be so. First of all, by our principle we recognize that in order for there to be two necessary beings, they would have to differ in some property or other. Then one necessary being would have to have a property that the other one lacks (or vice versa). Given our definition of a necessary being, such a thing is impossible. A necessary being is unlimited; it cannot lack any properties appropriate to it, and it cannot have any contingent properties extraneously tacked on. Consequently, to be a necessary being it must have all of the right properties, no more and no less. Therefore, since there are no properties in which they can differ, there can only be one necessary being.

A quick word about a point of confusion that sometimes arises in this connection. Does Christian theology not teach that there are three necessary beings—Father, Son, and Holy Spirit—in the divine Trinity? Thus does this doctrine not run afoul of the principle of the identity of indiscernibles? The answer is that the doctrine of the *tri-unity* does not teach that

there are three Gods. There are three Persons in the one
God—thus only one necessary being.[5]

6. *Unless there is a necessary being there cannot be any
contingent beings.* Now we come to the crux of the argument,
to show why we must in fact believe that a necessary being
exists. As you can see from the "unless" formulation of this
premise, we are now going to use transcendental logic. We
are going to show that the existence of a necessary being is a
necessary condition for there to be contingent beings.

1. Suppose you look at chandeliers suspended in a dim
Gothic cathedral. You cannot see the ceiling, and you are
wondering how the chandelier is mounted. If someone tells
you that it is hung from the lowest link of a chain, that
answer will not satisfy you. Pointing out to you that the last
link is hanging from a link above it will not help either. In
fact, you know that chains cannot hang from themselves.
Somehow the chain must be installed in the ceiling. It really
does not matter how long it is. Unless the chain is suspended
from a fastener that does not depend on the chain, the chain
could not hang.

2. Let us say you are interested in railroad trains. You are
riding along a highway that parallels a railroad track, about
to pass a long freight train. As you overtake the caboose you
wonder aloud what is pulling it. A friend riding in the car
with you tells you that the caboose is pulled by the car in
front of it. Of course you know that train cars do not pull
themselves, so you ask what is pulling that car. Again
pointing to the other cars ahead will not help you. You
know that there has to be a locomotive. Unless something is
pulling the train without being pulled by it, the train would
not be able to move at all.

3. Once again call to mind that coffee cups do not fill
themselves. If I have a cup of coffee and you want to know
where I got the coffee, telling you that the potential of the
cup to be filled was actualized will not satisfy you. How
would you feel about my answer that the coffee was in
another cup and I poured it into the present cup? You would
want to know where the coffee in the other cup came from.
Multiplying cups to create a virtually endless chain of

[5]I talk more about the philosophical issues involved with the doctrine of the
Trinity in *Handmaid to Theology* (Grand Rapids: Baker, 1981), 157-66.

pouring coffee from one cup to another will not help. It does not make any difference how long we want to go on sloshing coffee. There must be a source for it, such as a coffee maker or percolator. Unless there is such a source for the coffee, there cannot be any coffee to be passed from cup to cup.

These illustrations show that sometimes there cannot be a series of events or objects without something that founded the whole set. Without the original cause there would be nothing at all. Although we can imagine the chain, the train, or the succession of coffee cups going back an infinite number of times, in reality this cannot be true. An infinite number of railroad cars without an engine would still be stationary. An infinite number of chain links without a hook would still lie on the floor. An infinite number of coffee cups without the pot would still be empty. Philosophers say that *in these cases there cannot be an infinite regress.*[6]

The Uncaused Cause

Now consider another chain, this time a chain of contingent beings. By its very nature a contingent being needs to be caused by another being. It consists of actualized potential, and since a potential cannot actualize itself, it must be actualized by a cause outside of itself. Of course the cause must be actual. Then, if it is also a contingent being, it too must be a caused being. Now this chain of caused causes can theoretically go on for a long time, but it cannot go on infinitely. There cannot be an infinite regress of caused causes. Unless something started the chain of actuality without being actualized by it, there cannot be any actuality at all.

Why not? Why can this chain of contingent causes not simply exist as given without needing an external cause? The reason is that such an eventuality would make the total collection of contingent beings a necessary being, and this cannot be so for two reasons. First, it makes no sense to think that adding up a lot of contingent beings should yield a necessary being. Second, once again the very most we could gain if we said that the totality of contingent beings is

---

[6]Presumably, an infinite regress is possible in other areas, such as a self-referential function in mathematics. If so, it is not relevant to the examples or the point of our cosmological argument.

a necessary being would be pantheism—the contradictory worldview we had to dismiss earlier.

Thus there must be a necessary being, a being that not only exists but also causes all contingent beings to exist. The being itself, as necessary being, is uncaused. An immediate corollary of this conclusion is that you cannot give what you do not have. The cause of beings must have the positive qualities that it instills in its effects. Of course it still is infinite, so it is omnipotent, omniscient, omnibenevolent, etc.

Any intrinsically positive property encountered in creation ultimately reflects the nature of the creator. If there is love in creation, it came from the creator. If there is beauty, the creator must have instilled it. Consequently the creator is supremely loving and beautiful. Another such property derived from this cause is the possession of personhood. Personhood is a trait of the world that the creator has instilled in it. In fact, we value the notion that we are not just biological organisms but are persons. Thus the first cause must be supremely personal (in the sense of having personhood). From this point on we can use the personal pronoun "he" to refer to the uncaused cause.[7]

Professor Edwards' Confusion

The force of our argument may come out most clearly by defending it against a critique. A contemporary philosopher, Paul Edwards, has challenged one of the illustrative images we used in support of the argument.[8] He suggests that the picture of a freight train is out of place. Each individual cause has an integrity of its own. Consequently we should think of a series of locomotives linked together: we would not need a first locomotive, and the whole chain could move on its own.

[7]There has been a lot of debate lately as to the appropriate gender with which to refer to God. Why not "She" rather than "He"? Or both? Or something in between? Let me state my position. God is not male. The use of "He" to refer to God is not the glorification of human maleness or masculinity. In the Bible, however, God has revealed Himself through masculine images and with masculine grammar. Since this is the only revelation on the matter, I consider it to be binding. However, rather than exalting human masculinity, God sits in judgment of sinful human males.

[8]Paul Edwards, "The Cosmological Argument" in Donald R. Burrill, ed. *The Cosmological Arguments* (Garden City, NY: Doubleday, 1967), 100-123.

This suggestion reveals a common confusion on the matter. In order for the image to hold true, each causing being must then itself be uncaused—a necessary being. The picture of the whole world as a multiplicity of necessary beings is too problematic by now to need further refutation.

7. *A necessary being exists.* We stated that something exists. It must be either necessary or contingent. If it is necessary, our quest is over. If it is contingent, there must still be a necessary being since we just showed that there cannot be any contingent beings if there is no necessary being. Therefore, either way, a necessary being exists.

8. *Therefore, God exists.* Since we have shown that a necessary being is properly called God, we can affirm that God exists.

9. *Only one God exists.* We have shown that God, as necessary being, exists. We showed that there can only be one necessary being. Consequently, there can only be one God.

10. *The God of theism exists.* Unsurprisingly, the characteristics of the necessary being match the characteristics of the God of theism. Thus the God of theism, the one who is supposed to be the subject of this entire discussion, does exist. Or, to put it into a form that fits our announced methodology: *Given the existence of the world, it is more plausible to believe that theism is true than that it is not.*

What Have We Done?

Since the time that I began writing this chapter two weeks ago and the time that I am writing this line, I have heard people assert, "You cannot prove the existence of God!" at least a dozen times. At no point did anyone give any good reason why not. I would suggest that, within the limitations discussed earlier, we have indeed given a rational demonstration of God's existence. If there were no God, there could not be a world.

What is the practical worth of this argument? We have looked at a very careful and qualified argument which hopefully is sound in all respects. I cannot imagine many situations outside of a formal academic setting where I would present the whole argument premise by premise. So why occupy ourselves with all of this work? Let me suggest three reasons.

First, we have given a rational answer to a rational question. The question is: Is it rational to believe in the existence of God? In response we have provided an argument to show that it is. We have not made God exist; we have not deduced God's existence. We have shown that the evidence clearly supports His existence.

Second, we have tried to make this argument as complete as possible. Thus we have invoked such concepts as transcendental logic and the principle of the identity of indiscernibles. Usually those notions do not come up in our everyday conversations, and I am not suggesting that they should. Their contribution is to show that our argument can withstand very technical scrutiny. Should such technical issues come up, there is an answer. Where the issues would be irrelevant, we need not bring up those concepts either.

Third, we have exposed a fundamental trait about the world, namely that it needs a God. In a more likely conversation, it is this feature that I would point to. Suppose someone said, "Prove to me that there is a God!" Your first reply should be: "What would you accept as evidence?" If (and this is actually a rare occurrence) the person sincerely replies, "Give me a rational argument for God's existence," I might say something like this: "When I look at the nature of what exists in the world, it becomes clear to me that if there were no God to create it, the world could not exist at all."

Thus you see, I would not start with necessary being, contingent being, actuality, potentiality, pantheism, and so forth (except in a very rigorous environment). Rather, as the conversation proceeded and my friend questioned this point or that, I would be prepared to provide whatever explanation he or she requested. All of these concepts only help us to analyze the one basic truth around which the argument is built: if there is no God, there can be no world. Stated negatively, *if you think you can look at the world without finding God behind it, you are not looking at the world correctly.*

Take a moment to check whether you understand the point of the argument in this chapter. Before reading my responses to the opening vignettes, go back to them and see if you can figure out how I would answer them.

Response to Vignette 1: To my own surprise, once I explained to Helmut more carefully what I was doing, he no longer had a problem with it. Usually it does not go that easily. I find a great mystery in the fact that Christians resist so vehemently the idea that God's existence should be demonstrable to reason. Sure, there are the objections mentioned earlier, but this resistance seems to go beyond those points. All I can figure out is that they are afraid to risk their faith on the vicissitudes of reason. Let me assure these brothers and sisters that this same God who created the world also created our minds.

Response to Vignette 2: It is for situations such as this one that this chapter is intended. The cosmological argument will probably never bring anyone all the way from atheism to teaching Sunday School in ten easy steps. It gives a thoughtful response to the flippant dismissal of theism as unfounded. Most undergraduate courses in Introduction to Philosophy and their textbooks contain a section that may best be characterized as "laughing your way through the proofs for God's existence." Students are taught by skeptical professors to sneer at theistic arguments and assume that they will not work from the outset. At a minimum, we have tried to show that the shoe belongs on the other foot.

Response to Vignette 3: The objection brought up in this casual encounter points out a serious problem with some versions of the cosmological argument, but not ours. We never said that "everything needs a cause." If we had, it would certainly be irrational to plead an exception for God. What we did say was that each being must be either contingent or necessary. Then we showed that contingent beings need causes. A necessary being, by definition, is uncaused. Thus the argument never became vulnerable to this objection.

For Growth and Study

Mastering the Material

When you have studied this chapter you should be able to:
1. List five objections to being able to prove God's existence and show why they do not work.

2. Describe exactly what an argument for God's existence can and cannot do.
3. Define "transcendental logic" and tell how it provides a method for an argument for God's existence.
4. Summarize the cosmological argument in your own words.
5. Distinguish between a necessary and a contingent being.
6. Show why a necessary being is God.
7. Make a case why the world cannot be a necessary being.
8. Explain the principle of the identity of indiscernibles and how it functions in the cosmological argument.
9. Demonstrate why an infinite regress of contingent beings is not possible.
10. Identify the following names with the contribution to which we have alluded in this chapter: Thomas Aquinas, Gottfried Wilhem Leibniz, Paul Edwards.

Thinking About the Ideas

1. We have now encountered several arguments for God's existence. What do they have in common?
2. In this chapter I presented one particular version of the cosmological argument. Other formulations are possible. Can you come up with any, either through your own thinking or library research?
3. Make a detailed list of all characteristics of God that can be compiled simply by unpacking His identity as uncaused cause.
4. Through collateral reading, find some objections to the cosmological argument from other writers. See if the argument in this chapter stands up to them or not.
5. In this book the cosmological argument represents the attempt to make a case for the rationality of theism. Suppose someone finds a fatal flaw in this argument. Is theism forever defeated? Is there some other way of making a rational case for theism?

For Further Exploration

Donald R. Burrill, ed., *The Cosmological Arguments* (Garden City, NY: Doubleday, 1967).

Norman L. Geisler and Winfried Corduan, *Philosophy of Religion*, 2nd ed. (Grand Rapids: Baker, 1988).

John Hick, ed., *The Existence of God* (New York: Macmillan, 1964).

J. P. Moreland and Kai Nielsen, *Does God Exist?* (Nashville: Thomas Nelson, 1990).

7

God and Evil

The Holocaust

Vignette 1: My family moved to the United States from Germany when I was thirteen years old. My brother and I enjoyed getting to know and becoming friends with a number of Jewish classmates, which was a new experience for us. One such boy, Randy, used to ride his bicycle home with us from summer school. One day he invited us to his house for lunch. We had sandwiches and talked about each others' worlds. When the conversation ran to religion, Randy said, "We are atheists." I did not immediately recognize the English word, so he clarified: "We do not believe there is a God. If there were a God he would never have allowed the killing of the Jews in the war."

From the Depths

Vignette 2: When pastoring a small church, I was called upon to visit an elderly woman in the hospital. She had just had her second leg amputated. Needless to say, she was miserable. When I first entered the room, she had tears streaming down her face. She was staring at her large-print New Testament. She felt let down by the God she had served faithfully all her life, and she was wondering if God had broken His promises to her.

Adam and Eve

Vignette 3: Yet another Saturday night; yet another coffeehouse, this time the Pilgrim's Cave in Washington, D.C. I played the late set, sometime around midnight. I closed the usual melange of Peter, Paul, and Mary as well as Bob Dylan tunes with a few Christian songs I had recently written. In the jargon of the sixties I said to the audience, "If anyone would like to dialogue about what I'm singing, I'll be glad to sit down and rap with you." (Groovy!)

After my set, two couples about my age called me over to talk. They said that I had gotten them thinking about God, and they were stuck. Could I please tell them what I thought? If there were a God, why did He allow famines, earthquakes, diseases, and other natural disasters? Of course I was glad to oblige.

"Don't blame God," I said. "God created a perfect world. But when Adam and Eve turned against God, they brought the whole world down with them. It's all our fault, not God's."

Where Was God?

Vignette 4: A few years ago, Taylor University, where I teach, was numb from the shock of a real tragedy. Toni, one of our students, had apparently committed suicide by leaping out of an upper-story window. While her fellow students were still grieving, I came to the unit on the problem of evil in my apologetics class. I knew what might happen, so I laid out the nature of the problem as gingerly as I could. Nevertheless, I got the reaction I had hoped to avoid. After I had talked briefly about God's power and control over the world, Jackie, a student who had been close to Toni, blurted out with a mixture of grief, fear, defiance, and accusation in her voice, "Are you saying that God could have stopped Toni from jumping and He didn't?"

In the last chapter we made a case for the plausibility of theism (belief in God). Before going further, we need to make sure our house is in order and we do not suffer from similar maladies as the other worldviews that we have criticized. If theism contains an internal inconsistency, we have not made any progress after all.

Some people believe that they have found such a defect in the incompatibility between the all-loving and all-powerful God of theism, and the undeniable reality of evil in the world.

Sticking to the Point

A crucial matter needs to be clarified at the outset. What we are about to consider is the intellectual side of the problem of evil. We want to face in rational terms the question of whether the reality of evil is incompatible with the God of theism.

There is another side to the problem of evil—the emotional, personal side. As we go through life we experience various forms of suffering, and they may cause us to question the meaning of our lives and God's personal love for us. In passing through such a crisis, the answers to the intellectual problem of evil may be of very limited help. Such a time frequently calls for emotional, spiritual, and psychological support more than for rational discussion of conceptual issues.

However, that does not mean that our present undertaking is useless. It only means that its utility is limited by its intent: it is a rational answer for a rational question. I do not believe that a rational answer alone will provide emotional comfort; but how much real emotional comfort can there be in a falsehood?

An Example and a Methodology

The problem of evil begins as a problem of apparent inconsistency. Let us remind ourselves of the nature of an inconsistency (as described in chapter 5). We have an inconsistency when we try to affirm two statements that cannot both be true at the same time, though they could both be false. Here is a pair of statements that appear to be inconsistent:

1. I own a brand new Porsche.
2. I do not have a car to take to school in the morning.

Now it would appear that these two statements cannot both be true. If I own a Porsche, I can get to school; if I do not have a car to take me there, I must not have a Porsche.

How would one normally deal with such assertions? The easiest approach would be to show that one or the other is false. I do not have a Porsche, or I do have transportation. Then the inconsistency vanishes, and the problem is solved.

What if we have good reason to believe that both statements are true? Then we would do what most readers have probably done by now already, namely find some kind of explanation for how both statements could be true. We can call this explanation a "mediating context" and express it with some further statements, such as

    3. a. My Porsche is a model car;

or

    3. b. My Porsche was totaled in a wreck.

If such a third statement is true, then statements (1) and (2) can also both be true.[1] Then once again the problem is taken off our hands.

Still, inquiring minds might want to know more information. Did I really have a wreck in a Porsche? If so, is there evidence for it? Or, how did I come to have a model of a Porsche as my only car? In other words, we are not going to be truly satisfied unless the mediating context we provide is also plausible. A lot of statements can remove the logical inconsistency, but only a plausible one will begin to answer the intellectual inquiry.

Of course we are not interested here in the question of my transportation possibilities but in the much weightier issue of God and evil. The two propositions in question are:

    1. God exists as omnipotent and omnibenevolent being;

and

    2. Evil is real.

Let us dissect this problem. "Omnipotent" means "all-powerful" and refers to the fact that God can do anything in harmony with His nature. Presumably that would include abolishing evil. "Omnibenevolent" means "all-good and all-loving." It implies that if there is some good which God can do, then He will want to do it. Clearly the abolition of evil is a good, and an omnibenevolent God would want to bring it about.

As we saw in the previous chapter, these two properties are a part of theism. If theism is true, then there exists a being who can abolish evil and wants to do so. This last point would lead us to believe that, given theism, there can be no evil in the world.

The truth is, however, that there is evil in the world. I am a little nonplussed when people ask me to define evil at this

---

[1]Technically, what we have done is to find a third proposition that is consistent with one and implies the other. Cf. Alvin Plantinga, *The Nature of Necessity* (Oxford: Clarendon, 1974), 165.

point. I tend to think that the meaning is obvious. My first temptation is to say, "Whatever you don't like," but that would be a little too subjective. Instead I will supply a general list that includes sin, crime, disease, immorality, earthquakes, and flat tires. We need neither a comprehensive definition of evil nor an exhaustive list of all evil to know that evil is real.

If the above is true, theism must not be true after all. An omnipotent God can abolish evil; an omnibenevolent God would want to abolish evil; and yet evil is still present. God must either be unable to abolish evil or not want to. Then He is either not omnipotent or not omnibenevolent (or possibly even neither one). In either case, theism, which is premised on a God with both properties, is false. An all-good and all-powerful God cannot coexist with evil.

A first look at the situation appears to show not only that our two statements are inconsistent, but also that, of the two, the first one must be false. Apparently there cannot be an omnipotent and omnibenevolent God.

Our job is to show that God and evil can be compatible after all. This task may not be an easy one, but we should not feel restrained from using all resources at our disposal. At times defenders of theism feel that in dealing with the problem of evil they may use only such information as is granted to them by their opponents. This is nonsense that destroys the case for theism. The theoretical problem of evil arises specifically out of the supposition of theism. Take away God, and there is no problem of evil Thus, since the problem is caused by theism, we must solve it with theism. Consequently we are free to explore theism to its fullest and make use of any insight included by theism in order to protect theism. In short, an internal problem may be solved internally.

A Sideglance: Four Unsatisfactory Explanations

In our paradigm case about my nonexistent Porsche, we saw that the quickest and easiest move was to deny one or the other statement. This has frequently been done with the issues involved in the problem of evil as well. It is clear, though, that any such maneuver would be self-defeating for our intentions. It hardly makes sense to attempt to salvage theism by scuttling an integral part of it. Nonetheless, if only to keep the record straight, let us look at the way this has been tried.

First Explanation: God Does Not Exist

The most extreme form of denial pays the heaviest price for alleviating the inconsistency. True, if there is no God, we do not have to worry about why He should tolerate evil. But this only multiplies the problems with the given reality of evil. Without a God behind the world, suffering and evil can be no more than painful indicators of the futility of a meaningless life. Atheism certainly creates more problems than it solves (remember our discussion of atheism in chapter 5).

Second Explanation: God Is Not Omnipotent

If God *cannot* abolish evil, then there is no inconsistency between His existence and the reality of evil. Even God is not obligated to do what He cannot do. Such an approach is advocated by Harold Kushner in his popular book *When Bad Things Happen to Good People.*[2] Kushner places limitations on God. God cannot

- violate the laws of nature;
- contravene events that come about by chance; or
- go against decisions we made with our free will.

Since evil results from such causes and God cannot undo them, God cannot be held responsible for evil. In fact, Kushner's God would very much like to see evil abolished. He hurts with us when we hurt and cheers us on when we do something about evil, but His role is restricted to that of the cheerleader God of panentheism. We should not expect God to take a direct hand in clearing away evil for us. Kushner informs us that we need "to forgive the world for not being perfect, to forgive God for not making a better world, to reach out to the people around us, and to go on living despite it all."[3]

---

[2]Harold Kushner, *When Bad Things Happen to Good People* (New York: Schocken, 1981).

[3]Ibid., 147.

Aside from endorsing a finite God—we would be conceding the case against theism—it might be useful to point out once more how futile a worldview based on a finite God is. We saw in chapter 5 that panentheism is practical atheism since we cannot expect God to have a real effect on the world or our lives. If God is too weak to do anything about evil, any hope for a better world can only be wishful thinking. If it comes about, we deserve the credit, not God. In the final analysis, finite godism pays the same unbearable price as atheism.

Third Explanation: God Is Not All-Good

Another all-too-easy solution to the problem of evil is to deny the goodness of God. If God is not all-good, then there is no inherent incompatibility between Him and the evil that is in the world. Maybe He even sent it. This is a horrible notion, to think that perhaps we are in the hands of a deliberately malicious being. Remember that this notion was a part of our original dilemma: an omnipotent being who does not abolish evil could not be omnibenevolent.

Few writers have espoused this position, but we can mention two, both of them Nobel Prize winners. In his book, *The Plague*, Albert Camus depicts the story of the Algerian town of Oran, which is beset by a plague epidemic.[4] The Jesuit priest of the town, Father Paneloux, defends the idea that God sent the plague, both as a punishment and as a test of faith. In either case, we ought to submit to God. The protagonist of the story, Dr. Rieux, protests that if God sent the plague, then we must fight against God as well as against the plague. A broader message in Camus' later writings is that we must rebel against anything opposing humanity, even against a God who sends evil. Elie Wiesel also questions the goodness of God. After suffering through the horrors of the Nazi concentration camps,[5] he concluded that God is malicious for having allowed the holocaust to occur.

Again we see how the idea of an evil God alleviates the inconsistency. Still we recognize that, if we make this

---

[4]Albert Camus, *The Plague*, trans. Stuart Gilbert (New York: Modern Library, 1948).

[5]Elie Wiesel, *Night*, trans. Stella Rodway (New York: Hill & Wang, 1960).

concession, we have conceded the case for theism. Furthermore, we are entitled to wonder to what extent the idea of an evil God is a rational notion for anyone to hold. Leaving aside for a moment the two most obvious concerns (Can we worship such a God, and what would be the point of it?) what is left of the meaning of the word "God" as opposed to "Satan" if we are contemplating a highest evil being. To what extent is the minimum definition of "God" still intact, or is not an "evil God" like a "square circle"?

Fourth Explanation: Evil Is Not Real

Eastern thought (from India and China) frequently affirms that evil is an illusion which, if contemplated from the right perspective, will disappear. This notion is also a part of Christian Science and many forms of New Age thought. They believe that there is an absolute which stands beyond all rational categories, including the distinction between good and evil. If we can see things from the vantage point of this absolute, this distinction fades away. Evil is not real; it is merely the "dark side" of a force that also has a "light side." In the end, these are two sides of the same coin. Even Darth Vader turns out to be Luke Skywalker's caring father.[6]

The problems with evil as illusion are manifold. It attempts to hide the bitter hurts of human experience behind a philosophical doctrine—and a poor doctrine at that. If evil is only an illusion, what is the status of the illusion? Is it good or bad? Advocates of this view want us to get beyond the illusion of evil because we are causing ourselves pain by clinging to the illusion. Then the illusion itself is evil, and there is an objective standard of good and evil after all. Calling evil an illusion briefly postpones the problem, but we still have to deal with the fact that we are beset by an evil illusion.

Of course this approach has no place in theism anyway. The goodness of God is not just a one-sided perspective on something beyond good and evil. The theist intends to say that God is intrinsically good in the sense of the exclusion of

---

[6]The most galling thing about this ending, possibly one of the sappiest in all of movie history, is how easily one gets carried away by the emotional sentiments of the moment. *Return of the Jedi*, Lucasfilms Ltd., 20th Century Fox, 1983.

all evil. Christian theism in particular maintains that "God is light; in him there is no darkness at all" (1 John 1:5, NIV). Conversely, theism demands that the evil we encounter is not just the relative underbelly of an undifferentiated reality. It is intrinsically bad and opposed to the goodness of God.

Towards an Answer

Now we are back to the issue at hand. If there is this irreconcilability between God and evil; if God can do something about the evil, why doesn't He? It is one thing to impugn non-theistic answers; it is quite another to come up with a plausible response from within theism. In five steps we will build up to a promising answer. The first three steps are intentionally very limited.

Step 1: God Did Not Create Evil

Let us be clear on this: God might be responsible for evil even if He did not create it. However, did God create evil? This is not the form in which we most often encounter this question. Usually I hear it as, "*Why* did God create evil?" Yet is it true that God created evil?

This issue seems especially acute because of the argument of the last chapter. If God is first cause of the world, He caused everything in the universe. We emphasized this point by tracing all positive qualities back to Him. We said that if there is good in the world, then He must have caused it, and He must possess infinite goodness. Should the argument not also work the other way around? There is evil in the world; therefore, God must have caused evil, and God Himself must be evil.

There is a time-honored response to this consideration based on a suggestion of how we should picture the nature of evil in our minds. Both Augustine and Thomas Aquinas argued that evil is not something. *It does not have being in the same way in which positive things have being.* The first time you hear this your reaction may be the same as mine was: somebody made this up just to get out of a hole, but please give the following explanation a chance.

Consider the following analogy. I am carrying an umbrella on a rainy day. By and large the umbrella does a fair job of keeping the water off my head; that is good. However, there is a hole in the umbrella; that is evil. For our purposes, the question is, what does this evil consist of? The evil lies, not in the presence of something extra, but in the absence of something that should be there but is not, namely umbrella material. Umbrella material is good; a lack of umbrella material is evil. Let this analogy illustrate a preliminary definition: *Evil is the absence of good.* Philosophers prefer to speak of *the privation of good.* In order for this idea to make sense, we need to add a few explanations.

The privation is real. Anyone who has ever contended with a leaky umbrella knows how real the absence of umbrella material can be. Thus we are not saying that evil is unreal; it certainly is very real, so the privation theory of evil is not the same as the Eastern theory that evil is an illusion. The absence of something that should be there is a painful, objective reality. Think about how real and painful death is, yet its reality is the absence of the loved one.

Not every absence is immediately an evil. Thomas Aquinas talked about blindness, which for a blind person is an evil (not that the person is evil but that he or she has to suffer from the evil of blindness). Where there should be sight it is lacking. You would not think of a rock as blind and pity it for not having sight. A rock is not supposed to have sight, so the absence of sight in a rock would not count as the evil of blindness. That is why the term "privation" is better than "absence"; it implies that something is not only absent, but is missing when it should be there.

The privation theory of evil has very narrow applicability. It is logically possible to describe an earthquake as the absence of stability in the earth's crust, or the Holocaust as the absence of all human decency. However in doing so we have not gained much. It would be more helpful to invoke categories of natural evil and moral evil respectively to understand these things. The privation theory only becomes truly useful in a more remote metaphysical sense—such as asking if God created evil.

The privation theory helps us see that God did not create evil. Since evil is not something, but the privation of something, it does not need a cause. The question "Did God create evil?" makes no more sense than the question "Did you bake your term paper?" Term papers are not the kinds of things that you bake. In the same way, evil is not something that exists which must have had a cause for its existence. It does not have being; it is a cancer within being. Thus it could not have been created.

Somebody or something must still be responsible for evil. Even privations do not happen on their own. Something must be responsible for them. When we are talking about an omnipotent and omnibenevolent God, everything that occurs happens on His watch, and so He is still responsible for the fact that He permitted a privation to infest His creation. He allowed evil to occur, but He did not create it. The creation of evil was the issue for this section, and we have an answer.

Step 2: God Would Only Have Created the Best of All Possible Worlds

G. W. Leibniz (the same one who formulated the principle of the identity of indiscernibles) came up with a clever argument in response to the problem of evil.[7] It is within the basic concepts of theism. Leibniz's concern revolves around this question: Given what we know about God, what kind of world can we expect Him to have created.

In a manner of speaking, Leibniz has us looking over God's shoulder as God is about to create a world. At this point Leibniz reasoned as follows:

God is omniscient. Therefore He is familiar with all the possible worlds He could create. (We can consider a world to be "possible" so long as it is not logically self-contradictory or does not contradict God's own nature.) Furthermore, He knows which of all those possible worlds would be the best.

---

[7]Gottfried Wilhelm von Leibniz, *Monadology and Other Philosophical Essays,* trans. Paul Schrecker and Anne Martin Schrecker (Indianapolis: Bobbs-Merrill, Library of Liberal Arts, 1965).

God is omnipotent. Therefore He is able to make any of those possible worlds, and, of course, He is able to make the best one.

God is omnibenevolent. Therefore He would only make the best of all possible worlds. An all-good, all-loving being would not create anything not up to the high standards of His nature. He would not make one kind of world if He could make a better one.

Thus Leibniz argued that God knows which world would be best, is able to make it, and would only create the best. Then Leibniz triumphantly concluded that since this world, the one in which we live, is the world God created, this must be the best of all possible worlds.

But can this world really be the best? Most people immediately respond that it cannot be so. After all, it is easy to imagine a world with fewer earthquakes, less cancer, or not so many exams. A better world must be possible. However, the objection is made from the vantage point of finite human beings. We do not know the whole picture the way God does. Of course, God knows about earthquakes, cancer, and exams, but apparently He sees something else that we do not see, namely the big picture. Leibniz argued that somehow the total amount of goodness in the world would be reduced if some of the evil were reduced. Certainly it would be simple to cut back on some of the evil, maybe to avoid one earthquake. Leibniz argued that in the process the whole balance of good and evil would be upset, and the whole world would not be as good.

Thus Leibniz advocated the notion of a total cosmic harmony. Every silver lining must have a cloud. The amount of evil in the world enhances the total amount of goodness. We can express this idea with two equations:

- Nothing but good in the world = fixed degree of goodness;
- Good + some evil in the world = greater total degree of goodness

To summarize this complicated argument: *God would only create the best of all possible worlds. Since there is evil in the world, it must serve the purpose of making this world better.* Before raising our eyebrows too high and picking this argument apart, I want to make two points: (a) this is a logically valid argument, and (b) the basic idea that God would only create the best world possible seems plausible.

Can we swallow the idea that this present world with all of its apparent defects truly is the best that God could have done? Historically Christians have said no; we are still waiting for a better world, heaven.

Skeptics have poked fun at the notion that God could only make a good world by allowing for so much evil. The best example of this approach is Voltaire's novel, *Candide*.[8] It records the misfortunes of a young man named Candide, whose greatest trial may have been having to listen to his teacher instruct him that "all is for the best in this, the best of all possible worlds." In short, no one finds Leibniz's conclusion particularly convincing.

Note that Leibniz's idea meets all but our last criterion. If God did in fact create the very best possible world, and if that world must of necessity include evil, then the inconsistency has been eliminated. An omnipotent and omnibenevolent being and the reality of evil would then be compatible. However, few people are satisfied with the assertion that was supposed to remove the logical problem. Yes, God would create only the best world. No, this cannot be it (at least, not yet).

Step 3: Evil Must Be the Unavoidable Condition for the Highest Goods (Such as Freedom)

There is one way of salvaging Leibniz's considerations. That is to point out specifically how evil functions in enhancing the goodness of the world. We are all used to the idea that sometimes an evil is the unavoidable condition for a higher good. In that case *evil does not become good,* but it carries out a good function in facilitating the higher good. Consider an analogy: if you should have a gall bladder operation, you are in for a bit of pain. That pain is bad, but it serves a useful function. Without undergoing it, you would not get better

---

[8]Voltaire, *Candide or Optimism* (New York: Appleton-Century-Crofts, 1946). Voltaire lived from 1694 to 1778. Read this book. Of all the books you are supposed to read to become educated, this is the one you want to read. You will laugh and acquire a bit of culture.

and would have to suffer from chronic gall bladder problems. This illustration falls far short of dealing effectively with the problem of evil, but it puts into view the fact that sometimes a first-order evil facilitates a second-order good.

Can we make such a case on a more general basis? Many people have said so within the framework of the so-called *free will defense*. The basic assumption is that evil is the unavoidable condition to make human free will possible. Let us look at it in more detail.

The first step in the free will defense is to say that *God will actualize the highest values possible*. One such value is that creatures have freedom to make significant moral choices. Any unfree, constrained choice is not nearly as good as one made out of one's own free will. Consequently, God (whose nature it is to create the best) would make free creatures.

Two quick explanations need to be inserted here. Obviously, someone who does not believe in the reality of free will cannot go along with this defense. Calvinists and behaviorists, who do not accept this idea of free will, can hardly stipulate it as a high value in the world.[9] They can rejoin the line of argumentation with the next section. Second, let us, for simplicity's sake, think of human beings when we speak of free creatures. Perhaps similar lines of thought apply to angels, some of which are also fallen; but we know even less about angels than we do about humans, and at best it would only serve to push the argument back a step without gaining any ground. Thus the operative statement is that God would have created a world with free people in it because that would have been the highest value.

The second step in the free will defense is to say that *evil is the unavoidable price tag for freedom*. True freedom implies that God would not influence our choices. Free creatures are free to disobey Him as well as to obey Him. God knew that we would eventually disobey Him. He was willing to pay that price in order to promote the higher good of freedom. If God

---

[9]John S. Feinberg has written a clever article on this point. "And the Atheist Shall Lie Down with the Calvinist: Atheism, Calvinism, and the Freewill Defense." *Trinity Journal* 1 (1980): 142-52. I might mention here that, as a Calvinist, I have to exclude myself from this defense as well.

had interfered so as to prevent human misuse of freedom, freedom would have been lost.

In this way the free will defense attempts to clear up the original inconsistency. God as an omnipotent and omnibenevolent being would create the best world—one including free creatures. Evil came about because those creatures misused their freedom. That is too bad, but it cannot be avoided. It is not God's responsibility, and thus our problem is solved.

Beyond a doubt, the free will defense is the most used approach to the problem of evil. It is logical, fairly plausible, and it appeals to our sense of importance in the scheme of things; but it contains a serious problem that makes it less useful than a lot of people think.

The question is this: Was evil really unavoidable? Did God have to pay the price of allowing evil in order for us to have freedom? The answer, as surprising as it may seem at first, is no. The idea of freedom prohibits God's directly influencing our choices, but there is another way of making sure of the desired outcome, namely by limiting the circumstances within which we choose.

Let us take this slowly. Assume that I have genuinely free will. My choices are still limited by circumstances. I cannot sensibly choose to be a world-class oboe player or the olympic gold medalist in butterfly swimming; I just do not have what it takes. I cannot reasonably choose to spend next semester on Mars: the laws of the universe and the policies of my university will not permit it. In short, pure unbounded freedom of choice does not exist. If we do choose freely, it is still within the limit of options given us.

Thus it is possible to influence someone's choices simply by arranging for an environment of circumstances. Parents do so with children. They teach them to exercise their capacity for choices within restricted options. At some time as a teenager, a person may have to decide whether to smoke. Parents would not expect a four-year-old to make that choice. They would protect the child from making the wrong decision. That does not mean that the child does not have freedom of choice within the range of choices available to him or her; but, because the parents know the child would choose poorly, they do not allow him or her to make choices beyond his or her capacity.

Now we come to the crucial point of this objection to the free will defense. God could have done the same thing with human beings. There is no logical reason why He had to let us free creatures lapse into disobedience. God could have arranged our available choices in such a way that we would be free but would only freely choose to obey Him. An omniscient and omnipotent being should have been able to do that.

In fact, we have two good indications of how such an arrangement could have looked. I am introducing two pieces of Christian theology here, not to beg the question in behalf of Christianity but simply to make the point that these are believable possibilities.

First, within the stipulation of this defense, God created Adam and Eve as free creatures who freely loved God. God did not have to place the tree of temptation in the garden. Adam and Eve's freedom would not have been abrogated by the lack of a tree. It is beside the point that their free obedience is somehow more meaningful in the light of the tree. Adam and Eve's free obedience would still have been free obedience, and that is all that counts for the argument at hand.

Second, we can point to the Christian idea of heaven. People who believe in free will typically do not believe that such free will is lost in heaven (though I have witnessed some puzzling momentary conversions to Calvinism at just this point). There is no sin in heaven. In other words, heaven is supposed to be exactly the kind of environment to which I am appealing: free creatures choose freely only to obey and not to disobey. If God can arrange things this way at the end of time, why could He not have started out that way?

If our objection is correct, the free will defense does not work. The defense is predicated on the idea that once God gave His creatures free will, evil became unavoidable. If, as we have tried to show, evil does become avoidable even for creatures that have a free will, then the defense fails. Evil is not the necessary price tag for freedom. Thus we are back to where we started. By allowing evil into the world, God must have a purpose beyond giving us freedom. *God must have had a good reason for permitting evil to happen.*

Step 4: The Present World Must Be the Best Way toward the Best World

Let us start again with the atheists' argument at its worst. Here is what it might say:

1. An omnipotent and omnibenevolent being would abolish all evil.
2. There is evil in the world.
3. Therefore, there can be no omnipotent and omnibenevolent being.

This is clearly bad reasoning. Consider the analogous argument:

4. My cat will eat all the mice in my house.
5. There are mice in my basement.
6. Therefore, I do not have a cat.

Of course the correct conclusion, as long as I have reasonable grounds to believe that I have a cat, is:

6. a. My cat *will* eat all the mice in my basement.

Similarly, we do have good reason to believe that an omnipotent and omnibenevolent being exists (see the last chapter). Then the correct conclusion to the above argument must be:

3. a. The omnipotent and omnibenevolent being will abolish all remaining evil.

Now we have introduced the future tense into our consideration and are ready to pull a few points together.

- Given God's nature, we can expect God to bring about the best of all possible worlds—a world without evil.
- Since the present world is not yet the best, we can definitely count on God to bring about the best world in the future.
- There is evil in the present world. This evil must then serve the purpose of facilitating the coming of the best world. In other words, the present evil is the needed requirement for making a better world than would have been possible without it.

The last statement is entitled to two further explanations. First, the affirmation that the present evil is a needed requirement for making a better world than would have been possible without it is premised on the assumption that the future world is an improvement over anything in existence until now. We saw that this is a reasonable expectation given the nature of God. We might also add that this idea fits in well with traditional religious forms of theism (including Christianity, Islam, and Judaism) in which there is a future hope of heaven. This is more than the restoration to an earlier stage. For example, in Christian theology the future state of glorification is seen as something greater than simply a return to Adam and Eve's state before the Fall.

Second, the affirmation that the present evil is a needed requirement for making a better world than would have been possible without it is premised on the assumption that some good cannot occur apart from some evil. This fact represents the pattern of a lower-order evil being the necessary condition for a higher-order good. Let me once more illustrate the principle involved. These analyses are in no way intended to do justice to all of the realities involved but only to indicate the pattern. You cannot have courage without having danger; you cannot have pity without having suffering; you cannot have redemption without having sin. Certain values cannot possibly be attained without certain evils as logical prerequisites. Even God cannot do the logically impossible.[10] Thus it is reasonable and plausible that God (in bringing about the best of all possible worlds) is using whatever evil is logically necessary to do so.

We concluded our discussion of the free will defense by observing that God must have had a purpose in allowing evil to come into the world. Evil was not just an accident to have happened to God and the world. God did not *create* evil, but He *permitted* evil so that He could make something even greater than would have been possible without it.

---

[10]If you believe that this fact somehow impugns God's omnipotence, you do not understand the nature of His omnipotence. God's omnipotence does not mean that He can do anything you can express in words, no matter how ridiculous—for example, make a square circle, make Himself disappear, make a stone so heavy that He cannot lift it. It means that He can do anything in *keeping with His nature*. And His nature is nothing if not rational.

Please do not misunderstand: evil is still evil, but God is using it to make a higher good. In philosophical jargon, this is not the best of all possible worlds, but it must be the best way to bring about the best of all possible worlds.

Step 5. *This Is the Worst of All Possible Worlds*

I find it helpful to look at the flip side of the above argument. We just said that God uses evil in order to bring about the best of all possible worlds. Exactly how much evil would God use to accomplish His purpose? Exactly as much as it would take. No less, because God would put to use whatever it took to bring off the best of all possible worlds; but also no more, because useless gratuitous evil would still be contrary to God's nature.

Let us latch onto the idea that God would not allow any more evil than is absolutely necessary to accomplish His purpose. That means, in short, that it is as bad as it can get. Not that a far worse world is unimaginable. We can conceive of a world with more earthquakes, more cancer, and more exams. However, *there is a limit as to how much evil God will allow: only as much as is required to bring about the best of all possible worlds.*

This conclusion helps me grasp a few corollaries. First, it lets me look evil straight in the eye and recognize it for what it is. There is a lot of evil in the world, and it does no good to gloss over it. Second, it helps me focus on the point that evil is in the final analysis under God's control. It is never pointless or excessive in terms of God's over all plan, even if we do not understand it. Third, it allows me to embrace the good in the world. Leibniz was a very astute man, yet he could confuse the worst of all possible worlds with the best. That shows how much good there is even in the worst. Finally, it reminds me that there is a cosmic dimension to the problem of evil. I cannot (in fact I am quite sure that I should not) figure out for every individual occurrence of evil how it contributes to the higher good. I get bothered by the facile rationalizations with which people try to overcome difficulties. Does God really let people die of cancer so that one or two others wind up with an improved prayer life? I try not to lose sight of the fact that from God's perspective, the entire pattern fits together seamlessly. The best of all possible worlds is coming!

This has been a complicated chapter with a lot of back-and-forth argumentation. Let us summarize what we have tried to accomplish.

First, remember the purpose of the discussion. We are confronting a possible problem with the worldview of theism. To repeat an earlier statement, we are trying to provide a rational answer to a rational question asked by rational people. This endeavor is closely linked to the spiritual and emotional trauma caused by evil, but it should not be evaluated simply on the basis of how much comfort it provides.

Second, let us summarize the problem and its proposed solution. We set up the problem as a possible inconsistency between the existence of God as an omnipotent and omnibenevolent being and the reality of evil. We said that God did not create evil, but He must have a purpose in allowing it. That purpose must be that God is using evil as He is preparing the very best possible world. Thus there is no inconsistency between the two statements; they can both be true, and there is no fatal flaw in theism.

Now we can respond to the opening vignettes, plus one that I have saved for the end.

Response to Vignette 1: Randy was voicing the most commonly heard objection to theism. I certainly cannot deny the emotional force of his complaint. It can be very hard to maintain faith in God in the light of horrendous evil, but the objection still does not follow. Even an evil as incomprehensible as the Holocaust need not count against God's existence. I would not even want to try to find some specific good to have come out of it, but I do not see the whole picture the way God does. I am sure that even the most outrageous evil we encounter must somehow contribute to God's overall plan for the world. After all, it is presently the worst of all possible worlds.

Response to Vignette 2: Here we have the typical situation in which something is called for other than intellectual reconciliation of a potential inconsistency of two propositions. I read some Bible verses with this woman. We prayed together. I gave her as much comfort as I could, assuring her that God had not abandoned her. Within a day or so her faith had rebounded. Please think about this: I could not have given her emotional comfort if I had been plagued by intellectual doubts.

Response to Vignette 3: As you now know, I would no longer take this approach since I do not believe that the free will defense by itself gets the job done. Adam and Eve would not have lunched on the apple if God had not allowed it to be included in His plan. Put me into a similar conversation today, and I will not talk about human beings, but about God and what we can know about His nature and purposes. Then I would try to get the people to see that even though evil makes us wonder about what God is up to, it can very well fit into His plan.

Response to Vignette 4: If there was a really good way of answering Jackie, I did not manage to find it, and so she was upset with me. The whole problem of evil pivots around this very difficulty. An omnipotent God could have prevented the tragedy. From where we see things, an omnibenevolent God should have prevented it. So why didn't He? I do not know why God did not stop Toni, and I do not ever expect to. Still that is not the issue under consideration. The point here is that Toni's mistake, no matter how tragic, does not count against the reality of an all-loving and all-powerful God. It does make His ways less understandable to us.

God Is in Control

A Fifth Vignette: June and I were standing next to the hospital bed of our younger son, Seth. His little four-year-old body was doubled over with rheumatoid arthritis, his joints red, swollen, and too painful to move. A local pastor, whose church we had visited twice about a year earlier, recognized our names on the list and stopped by. After exchanging the usual superficialities he asked if he could pray with us, and of course we agreed. He closed with words something like the following, "Lord, please heal this boy so that his life may be back in Your will and plan for him."

After the pastor had left, June and I looked at each other and immediately expressed the same thought: This can't be. Nothing that happens can be outside of God's plan, even if we neither like it nor understand it. The idea that our suffering is included in God's purposes for us may not sit very well, but the idea that God could ever be out of control is too horrible to contemplate.

At the time we had no idea that this was only the beginning of a lot of hurt involving the health of both our boys. June and I have spent much time puzzling, questioning God, and even being angry with Him. Still we know that God has not let go of the reins, that nothing happens outside of His purpose. This has helped us to make sense out of difficulties and to continue to trust Him.

For Growth and Study

Mastering the Material

When you have studied this chapter you should be able to:
1. Sketch out the apparent inconsistency that gives rise to the problem of evil.
2. Describe four attempts at dealing with the problem of evil that deny an important part of theism.
3. State the privation theory of evil and tell why it is significant for the question of God's creating evil.
4. Defend Leibniz's "best of all possible worlds" theory; then show why it is not believable.
5. Make a case for the free will defense; then explain why it is inadequate.
6. Describe the "best-way" defense. Show how it combines elements from Leibniz's "best-world" defense and the free will defense.
7. Explain the "worst-world" concept and the benefits it includes.
8. Identify the following names with the contribution to which we have alluded in this chapter: Augustine, Thomas Aquinas, G. W. Leibniz, Albert Camus, Harold Kushner, Elie Wiesel, Voltaire.

Thinking About the Ideas

1. In this chapter we have focused on the intellectual side of the problem of evil. What other sides are there? How are they interrelated?
2. Consider the sub-theistic explanations of the problem of evil. Why is it that people are willing to sacrifice their concept of God in order to have an answer for evil?
3. To what extent could a concept of a limited God find a place in a genuine, possibly even biblical, theism?
4. Research arguments for and against human free will. Why is an answer not necessarily important for understanding the problem of evil?

5. Contrast the "best-way" defense with other theories, such as Eastern illusion theory, the "best-world" theory, a finite-God theory.
6. Distinguish between the following concepts: (a) evil counts against God; (b) evil counts decisively against God. Can one hold (a) without holding (b)?
7. Why does a good answer to the problem of evil still leave us puzzling, questioning God, and at times even being angry with Him? Why does the tension not go away?

For Further Exploration

Norman L. Geisler, *The Roots of Evil* (Grand Rapids: Zondervan, 1978).

Michael Peterson, *Evil and the Christian God* (Grand Rapids: Baker, 1982).

Nelson Pike, ed., *God and Evil* (Englewood Cliffs, NJ: Prentice-Hall, 1964).

Alvin C. Plantinga, *God, Freedom, and Evil* (Grand Rapids: Eerdmans, 1974).

8

Miracles: Liability and Asset

Clear Head

Vignette 1: It was lunch hour at the hospital where I was working as an orderly—one of a number of such jobs I held during the long years of pursuing degrees. We were talking about the fact that I had just finished my master's at a seminary and was getting ready to leave for Houston to work on my Ph.D. The nurses could not quite figure out if I was going to be a professor, a pastor, or something they had never heard of. One of them asked my replacement orderly, whom I was training at the time, "What about you, Jim, are you religious, too?"

"Well," said Jim, "there are times when I feel like I want to believe in God. But with a clear head, I can't bring myself to believe in resurrections, healings, and such supernatural things. After all, we live in the twentieth century."

Miracle Versus Science

Vignette 2: The professor was lecturing our class on the scientific method. "Science concerns itself with evidence—things we can see, measure, verify. In religion people accept impossibilities on faith. In science we have no use for the supernatural or other superstitions."

A student asked, "What if you had hard scientific evidence for religion? Like a miracle or something?"

The professor waved off the idea. "That's impossible. The two categories are mutually exclusive."

"But why?" The student persisted. "Say you have complete incontrovertible evidence that something happened that contradicts all laws of science."

"That still wouldn't prove you had a miracle. It would only mean that something very unusual occurred. Maybe we don't have a scientific explanation for the event yet, maybe we never will. That still does not mean that something beyond the laws of nature happened."

Experience with Healing

Vignette 3: Scott was on staff of the Natural High Coffee House; that is, when he showed up. One year out of high school, he spent a lot of his weekends going to Jesus People rallies in the pursuit of spiritual goose bumps. At times, he would call in sick, so that he could attend a meeting. His boss, after all, "did not understand Jesus People."

One evening Scott came to the coffeehouse, all excited about the rally of the previous night. "It was great," he told me. "They were healing people and driving out demons. There was one person whose one leg was two inches too short. They prayed, and the leg stretched out the extra inches."

But is it true? We have tried to show that theism is true. But is Christianity the true theism? In the next chapters, we will try to make the case that it is. Our goal is to show by the life and miracles of Christ that He is the Son of God. As anyone can immediately tell, this agenda raises many questions, such as whether we can know anything about the historical Christ or whether He did miracles. And, speaking of miracles, there is no point in this entire discussion if we do not, at the outset, settle the question of whether it makes sense for a rational person to believe in miracles. We are operating within the methodology of hypothesis testing. The hypothesis in question for this chapter is that it is possible to know and recognize miracles.

Miracles are a *three-edged sword,* if you can picture such a thing. They are both an asset and a liability; but even as an asset they can become a liability again. Some people say miracles prove the truth of Christianity. Others say they disprove it. If we allow their possibility, we need to contend with the fact that other religions have their miracles, which they believe prove their truth.[1] The following chart tells the story:

---

[1] A thorough study that will be of value throughout this chapter is Colin Brown, *Miracles and the Critical Mind* (Grand Rapids: Eerdmans, 1984).

Miracles Impossible	*Miracles Possible*	
liability	*other context*	*biblical context*
	liability	asset

There was a time when miracles were considered a major asset to Christian apologetics. Thomas Aquinas refered to the authority of Scripture as "an authority divinely confirmed by miracles."[2] In this vein someone might say; "Christianity must be true, just look at the miracles!" All of that has changed. With the coming of the Enlightenment and the rise of deism, fewer people believed in miracles. The Christian's claim to miracles became a liability. "Christianity must be false," someone might say. "Just look at the supposed miracles."

A simple argument rehabilitating all miracles is going to be less than helpful. Many religions other than Christianity also claim miracles, and they also use them to support their own truth. For purposes of this study, we are specifically interested in evidence for biblical miracles. Evidence for Buddhist miracles would not necessarily pull the rug out from under us, but it would certainly clutter our argument if we had to live with the fact that they were all valid.[3]

In fact, throughout this discussion ask yourself the following: How would I respond to the evidence for biblical miracles if it were presented on behalf of another religion? Suddenly you find yourself playing the role of the critic. Look at an example. Why do you believe in the resurrection of Jesus? Many students give me the well-memorized answer: there were eyewitnesses present. Even so, you were not one of the eyewitnesses, and you have not talked to any of them. All you have is their records in a two-thousand-year-old book. Would you accept that kind of evidence for Buddhist miracles?

---

[2]Thomas Aquinas, *On the Truth of the Catholic Faith (Summa Contra Gentiles)*, vol. 1, ch. 9, trans. Anton C. Pegis (Garden City, NY: Doubleday Image Books, 1955), 77.

[3]Of course miracles done in a Buddhist context do not prove that Buddhism is true. In the same way we are not simply going to point to miracles in a Christian context and say that Christianity is therefore true.

My point for now is simply to show how complex the issue of miracles is. In later chapters we will look at the factual questions about the historical accuracy of the New Testament and specific miracles, such as the Resurrection. In this chapter we will consider two questions: (1) do miracles happen? and (2) how can we recognize a miracle?

Do Miracles Happen?

The problem is not with giving an answer to this question; the problem is with giving an answer that is not simply arbitrary and question-begging. Let us look at the argument from the perspective of someone who rejects all miracles.

Hume's Argument Against Miracles

David Hume (the same one who brought up the criticisms against the teleological argument) contended that no miracles have ever been plausably known to occur. We will look at his argument in three stages.[4]

1. All knowledge is to some extent a matter of probability. You do not have to buy into a full-fledged skepticism in order to accept this premise. Hume is not saying that no one can know anything. He is saying that no matter what the subject of our knowledge might be, there is always the chance that we might be wrong. In other words, he is not denying the possibility of knowledge; he is including the possibility of error, be it ever so slight.

2. The knowledge with the highest probability is knowledge of the laws of nature. I might wind up being wrong about a good many things, but if I refer to the laws of nature, I am not going to be disappointed. They have never been known to work improperly. Consequently, for all practical purposes, the laws of nature cannot be violated.

3. For any alleged miracle, it is more probable that the supposed witnesses were mistaken than that the laws of nature were violated. Suppose I told you that the last time I was in Washington, D.C., I saw the Washington Monument move over by a foot and then move right back again. Would you believe me?

---

[4]David Hume, *An Inquiry Concerning Human Understanding* (Indianapolis: Bobbs-Merril, Library of Liberal Arts, 1955), 117-41.

Probably not. You would try to find some reason why I must have been mistaken. That does not mean that you would question my integrity or accuse me of lying. Buildings do not waltz, so something else must have happened. Maybe my bifocals jiggled.

David Hume applied this approach to any report of an alleged violation of the laws of nature. In each case he wanted you to ask yourself: What is more likely, that a law of nature was actually broken, or that a fallible human being, as sincere as he or she may be, made a mistake? Surely, Hume would submit, it is always more likely that the witnesses were mistaken. We rely on the laws of nature; we expect them to hold. If reasonable people have to choose between a violation of the laws of nature and human error, they will choose the latter as much more probable.

Take for example the Resurrection. Four people reported that a dead man, Jesus, has come back to life, but it is a solid law of nature that dead people stay dead. So we ask ourselves Hume's question: What is more probable, that a corpse was resuscitated or that these four people were sincerely mistaken? The odds have to favor the notion that the four people were wrong. A reasonable person would have to say that no matter how pious and saintly the four witnesses may have been, they could not have been accurate.

Note the subtlety of Hume's argument. He does not say that the Resurrection could not have happened. He says if it had, we could never know it. The same argument would apply to any other alleged miracle. Thus the conclusion of the matter is that for purposes of what we can actually know, we can rule out the occurrence of miracles.

Response to Hume

What appeals to me the most about Hume's argument is its common sense approach to the knowledge we use every day. We expect the laws of nature to hold. I do not expect you to believe that I saw the Washington Monument dance a jig. If I told you I just saw a resurrection, I would want you to be skeptical; in fact, I insist on it. I am allowing you the same degree of incredulity that I reserve for myself. Even so, the problem with Hume's argument is that he absolutizes it, going beyond what can be tolerably accepted.

1. *A theistic worldview softens the probabilities.* We have worked hard at establishing a theistic worldview. There is no reason why we should now have to forget about it. We spent three chapters making a case for theism, first by debunking other worldviews, then by establishing theism, and finally by fortifying it against the problem of evil.

The possibility of miracles should now be set within a theistic worldview. Whether it is possible to know miracles in a non-theistic worldview is relatively uninteresting to us here, though I am inclined to agree with Hume in that case. Other Christian apologists disagree; they believe it is possible to establish the existence of God beginning with the Resurrection. Nevertheless, I am not sure they could ever get around Hume's objection. For our purposes, having clearly established the existence of God, we need not focus on anything but a theistic worldview.

A central tenet of theism is that God is immanent in the world (remember our description at the beginning of chapter 5); God is conceived of as present and active within the world. That idea softens the status of the laws of nature as supposedly inviolable. Our basic experience of nature is still just as uniform and unbending; but we must allow for the fact that there is a higher power behind it, namely the God who created nature with its laws and who is not subject to those laws.

Thus the probabilities may shift. Is it always more likely that the witnesses were mistaken than that a miracle occurred? Not necessarily. Given a theistic universe, if we have reason to suspect that God may have intervened directly, it may be more likely that a miracle occurred. Rather than judging probabilities in advance, the final decision may have to depend on particular cases.

2. *Miracles do not violate the laws of nature.* It may be helpful at this point to seek to clarify the nature of a miracle. David Hume treated miracles as violations of the laws of nature, but Hume's understanding of what happens in miracles is clumsy and inaccurate.

In some miracles the laws of nature are superseded. When Jesus resurrected Lazarus, turned water into wine, and walked on water, He was defying our laws of science. Our understanding of the world says that such things should not happen, but nothing has been broken or suspended. The normal operation of the laws of nature has been superseded by the act of the Creator who made them.

Let us look at two analogies. You approach a traffic light in your car. It turns red just as you get there. You are about to stop, but there is a policeman in the middle of the intersection waving you through; so you proceed and cross against the light. You did not break any law; nor was the law concerning traffic lights suspended. The authority of the policeman superseded it at that moment.

Here is another analogy. You nimbly leap off the high dive board and in a graceful swan dive proceed downward. There is a law of physics that says that you will continue your downward progress until you either reach the center of the earth or chance upon a solid obstruction and smash to a pulp. (We have a euphemism for this scary reality called the law of gravity.) However, there is water in the pool, and happily the laws of buoyancy supersede the law of gravity; so instead you enter the water, and, after a few moments of submersion, you arc to the surface only to glide smoothly to the edge of the pool. You did not violate the law of gravity; it was not suspended; it was superseded by the laws of buoyancy. In the same way, we ought not to picture the laws of nature as self-contained and autonomous, so that God must break them to do a miracle. They are at all times subordinated to God (remember, He is first cause). Anytime that God wants to, He can manipulate events on the basis of His higher authority.

Some miracles consist of the unexpected configuration of events. Consider the following unlikely story.

At nine o'clock in the morning on Tuesday you have a term paper due. You actually get it done early Monday afternoon and take it across campus to show it to a friend. Unfortunately, a strong wind blows it out of your hands; you see it flutter into the back of a pickup truck speeding along the road on the edge of campus; and it is gone. Your graduation depends on your passing the course, and your passing the course depends on your having the paper in on time. There is no way you can redo it, so you pray for a miracle. The next morning you walk into the classroom, minus a term paper. The professor sees you, thanks you for dropping off the paper at her house in the morning, and tells you that you got an A. Your graduation is assured. You are left speechless, except to thank the Lord for a miracle.

What actually happened was that your paper traveled on the back of the pickup for a few miles and then fluttered off again. It lay on the sidewalk for a short time; then it was picked up by an eighth-grade boy and his friends on their way home from school. He wanted to make paper airplanes out of it, but his mother told him that he had to do his homework instead because they were going to the circus that night. Your term paper sat on their table for the remainder of the afternoon together with a sports magazine that had just come in the mail that day.

The boy decided to read the magazine on the way to the circus and scooped up your paper along with the magazine. He wound up carrying both into the tent, left your paper on his seat, and it blew into the arena. The elephants came out for late-night rehearsal; one of them stepped on your paper, and it stuck to his foot. It got scraped off right in front of his cage, where it spent most of the night.

When the milkman came into the circus village that morning, he saw the paper on the ground. Since he was a graduate student working his way through school, he was interested in the topic and picked it up. He straightened it out by putting it between two milk bottles and continued his rounds. Because this milkman had not slept for seventy-two hours on account of studying and delivering milk, he had a serious accident right in front of your professor's house. Your term paper got thrown out of the milk truck, and a breeze wafted it right to her front porch, where it nestled gently into the screen door. When your professor got up a little while later, she found your paper there and was impressed by your dedication in having the paper there for her that early.

Everything that happened was in complete accord with natural laws. Nevertheless, I believe you would be entitled to claim a miracle. The miracle consists of the coming together of many small events, each of which has a fairly high probability by itself, so that the chain of events strikes us as improbable. Combine this unlikely chain with the fact that you believe that the Lord carried it out, and you claim a bona fide miracle.

Many biblical miracles are such *configuration miracles*. They do not defy any known physical laws; the miracle consists of the fact that some natural events took place at one particular time in accord with apparent divine agency. An example would be the crossing of the Red Sea by the Israelites. The Bible tells us exactly what happened in terms of natural causes: an east wind blew the water away right in time for the Israelites to cross; when the Egyptians came, the wind let up, the water came back, and they drowned. The Bible unequivocally considers this one of its central miracles. The fact that these events came together in just this way takes it out of the realm of the natural into the supernatural.

Thus we see the other serious problem with Hume's understanding of miracles. There is not even an inkling of the violation of the laws of nature in these configuration miracles. If Hume tried to set up his scheme of weighing probabilities, there would be nothing to counterbalance the report of the witnesses because nothing occurred that stands in direct contradiction to physical laws. Hume's argument against miracles is unacceptable, not only because it is arbitrary but also because it does not do justice to a proper understanding of what miracles are supposed to be.

How Can We Recognize a Miracle?

The above observation takes us to the second major point of this chapter. *How can we be sure that this event was a true miracle?* Wouldn't somebody be justified in claiming that, remarkable as such coincidences may be, they are still nothing more than that—namely, purely natural events that just happen to come together in a most astounding way? Could we not say that there is nothing to make us think of it as a miracle? How do we recognize a miracle? Or is that at all possible?

The Critic's Case

A number of writers have argued that from the scientific point of view, there really cannot be such a thing as a miracle.[5] Antony Flew is one such critic of miracles.[6] Flew's argument runs like this:

1. *The whole idea of modern science is premised on the notion that we can approach nature as governed by uniform laws.* If we began with the idea that nature is unpredictable and that the laws work at some times but not at others, there would be no point to science.

2. *Science has had a lot of success, but there are still many things that scientists do not yet know.* The point is that we go on learning, probing, and experimenting. In the process we come to know more, and at times we have to revise what we thought we knew.

3. *An event that we cannot currently explain on the basis of scientific laws may not be considered outside of the realm of science.* We simply have not yet advanced enough in science to understand the event. At the heart of science is the assumption that the event is in keeping with some natural law. If you do not share that assumption, you have abandoned science.

4. *Science requires us to expect a natural explanation for unusual occurrences.* Suppose a dead person came back to life. Water was turned to wine. An iron axe head floated on water. The nature of science demands that you still expect there to be some natural explanation for this event. Such an explanation may be a long time in coming, we may not even have any idea what such an explanation would be like if we had it. If you are being scientific at all, however, you are committed to the idea that there still is a very unusual, but very natural, explanation somewhere within the universe.

5. *The essence of science is that there can be no miracles.* Divine interventions superseding the laws of nature would eliminate the basic presuppositions of science. Thus we will never be

---

[5]E. G. Patrick Nowell-Smith, "Miracles," in Antony Flew and Alasdair MacIntyre, eds., *New Essays in Philosophical Theology* (London: SCM, 1955).

[6]Antony Flew, "Miracles," in Paul Edwards, ed., *The Encyclopedia of Philosophy*, vol. 5 (New York: Macmillan, 1967), 348-49.

able to recognize a miracle as such. Somewhere there must be a natural explanation lurking in the background.

The Rules of the Game

As persuasive as Flew's argument is, there is something inherently wrong with it. It demands that we play by some unfair rules. It is as though someone told you: "I will play tennis with you. If you make a fault, it's a point for me. And if I make a fault, it's a point for me." In other words, the rules are written in such a way that the person cannot lose.

Christians, in their eagerness to communicate with non-Christians, have often adapted their argumentation to the rules as laid out by the non-Christian. This is commendable, but there comes a time when you have to realize that the non-Christian has boxed you into a corner. He or she has invented rules that are specifically designed to keep you from ever being able to make your case. "We will assume that there can be no God. Now prove to me that there is a God." Or, "Miracles are by definition impossible. Can you prove to me that miracles can happen?" This is fatuous, and there is no reason why we need to observe those strictures.

There is no argument available against the critic who has made up his mind that, by definition or by scientific presumption, miracles cannot occur. That is not the fault of the person who believes in miracles. The critic has decided to cut off dialogue on the issue. Since he or she has already informed us that no argument can possibly count against his or her position, it would be foolish to offer further arguments for miracles.

Science has to have reasonable explanations for phenomena we encounter in nature. We discover regularities, causes, effects, principles, categories. The point is to accumulate knowledge. When a critic like Flew appeals to yet-to-be-discovered, so-far-unheard-of, possibly-beyond-all-comprehension laws behind some apparently miraculous event, he is not being particularly scientific. He is inventing something unknown and obscure as well as unverifiable in order to avoid the supernatural. However, there is nothing natural or scientific about such an explanation.

Even so, many reasonable people are looking for evidence for miracles and are open to the possibility. We can direct our arguments to these people, hoping that these arguments will have something to say to the more severe critics as well.

Again we must not forget theism. When we scan the world to see if we detect a miracle somewhere, we are not looking at pure nature, we are looking at creation, put into place and governed by a Creator. This is not an arbitrary rewriting of the rules in our favor, for, as we already said earlier, we have earned the right to invoke theism. Thus the question becomes: Can we recognize miracles in a theistic context?

Definition and Flexibility

A miracle is an event so unusual that, given all the circumstances, the best explanation is that God intervened directly. We must now use this definition to help us identify a miracle if we should come across one.

Note how unspecific and subjective this definition is. It leaves room for disagreement, but that is precisely a part of the idea. There is no reason why we should be able to have an ironclad rule that in all cases allows us to identify infallibly that a miracle has taken place. Even Christians disagree among each other at times about whether a particular event is a miracle or not. For example, in John 10 we read the story of Jesus' escaping from a crowd of people by walking through their midst. Some commentators consider this event a miracle, but others only see it as Jesus' exercising authority over other people. There is a certain amount of room for interpretation when it comes to deciding which event is a miracle and which is not. Many other events, such as the Resurrection, are more definitely miraculous.

We have two components to this general definition. First, we see that the event must be highly unusual. As we saw, this unusualness can show up in one of two ways. Either the event appears to defy known physical laws (*the superseding miracle*), or a set of events seems too improbable to come together on the basis of coincidence alone (*the configuration miracle*). Somehow something happens that rational people, in touch with the normal workings of the world, would not have expected to happen.

Second, one would look for some intervention by God in the event. Coincidences and unusual things do happen; so, in order to be called a miracle, the event should be the kind of occurrence in which we might look for God's direct intervention. By "direct intervention" we mean that God is directly responsible for bringing about this unusual event. Christians recognize God's hand in providence (His everyday care for us) as well as in answered prayer, but we may consider God to have answered a prayer even if the answer consists of an otherwise normal event. Only when we are confronted with the "unusual" and see that God's action is the easiest explanation for it are we inclined to call it a miracle.

Not All Explanations Are Created Equal

All of the above sounds fairly arbitrary. One person looks at an event and says it is a miracle; another person looks at the same event and says it is not. Who is to say who is right? How can we recognize miracles on such a subjective basis?

I already conceded that there is some room for disagreement, but saying that much is a far cry from the notion that either option is equally as good an explanation for an event. Sometimes one explanation is clearly better than another.

Suppose that I am sitting in my office trying to concentrate on my writing. I notice my old gray floppy hat on the coat hook at the far end of the wall. How did it get there? Several explanations are possible:

a. I wore the hat to school this morning and hung it up when I entered my office.
b. I left my hat home this morning, but my wife, figuring I might need it later, drove out to bring it to me.
c. Last night a burglar stole my hat, repented of his deed, and hung it up in my office while I was not looking.
d. The dean of the university, in an effort to convince the board of trustees of the impoverished state of

the faculty, sent an associate dean to my house to pick up my hat and put it on display in full view in my office.

e. The Hindu god Shiva, who delights in playing pranks, miraculously transported my hat from my home to the office.

f. A group of extraterrestrial invaders mistook my hat for a hostile life-form and hung it on the hook to die a slow and painful death.

g. The object I am perceiving is not my hat at all but a clever hologram produced by some unknown fiend.

h. Who knows? The imagination has no limits.

Are all of these explanations equally likely? Of course not. The point is to show that different explanations have a very differing degree of likelihood. How we assess the probabilities depends on the circumstances, our knowledge of the world, and a dose of plain common sense. There is no formula to assess it, but none is needed.

Given my normal routine, (a) is by far the most likely. If I knew for sure that I could not have worn that hat to school (perhaps because I still had another one on my head) (b), (c), or (d) would become possibilities. For each of those cases I would want to have some more information before they become probable. (My wife and I agree that of these three, (b) is the least likely.)

I am not going to give (e), (f), or (g) a whole lot more thought. They are completely extraneous to my understanding of the world, and I have no evidence to reconsider that understanding. To accord those options any probability would demand, not only that the circumstances be drastically different, but also that they would have to be so different as to induce me to alter my worldview.

Thus we see that we would think in terms of a *reasonable presumption*. When confronted with alternative explanations, we immediately favor one over the others. It is the one most congenial to our understanding of the circumstances and expectations. Reasonable people can still disagree over which is the reasonable presumption, but it is not arbitrary. It cannot be decided on in advance of knowing the full story.

An Important Example

Now consider the following set of circumstances. Around the time of the Roman occupation of Palestine, there lived a very unusual man. Let us, for the sake of argument, assume that the historical records we have about Him are accurate. Then we see that this man taught about the God of theism, saw Himself as the agent of God, even as God Himself. He described all of His works as the work of God. In God's name He healed sick people, blind people, and others who were afflicted in various ways. He turned water into wine, fed thousands of people with five loaves of bread, raised people from death, predicted His own death and resurrection, which then occurred in accord with His predictions.

It is conceivable that all of this was coincidence. We cannot at this point in the book rule out the possibility that maybe some as-yet-unheard-of, unknown, natural law was at work. Is this the reasonable presumption? Everything in the accounts of the circumstances as we have them is geared in the direction of one presumption: that these are miracles occurring in a theistic context. Maybe that presumption will turn out to be wrong, but to rule it out a priori without considering the evidence is not the reasonable presumption. How far will a critic go in order to protect his presupposition?

Why, then, am I closed to the possibility that Shiva deposited my hat in my office? There is nothing in that statement to make it a reasonable presumption for me. I have no reason to adopt a worldview centered around Shiva. The circumstances do not point to Shiva as the agent in any other way. If those conditions were met, I might have to consider the possibility more closely. In fact, if I were even a little more open to the possibility of Shiva's existence, and if I were in a Hindu temple observing a Brahmin performing miracles in the name of Shiva before my very eyes, Shiva's agency would become a far more reasonable presumption. I am convinced that it would turn out to be false on further inspection, but I would be unreasonable if I would not bother considering it.

The Balance Sheet

How do we recognize a miracle? The circumstances must be highly unusual and set up in such a way that the most reasonable presumption becomes divine intervention. Thus the hypothesis for this chapter stands: *it is possible to know and recognize miracles*. With this conclusion we have made some gains, but we have incurred further liabilities.

The Gains

Miracles are possible; miracles are knowable; miracles are recognizable. Given a theistic worldview, Hume's argument loses its absolute force. Given an approach based on reasonable presumption, Flew's argument is shown to be an exercise in pure circularity. Thus the main two concerns of this chapter are answered.

The Liabilities

Looking backwards, I would not have much hope for this line of argumentation apart from an acknowledgment of theism. Most debates about miracles are beside the point. When someone has shut the door absolutely to every possibility of the supernatural, as unreasonable as such a foreclosure may be, it makes little sense to debate a particular miracle with him or her. The discussion needs to go back to the topic of theism. Why is theism true and why are other worldviews false? Unless there is openness to the possibility of divine intervention, a case for divine intervention in a particular instance cannot succeed.

Looking ahead, the issue becomes one of evidence. For any given claim, are the circumstances such that the reasonable presumption is divine intervention? After we investigated the claim, is the most reasonable conclusion that a miracle did occur? It comes down to cases. We have to reckon with the theoretical possibility that despite our openness to the possibility of miracles, no particular miracle can be verified in reality.

Since we are interested in biblical miracles, the liability becomes even greater. The only way we can examine these miracles is to concern ourselves with events that happened two thousand years ago. How such a task can be possible is the subject of the next chapter.

For now we can return to this chapter's vignettes.

Response to Vignette 1: Jim manifests a common attitude that gets more and more puzzling the longer one thinks about it. What do we really know about miracles in the twentieth century that people in other ages did not? Nothing, actually. We have had a lot of success explaining a lot of things, but it is a leap into the unknown to argue that there is no supernatural and that miracles are impossible. Every age has had its believers and skeptics to varying degrees of excess. If we are going to pride ourselves on being more scientific than other ages, we should be more willing to judge these matters on evidence rather than presupposition. The refusal to believe in anything supernatural is not the sign of a clear head but of a mind thoroughly made up.

Response to Vignette 2: I have a lot of sympathy with the attitude expressed by the professor. If we use God as an explanation anytime we get stumped, we are really not explaining anything. Somebody asks why frogs are green. We answer, because God made them that way. Then, why are roses red and the sky blue? Simply to bring in God again would be worthless. An explanation that explains everything explains nothing. Thus science is based on the idea that we look for the most immediate explanation that covers the item in question. Most of the time that will be a natural explanation.

Science is also premised on the importance of evidence. If all the evidence points in the direction of something supernatural, the scientist who rules out the supernatural from the start is no longer being scientific. The best, most immediate explanation may very well be that a miracle has taken place. I am not saying that a scientist should always embrace that option, but never to consider it may be just as unscientific as bringing it in too soon. Again, it comes down to cases.

Response to Vignette 3: God can stretch out legs if He wants to. He may have done so at that rally; but I was (and still am) dubious about Scott's account. Believing in miracles does not mean we have to be gullible and swallow every sensationalist account we hear about or see displayed in the papers at the supermarket check-out. Scott had already made it clear that he had no problem defining the truth in accords with his spiritual purposes. So I just smiled and said something about how interesting that story was.

Let me add a word of caution. As we proceed with our argument over the next few chapters, we will show that some important beliefs ride on the historic miracles of Jesus. These miracles are far more momentous than the special effects sometimes produced at revivals or rallies. *Do not let your personal faith ride on special healings and other momentary points of excitement, even if they are real.* God may have other things in store for you as well (see the last chapter). Let your faith depend on objective realities, and thank God for special miracles if He should provide them. Thank Him also for times of painful growth because He may also provide those.

For Growth and Study

Mastering the Material

When you have studied this chapter you should be able to:
1. Tell why miracles are a three-edged sword, that is, why there are two liabilities and one asset in the topic.
2. State the three points of Hume's argument against miracles and show why it is plausible.
3. Show why Hume's argument does not have full force within a theistic framework.
4. Distinguish between two different kinds of miracles and tell why they do not violate the laws of nature.
5. State Flew's argument against ever being able to recognize a miracle.
6. Explain the notion of reasonable presumption and show how it defeats Flew's argument.
7. State what, in general, would be necessary for us to recognize an event as a miracle.
8. Identify the following names with the contribution to which we have alluded in this chapter: Thomas Aquinas, David Hume, Antony Flew.

Thinking About the Ideas

1. Research the claims for miracles in other religions, focusing on the amount and type of evidence available for them.

2. Research various descriptions of the scientific method. To what extent would they rule out supernatural explanations?
3. We have identified two kinds of miracles, superseding miracles and configuration miracles. Can they be combined? Is a third type possible?
4. Distinguish between the following concepts: presupposition, hypothesis, reasonable presumption, conclusion. How are these distinctions crucial in approaching miracles?
5. Set up an ideal case in which all the evidence points to a miracle having taken place. (Here is your chance to be creative and funny.) Have someone else try to find a hole in it.

For Further Exploration

Colin Brown, *Miracles and the Critical Mind* (Grand Rapids: Eerdmans, 1984).

Norman L. Geisler, *Miracles and Modern Thought* (Grand Rapids: Zondervan, 1982).

C. S. Lewis, *Miracles* (New York: Macmillan, 1947).

John W. Montgomery, *Faith Founded on Fact* (Nashville: Thomas Nelson, 1978).

9

Back to the Past

Nobody Really Knows History

Vignette 1: Todd was a philosophy major when I was an undergraduate at the University of Maryland. He attended one of our campus evangelistic meetings, more from curiosity than anything else. He and I wound up chatting afterwards. It turned out that he identified with an understanding of Christianity that had more to do with existentialist philosophy than the Bible. After our brief discussion, we agreed to talk some more.

A few days later we ran into each other when both of us had a few minutes to spare before our next classes. Todd gave me the opportunity to tell him about the objective work of Jesus Christ for our salvation. His response was that I was giving one interpretation of Jesus, but others were possible.

"I guess the only way to resolve this," I allowed, "is to check the facts of history."

"History?" was Todd's immediate answer. "That's only so much of what people say must have happened. Nobody really knows what did happen."

Challenge of Differing Accounts

Vignette 2: When my older son, Nick, was thirteen, he undertook an in-depth study of the story of Roanoke, the British colony in Virginia that disappeared without a trace early in the seventeenth century. He made many trips to the library and consulted different sources, most of them going back to the colonial British themselves. Slowly he began to piece together the puzzle of what happened to these settlers.

165

Then one day he came across a completely different account. This one was from a Native American. It not only called some of the standard interpretations of the event into question but some of the facts as well. Whom was Nick to believe? There was no readily available way of deciding who was telling the truth, so he shelved the project for the time being.

Eyewitness Testimony

Vignette 3: One spring I gave my standard lecture on the Resurrection. I discussed the available evidence and how Christ's resurrection from the dead is the best theory to fit that evidence. When I was done, Jack, a bright student, came up to me and said, "Let me double-check. You are saying that there were no eyewitnesses. No one actually saw Jesus coming out of the tomb."

"That's correct," I replied. "If there were any, we don't know of them."

"Then I don't see how you can believe that it happened. I think we should only accept those facts as historical that are based directly on eyewitness testimony."

Male History

Vignette 4: The guest lecturer was facing the class, a smile on her face but a note of stridency in her voice.

"What you have to face is that we are all caught in one big circle. What most of you consider Christianity is Christianity as developed by the male half of humanity for the advantage of males. It has a long history, but it is a history written by males for the advantage of males. In fact, almost all so-called history is simply the propagation of a male point of view."

Just because miracles are possible, does not mean that a miracle has ever occurred. To be more specific, it is one thing to say that in a theistic framework a case can be made for the reality of the Resurrection, but it is another thing to evaluate the case. Did the Resurrection actually happen? We cannot decide that matter simply by wafting philosophical arguments back and forth. Sooner or later we have to look at what actually happened in history.

Is it possible to look at the facts of history? Many people say that you cannot. You can look at theories and interpretations of history, but it is impossible to get back to the facts themselves. A bedrock set of historical events is not available to us. Consequently there can be no way of checking on our conclusions about history by appealing to "what really happened."

In that case, we are in serious trouble with the rest of this project. If there is no hope of ever checking whether the Resurrection happened, it hardly makes sense to use the Resurrection to make a case for Christianity. Thus we need to expend some effort in exploring the nature of history. What can we know? How can we know it? The hypothesis we want to test in this chapter is the following: *it is possible to have genuine knowledge of historical events.*

This chapter proceeds in two parts. The first part will have a rather pessimistic tone; it will describe the obstacles to writing history. In the second part we can hopefully work our way out of the problem and show how it does become possible to have genuine historical knowledge.

The Problems of Writing History

How does a historian do research? A chemist goes into a lab; a biologist might go out into the field; but what does a historian do?

The historian cannot travel back into the past. Some of my favorite movies involve the notion of time travel, but flux capacitors do not actually work in reality. If a historian wants to do research on Thomas Jefferson, she cannot simply dial in 1776 and go back for an interview.

Instead, the historian studies *documents*. These are written records of many different types that somehow shed light on the historical events in question. The historian's task is to study the documents, evaluate them, and somehow build a coherent story from the information contained in the documents.

The Nature of Documents

If the word "document" brings to your mind images of officially sanctioned, meticulously checked transcripts, you are in for a disappointment. Even though the historian may on occasion work with official transcripts, more often than not the documents under her consideration are going to be far less imposing than that. What we now consider to be historical documents can be anything written that helps us understand the story. This can include letters, news accounts, court testimony, folk tales, sermons, food orders, graffiti, and many other types of materials.

Often, the historian does not have the original of the document in question. All that may be left is a copy of the lost original. By "copy" I do not necessarily mean something directly copied. It could be a quote taken out of context inserted into another document. We must also recognize that no document depicts everything that was said and done involving a particular event. This would be patently impossible.

According to a wide-spread story, Marie-Antoinette, Queen of France, when told that the peasants had no bread, said, "Let them eat cake!" Let us say you are a historian wanting to find out if she really said that, and if so why, and what its effect was. Where would you look? Chances are nobody was following the queen around that day, writing down every last word that she uttered. Somebody wrote it down later, to make a point: somebody was trying to illustrate exactly how obtuse Marie-Antoinette was.

This hypothetical example illustrates three problems with historical documents.

1. *Historical documents are incomplete.* Even if they are remarkably well preserved, they never tell the whole story. They all begin too late and end too soon. They only give us one piece of the puzzle.

2. *Historical documents are removed in time.* Except for rare exceptions, there is going to be a gap in time between the event and the recording of the event.

3. *Historical documents are biased.* All historical records reflect a point of view. In fact, it may not be an overstatement to say that everything ever written had some kind of purpose, and the purpose affected the writing. Consequently the historian needs to keep in mind that any document must, by its very nature, bear the imprint of the person who wrote it. It may be difficult to sort out factual information from personal opinions.

This last point deserves further consideration. There is such a thing as systematic bias. I saw some of it in action recently when I was doing research on a spiritual writer from the fourteenth century. Back in 1310, Margaret Porette was burned at the stake in Paris (for believing much of what I believe). Church officials had decided that she was a heretic, and she suffered the traditional penalty for heresy. She had become known as a leader in a heretical group known as the Brethren of the Free Spirit. Now if you begin to read the official church records about this group, you are in for some hair-raising descriptions. Apparently the Free Spirit movement consisted of blaspheming pantheists who used every available opportunity for the worst kinds of sexual immorality.

A more careful look at the evidence makes it clear that these charges were unsubstantiated. Margaret's and the movement's major "crime" may very well have been their failure to acknowledge the authority of the official church powers, and it is very likely that the official records were *ex post facto* descriptions of what anyone outside of the church was presumed to be like according to the authorities. These were not actual descriptions of what they *were* like.[1] A particular "official" version had become standard information and was simply being copied from document to document without being questioned. If the historian is aware of systematic bias of this nature, she can take it into account in her evaluation of the evidence; but if she does not realize that systematic bias is at work, she is going to be a part of the unconscious propagation of falsehood.

Bias may also have the best of motives. Frequently in the Middle Ages, chroniclers believed that glorifying God and His servants was far more important than recording the facts. Barbara Tuchman (possibly my favorite historian) tells us of the exploits of the great knight Coucy as related by the chronicler Froissart. Just when we are thrilled by the depiction, Tuchman explains that "nothing of the kind happened."[2] The modern reader wants the facts, but the

---

[1] An excellent book on this subject is Robert E. Lerner, *The Heresy of the Free Spirit in the Middle Ages* (Berkeley: University of California Press, 1972).

[2] Barbara W. Tuchman, *A Distant Mirror: The Calamitous Fourteenth Century* (New York: Ballantine, 1978), 277.

medieval listener preferred Froissart's glorious fiction. In short, not only are all historical documents biased in some way, sometimes they are deliberately and systematically biased. Somehow the historian has to see through all of that.

Telling the Story

What does a historian do with the documents she has studied? Her job is not simply to string all of the facts together or to mindlessly amass as many details as possible about any one event in the past. The historian is supposed to tell a story.

The story must contain a coherent sequence of events. We must be able to discern what caused an event and what the effects of an event were. We must be able to sort out important from unimportant events. The story has to make sense.

Thus the historian begins with the imperfect documents we described above; then she fills out a coherent picture that makes sense out of them. Obviously she may inject her personal bias into the procedure. This is inevitable. Every step of the way, she must interpret the documents; and the history she writes becomes *history as she sees it*. There appears to be no way around this.

The Dilemma

We seem to be in a catch-22 situation; regardless of how we approach the project of writing history, we wind up with skepticism. Apparently there is no way of actually getting back to the events as they really happened. There are two options on how to set up a historical investigation, but both of them wind up at a dead end.[3]

Option 1: The documentary approach. We can stick exactly to the information in the documents—nothing more, nothing less. Whatever we read in the documents goes into our story; whatever is not there must not be filled in. We tailor our conclusions to exactly what our data say, and we avoid exceeding our data in any way. It is tempting to think that this is the only way to proceed with integrity.

---

[3]A good summary of all of the issues and attempted resolutions is provided by William H. Dray, *Philosophy of History* (Englewood Cliffs, NJ: Prentice-Hall, 1964).

The problem with the documentary approach is that it does not work. As we saw above, the documents are incomplete, biased, and removed in time. Sometimes they even contradict each other. If we stick to the documents alone, we are left with a box full of puzzle pieces without any hope of ever putting them together. In short, if we try to stick to this approach, the result is historical skepticism.

Option 2: The Theoretical Approach. The only alternative left seems to be to begin with some kind of theory and then to accommodate the documents to our preconceived ideas about what must have happened. Although this approach may appear to lack scholarly integrity, in practice this is what historians do. They have a notion of what must have happened, and they fill out their theory with the documents they read.

Sometimes this approach manifests itself on a large scale. Communist countries, such as the East German state, used history books written from the Marxist perspective in their schools. When the East German regime collapsed in 1989, a crisis hit the schools because they did not have history books written from a capitalist point of view. They had to stop teaching history for a few months! Thus we see how the theoretical approach to history is a normal way of operation.

There are obviously problems with the theoretical approach. If we subordinate the documents to our theories, we may wind up learning more about our theories than about the records of the past. History that is written in that way becomes *history of what we think happened,* but not history of what really happened. We do not have access to the facts, only to our theories about the facts, and so the result is, again, historical skepticism.

How to Write History: The Solution

Everything we said above is correct, but it is overstated. In order to rescue ourselves from the shoals of skepticism and come up with a workable solution to the problem of history, all we need to do is rethink what is involved in communication at any given time. How do we interpret written records, historical or otherwise?

The Hermeneutical Circle

In Greek mythology, *Hermes* was the messenger of the gods. The study of how to interpret communications is named after him: *herme-neutics*. Hermeneutics is also sometimes called the science of understanding. How do we understand what someone is trying to communicate to us? The nineteenth-century German theologian Friedrich Schleiermacher said that the process of understanding is always circular. That is why it is sometimes called the *hermeneutical circle*.

Imagine you receive a letter from a close friend. As you slit the envelope, you have certain expectations of what you are about to read. You do not expect to be billed for so many cubic feet of gas or to read a formal notice telling you that your job application has been rejected. You expect to read certain personal information having to do with the circumstances in which you and your friend live, as you are familiar with them.

You read the letter. Some of your expectations will be met: "I knew he was going to say that!" There will be some surprises: "That's the last thing in the world I would have expected him to write!" Then you put the letter aside.

A few days later you get around to answering the letter. You get it out to refresh your memory. Now your expectations are much more refined. You have fairly detailed advance knowledge of what you are going to read, but as you read, you may notice more details and connections that escaped you the first time. If you decide to read the letter a third time, you come even better prepared, but you may pick up even more insights.

Each time that you go through the process you learn more. Now you are obviously not able to read your friend's mind. He may have intended to convey something in the letter that you keep missing even after reading it quite a few times. For that matter, you may be constantly reading something into the letter that your friend never intended. In other words, communication is not perfect, but *just because your communication is imperfect does not mean that you are not communicating at all.*

This is what happens every time communication takes place, including any time we try to understand a written text. Thus we get the picture of the hermeneutical circle:

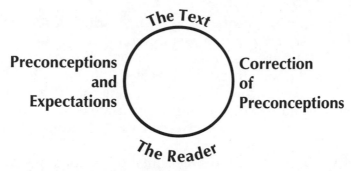

Each time you try to understand a piece of literature, a homework assignment, a movie review, or anything else, you move around this circle. You cannot break out of it, but there is no reason why you should want to since you gain new information by moving around it.[4]

We can also apply the same model to the work of the historian:

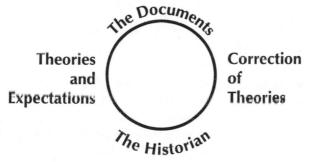

The point of this model is to show that the work of the historian is much more dynamic than our earlier dilemma allowed. Yes, the documents are imperfect; yes, the historian brings theories to her work; but we do not have to think in terms of one dominating the other. A much better picture is

---

[4]This model also applies to biblical interpretation. In fact, that is actually where it arose, and it is a much-debated topic. I have summarized the issues in an article, "Humility and Commitment: An Approach to Modern Hermeneutics" *Themelios* 11 (April 1986): 83-88.

one in which we think of interaction between the historian's theories and the documents.

Evaluating the Documents

The purely documentary approach to writing history leads to skepticism only on the assumption that it is inherently impossible for the historian to judge which documents are more reliable than others. This is clearly not the case. Often one document's word is as good as another's, and there seems to be no way of figuring out which to believe. Yet that does not mean that no one can ever decide between documents. Sometimes we can.

What are the criteria by which to evaluate historical documents? There are no esoteric rules established by professional historians for exclusive use by initiates into their guild, but there are some guidelines grounded in common sense.

Imagine that two friends tell you contradictory versions of the same event. You might not know which one to believe. Then again, let us say that one of the two has an immaculate record for truthfulness. She has a reputation for an accurate memory, has nothing to gain by falsifying the story, and everything she says fits into what you already know. The other friend has been caught in several lies before. He is known to suffer from occasional memory lapses, would come out way ahead by fabricating the story, and the story does not fit with all other facts as you have them. Do not tell me that it is a toss-up as to whom to believe!

The situation is the same with historical sources. Not all documents are equally credible. Here are some simple criteria that a historian would use in evaluating a document:

- How close in time is the document to the event in question?
- Does the author have a reputation for truthfulness?
- Is the document internally consistent?
- Was the author a direct participant in the event in question?
- Does the document report events that are clearly impossible?

- Is the document consistent with other documents?
- Are the events mentioned in the document referred to anywhere else? This is known as multiple attestation.
- Does the document show evidence of systematic bias? Is there some other reason to suspect deliberate distortion?
- If we have only a copy of the original document, is the copy an accurate reproduction of the original?

In a typical brainstorming exercise, my students who are not history majors came up with these criteria, and they are the criteria used by historians as well.

Clearly not every criterion mentioned here is appropriate in every case. This is not a simple checklist with an easy "yes" or "no" for which you add up the scores and assign a reliability factor to a document. When it comes down to cases, historians frequently disagree in their application of the criteria, but clearly there are criteria.

Even though historians can and do disagree, it is inconceivable that a historian will say: I prefer document A over document B because document A was written a long time after the event; document A was copied so poorly that we do not know what it really must have said; it is self-contradictory: it was obviously written without regard for the truth but only to achieve certain political ends. Therefore, I believe document A. That is not going to happen.

So there are criteria to decide between documents. They are not infallible, and they are not always decisive; but they are available, and, as often as not, they get the job done.

Interpretive Realism

Once we put all of this together, we come up with what the respected Christian philosopher Arthur Holmes has called "interpretive realism."[5] The historian must judge and interpret. There is an inescapable subjective factor in historical writing. However, that does not exclude all reference to reality.

---

[5]Arthur F. Holmes, *Faith Seeks Understanding* (Grand Rapids: Eerdmans, 1971), 78-84.

Somewhere within the process of interpreting, the historian will probably hit bedrock. She encounters some basic events that are not subject to interpretation. There is a reality underneath the theorizing, and sooner or later she may find it.

Martin Luther was a monk who took his spiritual quest seriously. He went through all the disciplines and regimens prescribed in those days for someone seeking salvation, but he still felt inadequate. Finally he discovered that God Himself would give him righteousness through faith in Christ. Luther called public attention to his discovery in response to the monk Tetzel, who was selling time out of purgatory for money. Luther posted his Ninety-five Theses, and the Reformation was underway. Obviously, the above description is only one way of looking at the Reformation. It emphasizes Luther's spiritual quest and theological discovery, but other points of emphasis are possible. An economic interpretation would focus on the massive expense of the Renaissance papacy. The popes were forced to raise funds in Germany, and Tetzel became their agent. The German princes resented having their own territories milked dry by the Italian prelate. When Luther raised questions about Tetzel's activities, the princes jumped on the theological bandwagon. Identifying with Luther's protestantism gave them the opportunity to become independent of Roman taxation.

Further interpretations are possible. A Marxist understanding of the Reformation sees the whole event as one phase of the struggle between the peasantry and the aristocracy. Luther provided the peasants with the opportunity to spite the nobility, though, when it came down to the serious confrontations of the peasant war, Luther supported the nobility.

Thus there are different theories that attempt to pull together the events of the Reformation. You may say, "Why does it have to be one of those three? Can't it be a combination of them all?" Of course it can, but you have a theory at that point. You have traded a simple theory for a combination theory, but the theory is still there.

In all this discussion of theories and interpretive schemes, however, some facts become obvious. There was a

Reformation. There was a Martin Luther who opposed the church's doctrine on salvation. There was a monk Tetzel, who sold indulgences. There was a pope. There were princes and peasants. The list could go on. In the process of sorting through various interpretations, certain historical facts emerge as beyond dispute.

The same pattern applies in other historical investigations. Even though there is room for sorting out *facts* and *interpretations,* some basic facts provide a reference point that is not reasonably put in question. These are the data that historical interpretation seeks to explain, and they are not subject to interpretation.

Back to Basics

At this point, someone might want to ask, "But can you be *really* sure that those things happened? These conclusions result from historical investigation, but this does not mean that the events *really* took place."

Now this objection ought to have a familiar ring to it. It is actually only a specialized version of the matter we discussed in chapter 2 when we made a case for the possibility of knowledge in general. We said that we are entitled to claim knowledge for a belief when it has passed the appropriate tests for truth. What are the tests for truth? This depends on the type of belief in question. Whenever the belief has been justified by the proper procedure, we can say that it has become knowledge.

The distinction between knowledge as construed in this way and "real" knowledge is spurious. There is no such thing. Knowledge apart from what counts as knowledge is a meaningless use of words. The only possible outcome of raising a demand for knowledge beyond knowledge is to get lost in skepticism, which is the denial of any knowledge, including the knowledge that skepticism is true. Skepticism is an impossible position because it denies the possibility of any thought at all.

The situation with regard to historical knowledge is the same. Although serious difficulties are attached to finding out what happened in history, we must be willing to accept whatever knowledge does emerge. The appropriate test for truth in history concerns the proper evaluation of the documents. If a conclusion passes muster on the best kind of examination, we have no reasonable alternative but to accept it as true. To seek refuge in any further appeal to subjectivity is the same thing as looking for knowledge behind knowledge. *The point of historical investigation is to find out the facts beneath the subjective factors.* Once we have done that it is unnecessary to invoke the subjective factors once more. It is asking for historical conclusions without historical conclusions.

You read about the difficulties with historical research earlier in this chapter. They do not go away. I am not now taking with one hand what I gave with the other. I am saying this: *the same procedures that cause us to doubt some historical conclusions also confirm many other historical conclusions.*

Someone might still be dissatisfied with my arguments here. He or she might say, "I am not advocating skepticism. All I want is better tests. I would be a lot more inclined to accept historical facts if they were based on direct eye-witness accounts written by several observers at the immediate point of occurrence. What is wrong with wanting *better* knowledge?"

This objection seems harmless, but it is asking for something that we have no right to request. It still comes down to wanting historical knowledge without historical methodology, and so it is asking for a test for truth that is not appropriate. As an analogy, it would be the same as having someone say, "I will only believe in atoms if you can show them to me with the naked eye." That would not be a reasonable request. Atoms cannot, by their very nature, be seen with the naked eye, and so to demand to see them that way is really to set up skepticism. Similarly, to expect historical conclusions without the normal procedures of evaluating what there is in the documents is in effect arbitrarily to shut the door on historical knowledge.

At the risk of overstating the issue, it really comes down to skepticism versus knowledge. If you arbitrarily deny whatever facts can be uncovered by historical methodology, you are really slurring the whole idea of knowledge as we have delineated it. Why would you believe anything that you have read, heard, or seen? Because of evidence. The same arguments made against any historical knowledge whatsoever would ultimately also hold against any other type of knowledge.

Thus we can conclude this chapter on a positive note. The hypothesis in question was whether it is possible to know what really happened in the past. Our response is that it is. The process is not easy; we may not know all of it, nor all the details of it; but we can know some of it, and that is all that is required.

Our next question is whether biblical history is among the knowable parts of history. For now, we can take a second look at the vignettes for this chapter.

Response to Vignette 1: It's almost impossible to argue with such broad, unqualified overstatements. As I recall, I said something like, "Well, we'll have to talk some more." That was not exactly helpful, but it was probably as helpful as any statement would have been at that point in the conversation.

According to this reasoning, someone could argue that "Neil Armstrong was not really on the moon. John F. Kennedy and Elvis are alive. World War II really did not happen. Reality is only what people have agreed must be real. I am only what people have agreed I must be." Where is it going to stop? There is only one way of deciding any factual matter, and that is on the basis of the appropriate evidence. To attempt an end run around the evidence is to succumb to skepticism.

If I were now given the luxury of sitting down and conversing with Todd about this issue, I would point once again to the viability criterion. Todd lives by the fact that he can know things about the past. All of us do. The only issue left is *what* we can know, not whether we can know anything.

Response to Vignette 2: There are criteria for deciding between historical documents. Sometimes they do not work. It may have been Nick's lack of expertise that kept him from figuring out whom to believe, or it may have been that this truly was one such difficult case. I am inclined to believe the latter because both sides of the debate were represented by competent professional historians. For our purposes, the point is that one such case, even a million such cases, does not impugn all historical inferences. Some historical events are shrouded in mystery,[6] but it would be a leap in logic, of olympic proportions, to say that, therefore, no historical questions are decidable.

Response to Vignette 3: Jack thought he was being rigorous, but he was really being arbitrary. As mentioned above, what he was saying was really no different from persons who say they will not believe in atoms unless they can see them with the naked eye. All of us, including Jack, believe a lot of things apart from direct eyewitness testimony.

In any event, the eyewitness criterion is a red herring because it leads us in the wrong direction. Everybody knows the eyewitness accounts can be unreliable; for example, there are contradictory accounts of car accidents. Even so, historical eyewitness testimony still comes down to us one way, namely through the documents.

Every once in a while someone wistfully says, "If only we had video cameras and television coverage back then. Then we would not have all this uncertainty." Actually, as good as that wish sounds, it is not so helpful as one might think. Just consider all of the controversy concerning who killed John F. Kennedy and why.

Response to Vignette 4: The speaker is by and large right, of course. Make no mistake about the fact that the writing of history is always subjective. Since most of what we currently consider history has been written by white males for the sake of other white males, that viewpoint is bound to come across.

Does a strong bias rule out the factual basis of what the bias is all about? Consider one further example. Last Monday night the Washington Redskins trounced the Philadelphia Eagles. I am a Redskins fan; if I discussed the game, I would do so in glowing terms, emphasizing the brilliance of the Redskins. If I were to associate with an Eagles fan, he would give a different description of the same game, probably in the tone we usually reserve for painful funerals. Our biases would come through, but we would be referring to the same game.

Just because there is bias in the writing of history does not mean that it is all up for grabs. There still is evidence in the documents with which the historian must cope. She is not free to say that since all history is subjective anyway, she can rewrite what happened as she feels it should have happened; and any revision is as good as any other. A few years ago, Marion Zimmer Bradley rewrote the story of Camelot from the point of view of a woman committed to the ancient worship of the goddess.[7] It may make for good reading, and even shed light on our collective

---

[6]In fact, the issue of the Shroud of Turin may be another one.

[7]Marion Zimmer Bradley, *The Mists of Avalon* (New York: Knopf, 1982).

prejudices, but it does not qualify for historical writing because it is not based on scholarly research of the sources.

When historical writing is nothing more than a tool to express an ideology, it quickly becomes the tool of political power. One of the first moves of any totalitarian regime is to rewrite history to fit its purposes. In his novel *1984*, George Orwell described this as the Ministry of Truth, which revised history daily in order to accommodate the ever-changing needs of the dictatorship.[8] Our only defense against that sort of manipulation is to insist that at the bottom of history is an accessible bedrock of facts.

For Growth and Study

Mastering the Material

When you have studied this chapter you should be able to:
1. Give a general description of historical methodology.
2. Tell why historical documents are inherently imperfect.
3. Show why the work of the historian is always subjective.
4. Delineate criteria for deciding between historical documents.
5. Explain how the work of the historian is akin to the hermeneutical circle.
6. Define interpretive realism and tell how this idea restores the possibility of knowing historical facts.
7. Make an argument for why the alternative to knowing what happened in history is skepticism (and show why that is not an acceptable alternative).
8. Identify the following names with the contribution to which we have alluded in this chapter: Barbara Tuchman, Arthur Holmes.

Thinking About the Ideas

1. What can count as a historical document? Distinguish between direct and indirect documentary evidence. Can religious writings be historical documents?
2. Talk to a historian. Find out about the documentary evidence for some event in history few of us would question. Do you find it convincing?
3. Undertake a study of systematic bias in the writing of history. To what extent do you find systematic bias in history as it is currently being written?

---

[8]George Orwell, *1984* (New York: New American Library 1983, orig. 1949).

4. To what extent can bias in the writing of history be a good thing?
5. React to the statement, "In order for an event to count as bedrock historical fact, it must not be questioned by anyone."

For Further Exploration

William H. Dray, *Philosophy of History* (Englewood Cliffs, NJ: Prentice-Hall, 1964).

Mircea Eliade, *Cosmos and History* (New York: Harper & Row, 1959).

Arthur F. Holmes, *Faith Seeks Understanding* (Grand Rapids: Eerdmans, 1971).

John Warwick Montgomery, *The Shape of the Past* (Ann Arbor, MI: Edwards Bros., 1962).

10

The New Testament and History

Skeptical of Biblical Authenticity

Vignette 1: One of the required English courses at the University of Maryland included a unit on the Bible as literature. I found it to be interesting and a good jumping-off point to share the gospel with my fellow students.

I remember leaving the classroom late one afternoon after the lecture. We had just heard about the prophets' condemnation of sin.

"What do you think about all this?" I asked Karen, the girl who had sat next to me.

Without missing a beat she answered in complete confidence, "Oh, I think a bunch of people got together and simply made up the whole Bible."

The Missing Originals

Vignette 2: At conferences, scholars tend to have conversations as free-wheeling as any dorm discussion late into the night. During one such session, the conversation turned to the nature of the Bible. I mentioned that I believed in the complete truthfulness of Scripture.

"When you say that, you refer, not to modern translations, but to the originals, right?" an acquaintance asked.

"Yes," I responded. "There's no arguing with the fact that scribes and translators may have introduced some variations into later versions."

"But we don't have the originals," he responded. "So you're telling me that you are convinced that some hypothetical documents, that nobody has seen in two thousand years, are completely truthful. Sounds a little fantastic to me."

Who Is the Real Jesus?

Vignette 3: I was talking to Ibrahim, a Muslim student from Kuwait. He had come to Taylor University specifically in order to study at what he considered to be a typical American Christian college. I first met him in my class on New Testament survey. After a few weeks, we were sitting in my office chatting. If there is such a thing as a respectful snicker, he managed to bring it off at my feeble attempts in Arabic.

"You sound North-Egyptian," he commented. Apparently that was a bad thing to sound like where he came from.

Then the conversation got more serious. I asked him (in English, of course, since I wasn't ordering cheese or asking directions to the hotel) what he thought of Jesus, now that we had studied about Him in class.

"You see," he began to explain to me, "we learned about Jesus from the gospels. But the gospels were written by people who wanted to believe that Jesus is God, so they made up such stories about him. We Muslims believe that Jesus was a prophet, but only a man. In the gospels we read about what the Church believed about Jesus, not about the real Jesus."

But is it true? Now the question is whether we can consider the New Testament to be a reliable historical document. Only if we can make the case that it is reliable, does it make any sense at all to talk about the historical Jesus, His teachings, miracles, and identity. So our hypothesis for this chapter is this: *the New Testament is a reliable historical document for information about Jesus.* Since the four Gospels—Matthew, Mark, Luke, and John—are the books that give us the most content in this respect, we will focus on them.

I need to add a disclaimer here. Clearly this subject is far too broad for a chapter in a textbook on apologetics. The various branches of biblical studies are fields of academic inquiry in their own right with many issues and answers. All we can possibly do in this chapter is summarize the crucial issues for us and try to provide the best answers. There are many more details that could be expanded. My conviction is that filling out the details would not change the answers; it would only make them stronger.

Is the New Testament a Historical Document?

Before proceeding with our analysis, we need to clear the air on the important issue that it *is* legitimate to undertake such an analysis. Some people say that it is not. They argue that the New Testament is a piece of religious literature and that, as such, it may not be used as a source of historical information. This idea is based on the assumption that religious ideas are intrinsically divorced from historical facts. They are two different worlds of thought, expressed by two different literary genres, and should remain separate.

Let me respond to this objection with two comments. First of all, it is arbitrary. It is based on one particular assumption about the nature of religious truth, and a highly questionable one at that. This idea supposes that the world of religion and the world of historical facts cannot have anything in common. Therefore it not only passes judgment on the literary nature of various writings, but it also has to decide what may or may not count as religious truth. Surely these are things that should not be decided in advance.

Second, it is very clear that the New Testament claims to be a source for historical information. Luke says the following at the outset of his Gospel:

> Many have undertaken to draw up an account of the things that have been fulfilled among us, just as they were handed down to us by those who from the first were eyewitnesses and servants of the word. Therefore, since I myself have carefully investigated everything from the beginning, it seemed good also to me to write an orderly account for you, most excellent Theophilus, so that you may know the certainty of the things you have been taught. (Luke 1:1-4, NIV)

What Luke says here also applies to the other narrative passages throughout the New Testament. There is every indication that we are to accept them as factual and none that we should reject a factual interpretation.

Thus it is legitimate to read the New Testament as historical writing. That statement says nothing about the quality of the writing. It may be very poor history, perhaps nothing more than fiction passed off under a thin veneer of historical style in order to make it believable. These judgments still need to be made. For now we have argued for the legitimacy of even deciding if it is good history or bad history. At least it may be treated as history.

Criteria and the Burden of Proof

In the last chapter we listed a number of criteria that historians use to assess potential documents. In order to suit them to the discussion at hand, I will streamline them into five questions.

- Are the accounts written by people closely associated with the event?
- Are our present versions of the Gospels what the original authors wrote?
- Do the accounts contain impossibilities?
- Are the accounts so biased as to be unbelievable?
- How do the Gospel accounts fare in distinction to references to Jesus outside of the New Testament?

We need to add an observation here about the burden of proof. If a historian works along the guidelines of her field (as described in the last chapter), she is not free to disregard documents that do not appeal to her. For example, if she is writing about Marie Antoinette, she must take into account the relevant sources. Let us say that she comes across a document that was written by a person closely associated with Marie. The version of the document the historian has is a faithful replica of the original.

At this point the document must be allowed to stand on its own merit. The last three criteria become negative in the sense that unless they reveal serious problems with the document, the document must be allowed to speak for itself. In other words, the document assumes the status of innocent until proven guilty, or, better, authoritative until proven unreliable.

In the same manner, if we can establish that the Gospels are an accurate record of the recollections of Jesus' associates, then they must be given standing as historical documents with their own integrity. If we can then show that they are *not* reporting impossibilities, are *not* too biased to be believed, and are *not* contradicted by other sources, they become authoritative. The historian working with integrity is not free to disregard them and must accept them as bona fide data.

The Authors

Little needs to be said about the traditional authors' qualifications to write historical accounts. Matthew and John were disciples of Jesus. Mark was a native of Jerusalem and present at the gospel events; in addition, there is a strong tradition that Mark reported the reminiscences of Peter. Luke, of course, was a Gentile; he was not a disciple, and he was not present at the events. Yet Luke tells us of the research he did (remember our quotation above), and we can be fairly certain that he lived in Jerusalem for two years in close fellowship with those who had taken part in the events.[1]

Did these people really write the Gospels that bear their names? It is currently popular for biblical scholars to "suspend judgment" on the question of who wrote a particular book and then to establish on independent grounds who might conceivably have been the author. The document's own direct claim for its authorship does not bear particular weight in this investigation. This approach is bolstered by the fact that there are ancient pseudonymous books, books written under assumed names. A famous example is the Book of Enoch (which Jude actually quotes in his epistle); this clearly was not written by Enoch.

The historian is not free to suspend judgment with regard to the data at hand. In some cases it becomes evident that a certain person could not have written a particular account. Such a conclusion should result from careful investigation of the text, beginning with the claims that the text makes for

---

[1]Luke also wrote the Book of Acts. In Acts 21:15, he included himself among those who went to Jerusalem with Paul. Paul was arrested and spent two years in prison, first in Jerusalem, then in nearby Caesarea. When, after this time Paul was sent to Rome, Luke again included himself. It is a reasonable hypothesis that during this time Luke had contact with people who could give him firsthand accounts of the events of Jesus' life and that during this time he wrote his Gospel.

itself. To say that the claims of the document as to who wrote it count for nothing, and then to attempt to establish the supposed authorship apart from the documentary claims, reveals more arrogance than historical methodology can accommodate.

In short, there is nothing a priori to force us to reject the claims that the ancient manuscripts themselves make for the authorship of the Gospels. It is true that the names of the authors do not appear in the text, but they are always included as the headings of the manuscripts. That is where the historian has to start. We may begin, with the assumption that the Gospels were written by people who would have been in a good position to know the events of Jesus' life.

The Manuscripts

As you read this book, you may not read in every instance exactly what I wrote the way I wrote it. Modern publishers employ editors whose job it is to help authors get their point across by polishing their writings. They may correct grammar mistakes or clarify the language of a technical author so that lay people can follow it. On the negative side, it is possible that, in the process of producing the final printed copy, a typographical error may have slipped in unnoticed. Thus what you are reading may not be word for word what I first wrote out on a yellow pad and then entered into my computer. Of course, you can always borrow my disks and do a comparison if you really care what my original formulations were.

When we read the Gospels, do we read exactly what the original authors wrote? This is an important question. After all, if the Gospels as we have them now are seriously distorted from what was originally written, we cannot hope to get reliable information out of them, and our quest would be over.

So let us compare our present copies of the Gospels with the originals. *However, we do not have the originals.* They have long been lost. Fortunately somebody thought to make copies of them, but we do not have these direct copies of the originals either. Nor do we have copies of copies. What we do have are copies of copies of copies of copies, and on into further generations of copies. Then a second bad surprise awaits us: *these copies do not all agree; they differ from each other at many points.* The variations among copies come in many forms and sizes. The vast majority of them are decidedly minor, a different word being used or a slight alteration in grammatical construction. A few differences occur on a much larger scale; for example, some manuscripts leave out entire passages, such as John 8:1-11 or Mark 16:9-20.

Which manuscript is right? That is to say, which manuscript is faithful to the writing of the original author? Unless we can answer that question, we are stuck. A number of people say that, since we do not have the originals, the question is unanswerable. Hence we cannot use the Gospels as historical documents about Jesus; we do not know what the original Gospels said about Him.

Before proceeding with a response to this problem, it will be helpful to introduce some clear definitions.

A *manuscript* is a handwritten copy of a document in the original language. What we have called "document" throughout this discussion refers to one particular historical source, of which we may have many manuscripts. For example, the Gospel of Luke is one document; but we have thousands of manuscripts of Luke.

Autographs or *originals* refer to the book as it was written by the author, either in his own handwriting or as the result of his direct dictation. As we mentioned above, we do not have any of these autographs.

Textual criticism is the science of manuscript study. More often than not, it constitutes the attempt to reconstruct what the originals must have said on the basis of the available manuscripts.

Our task is to engage in a little rudimentary textual criticism. Can we, on the basis of the manuscripts as we have them, draw inferences about what the original autographs must have been like? Of course, my answer is going to be, yes.

Reading the next few paragraphs should feel a little like deja vu to you. The same line of thought that we used for historical documents also applies to manuscripts. Given some criteria that are essentially rooted in common sense, it is definitely possible to draw conclusions about what the original must have said.

Suppose a dozen people tell you the same story that they heard from another person. There are slight variations in the way in which they tell the story. Is it impossible for you to tell what the original version of the story must have been like? Not necessarily; with a little detective work, it is not going to be all that hard in many cases to decide what the first storyteller must have said.

You would probably take into account some of the following factors:

- What you know about the person who told the story originally;
- What you know about the individuals retelling the story, including:
  (1) their overall reliability; (2) whether they might have heard the story directly from the original teller or indirectly by way of intermediates; in the latter case, how many links there may have been in between; and (3) whether they might have had good reason to make some changes in their version of the story, possibly so that they could understand it better themselves or adapt it to their audience.
- Where the consensus of the group seems to lead.

Thus figuring out what the original might have said is not like the party game of "telephone." In that game, you remember, a chain of people take turns whispering a certain phrase from one person to the next in line to the third, and so forth. The hilarity of the game comes into play in that, by the time the chain is done, the phrase that comes out usually has little or no resemblance to the original. The last people have no idea what the first person heard.

The case of the New Testament documents is different. There are controls and criteria. We would have to think of many such chains in which the phrase is *spoken out loud* and where we have *reasonable expectations of what the original might have been and how it might have been altered.*

   As in the case of deciding between historical sources, we have the same provisions in the case of deciding between different manuscripts of one source: *there are criteria, and there are procedures for deciding.* Once again, even a novice to the field of textual criticism can figure out what the criteria would be. Let us phrase them the following way. Each of them is based on an all-things-being-equal assumption; that is to say, any one criterion could be overridden by a strong combination of the others.

1. Is the manuscript reading in harmony with others?
2. How old is the manuscript in question?
3. Given what we might know about the origin of a particular manuscript, are there reasons to suspect changes, such as substituting a more commom term in order to address a particular culture?
4. What is the physical shape of the manuscript in question? Is it tattered and full of holes?
5. What appears to be the overall accuracy of the manuscript? For example, are there obvious spelling and grammatical errors?
6. Are some of the variations in the manuscript easily explained as resulting from scribal error? Compare how in English it would be very easy accidentally to write "their" for "there."
7. Can we recognize an obvious motivation for why an easier reading might be substituted for a harder-to-understand one? If two manuscripts have different readings of the same passage, one of them must have changed it from what the original said. It is more likely that a scribe might have changed a passage that he could not understand to a more obviously understandable way than the other way around. Why would one change a perfectly intelligible reading into an obscure one? Thus (once again, all things being equal) the manuscript with the variant that is more difficult to understand probably has it right.

   This is not an exhaustive list, but it makes the point we are after: there are criteria; there are ways of deciding between manuscripts. We are not left in the dark as to what the original might have said.

Nobody is saying that this process is easy. Even with the best of criteria, there are some passages, such as the ending of Mark 16, for which we cannot decide what the original must have said. A few passages made their way into some English translations that apparently never were part of the originals; 1 John 5:7 in the King James Version, for example, is not found in any ancient Greek documents. The bottom line of all of this investigation is this: *the same criteria that cause us a few (mostly minor) problems make the New Testament look incredibly good on the whole.*

Let us compare the textual preservation of the New Testament with that of other ancient documents.[2] Take, for example, the status of the manuscripts of *Gallic Wars*, written by Julius Caesar in about 50 B.C. Today there are ten known manuscripts of this book, none of which comes from before A.D. 900. Thus we have ten manuscripts, all of which are about a thousand years removed from the original time of writing. That is not bad; it is typical of ancient historical sources.

By comparison the New Testament was written in the first century A.D.[3] The very first undisputed manuscript, the John Rylands Fragment, stems from the first part of the second century.[4] Most of the other manuscripts are dated within just a few hundred years of the original writing.

---

[2]See F. F. Bruce, *The New Testament Documents: Are They Reliable?* (Grand Rapids: Eerdmans, 1943), 15-18. F. W. Hall, *A Companion to Classical Texts* (Oxford: Clarendon, 1913), 199-285. Bruce M. Metzger, *The Text of the New Testament* (New York: Oxford University Press, 1964).

[3]Some more liberal scholars give a later date for some of the New Testament books. The interesting thing is that such a judgment would only make the textual connection look better. The later the writing of the book, the smaller the gap between the original and the first copies.

[4]There is an even older but highly disputed manuscript known as 7Q5. It was found among the so-called Dead Sea Scrolls at Qumran. It is a mere shred of papyrus, containing just a few letters; but the case has been made that it is a part of Mark 6:52-53. If so, due to known data about the age of the cave it was found in, this fragment would have to be from a copy of the Gospel of Mark dating no later than A.D. 70. Because of prophetic passages in Mark 13 predicting the destruction of Jerusalem in A.D. 70, it has become conventional wisdom among liberal scholars that Mark must have been written sometime after the event (since they reject predictive prophecy). The authenticity of 7Q5 as coming from Mark would, of course, shatter that theory. Consequently there has been a heated, and at times acrimonious, debate about this fragment. For our purposes, the textual transmission of the New Testament is remarkable, even if 7Q5 should prove to be inauthentic.

About five thousand Greek manuscripts of the New Testament are known today. No other ancient document equals the New Testament when it comes to the preservation of manuscripts, both in terms of number and closeness in time to the original autographs.

The sheer number of manuscripts makes it virtually certain that we have all of the major variations of the text. The probability that a new and much better manuscript with radically different readings will appear is by now low. This means that, for all practical purposes, even though we may not yet have an accurate reconstruction of the entire original autographs, chances are good that all of the readings of the original are represented in either the text as it has been reconstructed by now or, at least, in the available manuscripts.

Thus the manuscript heritage of the New Testament does not pose a serious problem after all. We can know, within the limits of reasonable textual methodology, what the originals said and that what we read in our English Bibles is, for the most part, exactly that. What started out as an apparent liability turns out to be one of the New Testament's greatest assets. An objective evaluation of the manuscripts can give us every confidence that we do know what Matthew, Mark, Luke, and John wrote about Jesus. No other ancient document can boast the same degree of textual accuracy.

Impossibilities and Incredulities

If an otherwise flawless manuscript reports clearly impossible matters, it would still have to be disregarded. Thus our next question is whether the New Testament contains accounts of impossibilities, so that we would not be able to use it as a historical source.

Many people would say that it does. The Gospels have stories of water being turned to wine, people walking on water, and even dead people coming back to life. Consequently, the historian can clearly not rely on the Gospels for factual information about Jesus.

At this point we may remind ourselves of our discussion of miracles in chapter 8. We tried to show that within a

theistic worldview miracles become both possible and
believable. The New Testament is written from the vantage
point of theism, and we have shown that theism is true.
Hence, we can be open to the accounts of miracles as they are
given to us in the Gospels.

There are two kinds of uses of the word "impossible."
One is logical impossibilities, such as square circles or being
a kangaroo and not being a kangaroo at the same time.
These impossibilities can never be believed, and even a
theistic framework would not rescue us from them. These
are not the kinds of alleged impossibilities we encounter in
the New Testament. What we read in the Gospels are
apparent physical impossibilities, but as we showed in
chapter 8, we can allow for these as long as we have
evidence that they might be the work of God who is free to
supersede His created laws.

Of course, the historian needs to proceed carefully in
dealing with the Gospels. Claims for the miraculous ought
never to be accepted lightly, but we are looking at
improbabilities, not impossibilities. As Sherlock Holmes was
fond of saying, "When the impossible has been ruled out, the
improbable must be true."

The Question of Bias

Are the Gospel accounts of Jesus so biased as to be
unbelievable? In the last chapter we talked about systematic
bias: sometimes one simply cannot believe a source because
the authors were obviously willing to go to any lengths to
defend their point of view, feeling free to sacrifice truth for
expedience.

Many people maintain that this is the case with the Gospels.
The authors were obviously believers in Jesus, so they wrote
these accounts with the single purpose of promoting their
point of view. Everything they wrote was written from their
biased perspective, intended to spread their faith in Christ.
Consequently the objective historian cannot use the Gospels as
a reliable source of factual information.

Given all we said in the previous chapter, this objection
ought to strike you as curious. There is no such thing as

historical writing that is not biased. Thus, simply pointing out that the Gospel writers had a definite bias, says nothing about their reliability as historical reporters. If we should disregard every piece of writing that contained a known bias, we would have to throw out, not only all historical documents, but also all other writings, including newspaper accounts, the last letter from your mom, and your electric bill.

The relevant question is not whether the Gospels contain a bias—which they do—but whether they are so biased that we have evidence of their forging the facts to suit their prejudices. Many people assume that this is also the case,[5] but is there good reason to suppose this kind of systematic bias?

It is helpful at this point to take a brief look at the nature of historical writing in the ancient world. In my earlier reference to Julius Caesar, I mentioned that he authored the history of the Gallic Wars. This fact counts for standard procedure in ancient history. The chronicles we have of Egyptian pharaohs, Mesopotamian kings, or whoever, were written by themselves about themselves in order to glorify themselves. According to their accounts, they had only victories, never losses; only successes, never failures. It is lucky for us that we can figure out that if King A beat Pharaoh B, Pharaoh B must have lost, and vice versa, but you would never know it from what Pharaoh B wrote.

In contrast, biblical storytelling is remarkably objective. None of the Bible's heros—Abraham, David, Peter, Paul—are shown without serious flaws. This kind of relative objectivity also carries over into the Gospels' portrayal of Jesus. If the Gospel writers had intended to present nothing more than propaganda for their belief in Jesus, they might have served their case better by leaving out phases of their description of Jesus that turn off the unbelieving reader. The twentieth-century philosopher Bertrand Russell lists what he considers to be defects in Jesus' character as part of his

---

[5]So, for example, the German New Testament scholar William Wrede taught that we must understand the Gospels, not so much as records about Jesus, but as records of what the Church wanted to teach about Jesus. The supposed sayings of Jesus then would only be words the Church later put into His mouth. William Wrede, *The Messianic Secret*, trans. by J. C. G. Greig (Cambridge, England: J. Clarke, 1971).

reasons for not being a Christian. He includes Christ's colorful condemnations, His cursing of a fig tree for not bearing fruit out of season, and His drowning the Gedarene pigs among the items that he finds objectionable in the Gospels' portrayal of Jesus. Russell concludes, "I cannot myself feel that either in the matter of wisdom or in the matter of virtue Christ stands quite as high as some other people known to history."[6]

Of course, I do not agree with Russell, and I am loathe to cite him as an authority on biblical interpretation. The important consideration is that Russell expresses his personal reaction to the Gospels themselves. Clearly, a set of writings that can turn off someone from the main character cannot be so biased in His favor as not to be believable. You cannot have it both ways. Thus, by normal historical standards, the bias of the Gospels is not so strong that we cannot trust their factual reports.

The Gospels and Other Accounts

How do the Gospel accounts fare in relation to references to Jesus in other literature? Before giving a direct answer to this question, I want to resurrect the matter of burden of proof which I touched on earlier. I am doing this for clarification, not as a defensive maneuver, for there is nothing to fear here. The short answer will be that the Gospels fare exceedingly well.

Sometimes people ask me if there is historical evidence for Jesus. What they mean by this question is whether there are reports about Jesus outside of the Gospels. There are. The intriguing thing about the way the question is phrased is that it assumes that only information outside of the Gospels can count as truly historical. We have tried to show that such an opinion is unacceptable; the Gospels themselves are historical accounts. Fuel is added to this misconception by an assumption that seems to be prevalent in scholarly circles: an assertion made by a pagan writer with his biases is

---

[6]Bertrand Russell, "Why I am not a Christian," in *The Basic Writings of Bertrand Russell*, ed. Robert E. Egner and Lester E. Dennon (New York: Simon and Schuster, 1961), 594.

somehow intrinsically more believable than an assertion made by a biblical writer, despite the obvious high moral standards of biblical teaching. What it boils down to is that they consider nothing in the Bible believable unless it is confirmed by non-biblical writers. This misunderstanding flies in the face of sound historical methodology.

Thus the issue is not whether we can prove the Gospels to be true because they are corroborated by non-Christian writers: that would surely be a strange methodology. Instead, what we need to do here is to test the reliability of the gospel documents by checking whether they are contradicted by other documents. At this point, having shown that the Gospels are acceptable historical documents on all other criteria, we are free to accept them as reporting truth *unless they are refuted by documents as good as, or better than, the Gospels themselves.*

In point of fact, the Gospels look extremely good in comparison to non-Christian references to Jesus. Let us look at three such reports.[7]

Tacitus

The Roman historian Tacitus recorded the story of the great fire of Rome (A.D. 64), which some people blamed on the Emperor Nero himself. Tacitus wrote:

> Consequently, to get rid of the report, Nero fastened the guilt and inflicted the most exquisite tortures on a class hated for their abominations, called Christians by the populace. Christus, from whom the name had its origin, suffered the extreme penalty during the reign of Tiberius at the hands of one of our procurators, Pontius Pilatus, and a most mischievous superstition, thus checked for the moment, again broke out not only in Judaea, the first source of the evil, but even in Rome, where all things hideous and shameful from every part of the world find their center and become popular. Accordingly, an arrest was first made of all who pleaded guilty; then, upon their information, an

---

[7]For a complete treatment of all of the available evidence, see Gary R. Habermas, *The Verdict of History: Conclusive Evidence for the Life of Jesus* (Nashville: Thomas Nelson, 1988).

immense multitude was convicted, not so much of the
crime of firing the city, as of hatred against mankind.[8]

Why was Tacitus so mad at Christians? The answer is that
most Romans did not really understand Christianity. They
had heard about the Christian celebration of the Lord's
Supper—the eating of the Son's body and drinking of His
blood—and thought Christians sacrificed babies and then
made a feast of them. Would you object to such a cult?

More importantly, Tacitus mentions the core events of the
life of Jesus. There was a man called Christus who was
executed under Pontius Pilate, but whose followers
continued to believe in Him (at a minimum an indirect
reference to at least *belief in* His resurrection). There is
nothing here to cause us to reconsider our view of the
Gospels.

Josephus

Flavius Josephus was a Jewish historian writing accounts
of Jewish history for the Romans. We read in his work called
The Antiquities of the Jews:

> Now there was about this time Jesus, a wise man, if it be
> lawful to call him a man; for he was a doer of wonderful
> works, a teacher of such men as receive the truth with
> pleasure. He drew over to him both many of the Jews,
> and many of the Gentiles. He was the Christ. And when
> Pilate, at the suggestion of the principal men among us,
> had condemned him to the cross, those that loved him at
> the first did not forsake him; for he appeared to them
> alive again the third day; as the divine prophets had
> foretold these and ten thousand other wonderful things
> concerning him. And the tribe of Christians, so named
> from him, are not extinct at this day.[9]

Certainly all of this information is in complete harmony with
what we read in the Gospels.

This quotation may be too good to be true. From all the
other information we have about Josephus, it seems highly

---

[8]Tacitus, *Annals* 15.44, written about A.D. 115, cited in Habermas, *Verdict of History*, 87-88.

[9]Flavius Josephus, *The Antiquities of the Jews*, 18, 3; in *The Works of Josephus*, trans. William Whiston, vol. 3 (New York: A. C. Armstrong and Son, 1889), 148.

unlikely that he actually believed that Jesus was the Messiah or that Jesus was resurrected. Consequently scholars have attempted to do textual criticism on Josephus' writing with the assumption that some Christian scribes may have altered what Josephus actually said.

On this basis, the following reconstruction of what may have been the actual words Josephus wrote has been put forward.

> At this time there was a wise man who was called Jesus. And his conduct was good and he was known to be virtuous. And many people from among the Jews and other nations became his disciples. Pilate condemned him to be crucified and to die. And those who had become his disciples did not abandon his discipleship. They reported that he had appeared to them three days after his crucifixion and that he was alive; accordingly, he was perhaps the messiah concerning whom the prophets have recounted wonders.[10]

These statements are toned down, definitely more in line with what one would have expected someone in Josephus' position to have written, but note that the basic story of Jesus and His disciples is still there, and there is nothing contradicting the New Testament.

The Talmud

The Talmud is a collection of Jewish writings. It includes interpretations of the law, anecdotes, historical references, parables, and much other information that has come to shape Judaism over the centuries. Jesus is mentioned in the Talmud at least once, in a section composed early in the second century. Because this time period is still close to the official Jewish condemnation of Jesus, one would expect this reference to be hostile to Him. Unsurprisingly it is; it portrays Jesus in a way that is not supposed to leave room for doubt as to His guilt. We read as follows:

> On the eve of the Passover Yeshu was hanged. For forty days before the execution took place, a herald went forth and cried, "He is going forth to be stoned because he has practiced sorcery and enticed Israel to apostasy.

---

[10]Reconstruction by Schlomo Pines, cited in Habermas, *Verdict of History*, 91-92.

> Any one who can say anything in his favor, let him
> come forward and plead on his behalf." But since
> nothing was brought forward in his favor he was
> hanged on the eve of the Passover![11]

This quotation adds some wrinkles we had not encountered before. It supplies information on a herald who supposedly attempted to summon any supporter Jesus might have had, but the herald did not find any. Of course we cannot approach this Talmudic fragment less critically than the Gospel's report without any herald, and so we need to ask ourselves which is the more believable. The simple answer is that the Gospels are more believable and that the Talmud cannot be trusted on this point. All textual reasons aside, an obvious point is that if Jesus had had no supporters, where did they all of a sudden come from?

In all other respects this report is in harmony with the Gospels. We even glean some new information, namely the Jewish perspective on why Jesus had to die. His crimes are listed: enticing the people to apostasy and practicing sorcery. These are negative words, but they translate well into the perspective of the Gospels, for they corroborate the Gospels' witness that Jesus claimed to be God and that He did miracles. This point is worth pondering for future considerations: the most hostile of the early non-Christian sources about Jesus does not deny that He did miraculous deeds.

Tacitus, Josephus, and the Talmud are the three clearest references to Jesus outside of the New Testament. When we approach them with appropriate historical methods, we find that they do not take away from the historical integrity of the New Testament Gospels.

We have now responded to the five criteria brought up at the outset of this chapter. We have shown that it is acceptable by normal historical methodology to treat the Gospels as reliable historical sources. Anything less would constitute special pleading against them.

---

[11]*The Babylonian Talmud*, trans. I. Epstein (London: Soncino Press, 1935), vol. 3, Sanhedrin 43a, 281, cited in Habermas, *Verdict of History*, 98.

What About the Errors and Contradictions?

Are the Gospels really reliable? What about all the errors and contradictions everybody knows are found all through the Bible, including the Gospels? How can anyone call a document reliable when it is full of mistakes?

These are difficult questions for me to bring up at this point, because in a sense I am going to restrain myself from answering them. My inclination has been to list two or three examples of such supposed errors and then to show that, with a little sympathetic understanding, there is no contradiction at all. The problem is that immediately someone else would think of another supposed contradiction, and if I resolved that, a third person would find a few more puzzlers. Numerous sessions of "stump-the-professor" along this line have taught me that the only way to surmount this hurdle is from a more general perspective.

Let me be brash and simply state that, as far as I know, there were no errors in the original autographs of the Bible, including historical material. To substantiate this point, one would have to cover more ground than is either possible or desirable for a chapter in a book such as this one. Many scholars have devoted considerable energy to this issue.[12]

For our purposes, we need to remain with the goal we have set for ourselves, namely to see if the Gospels meet the normal criteria for historical documents to be reliable. It is not a normal criterion for such a document to be totally free from error. Certainly the believability of a source is impugned if we find serious mistakes and enhanced if we can show that it contains no mistakes whatsoever, but that is no requirement before we can use that source for historical evidence.

Obviously the particular problem passages need to be sorted out and accounted for. I already indicated that I have every confidence that such a project would be successful, but we need not wait for the last possible difficulty to be cleared before we can use the Gospels as historical sources. If we were to undertake a deeper study of the life of Christ than is necessary

---

[12]See for example, Gleason L. Archer, *Encyclopedia of Bible Difficulties* (Grand Rapids: Zondervan, 1982).

for our purposes, we would have to work our way through more detail than is required for us to go on in this study.

All We Have

Now for a mind-boggling statement: *you now have information on all of the basic documents needed to assess the reliability of the Gospels.* What you have is what anybody has. That does not mean that you are now an expert. It also does not deny that there are many other documents that can help us understand the Gospels better. For instance, there are pagan sources that have nothing to do with Jesus but which give us information about His times. The same thing is true for Jewish sources. There are also the much later, but spurious gospels, such as the Gospel of Thomas. These are of no particular historical help, for they were written in the second century or later and show such obvious systematic bias that we cannot treat them as valid historical sources. However, they do show us how some people conceived Jesus later on. None of these sources gives us any further historical information to amplify the records as we presented them above.

My point is that a collection of other sources that only scholars know about does not exist. The work of the scholar comes into play in the task of analyzing and evaluating what is there, but you have essentially the same documentary data that the scholar has. He or she only knows more about it than you do.

Sometimes in the course of analyzing a source, scholars have concluded that there was another source behind it. For example, some New Testament scholars have stipulated that the sayings of Jesus found in Matthew and Luke but not in Mark must come from a common source, which they have called Q (abbreviated from the German *quelle*, which means "source"). If that is the case, I do not see anything particularly pernicious about it, as long as that insight is used to help us understand Matthew and Luke. Yet we need to remember that Q is a purely hypothetical construct based on material extracted from Matthew and Luke. No one has ever seen Q, and we do not have any separate witness to it.

To use it as an independent source for the life of Jesus would be the height of folly.

Consequently, to gain information about Jesus, there is only one reasonable place to turn, namely the Gospels as they are contained in the New Testament. Every once in a while statements appear in popular news magazines suggesting that contemporary scholars have inside information about Jesus, information that is only imperfectly reflected in the Gospels. That is nonsense. Take away the Gospels, and we have virtually nothing.

All we have is all we need. We have shown that the Gospels are acceptable historical documents in their own right. Thus it is not a concession for us to start an investigation of Jesus with the Gospels. That is where we would want to start as well as where we ought to start.

Let us then respond to the vignettes for this chapter.

Response to Vignette 1: In some ways, statements like Karen's are the hardest to respond to. It is unfounded opinion; she obviously has no idea of what she is saying, other than something she may once have heard that helps her cope with whatever religious convictions she is trying to hold or to avoid holding. For that matter, she may only have been signaling that she is not in the mood for theological discussion, a signal that ought to be respected.

If there is reason to believe that it might make sense to carry the discussion further, two possibilities exist. If you feel it is necessary to confront the person, you might want to ask how he or she knows that that is how the Bible came about, hoping that, as they fumble around for an answer, they might eventually ask you what you think. More likely though, it might be time to tell the person briefly what you believe the Bible is and how God has used it in your life. When people obviously are not ready for an intellectual inquiry, we ought to tell them how Jesus has saved us, and how He is real in our lives now, instead of forcing a conversation about textual criticism.

Response to Vignette 2: How can one possibly make assertions about original manuscripts nobody has seen for almost two thousand years? The answer, as we showed above, is clear: by reproducing the originals on the basis of the manuscript evidence we have. We saw that this evidence is excellent.

I have discovered that in connection with the original autographs of the New Testament, many people have erected a wall that they would never raise in other areas. Of course, we are entitled to discuss things we have never seen directly. I have never seen the current president of the United

States; does that fact imply that I may not assume that he exists or that I may not assess the merit of his policies? Surely not, I have good reason for both, even without ever having directly seen him. Similar things can be said for atoms, black holes, and music recorded on a tape. If I follow the correct procedure for establishing their reality, I am entitled to evaluate them. That is all I am asking for on behalf of the original autographs for the Gospels.

Response to Vignette 3: Did the Gospel writers believe that Jesus was God? Beyond the shadow of a doubt. Did they write their Gospels in such a way that their point would become clear? Certainly they did. Does that fact automatically impugn the historical believability of the Gospels? No, why should it? The only reason one would assume that the bias of the Gospel writers eliminates their historical reliability is if one had decided in advance that they were wrong.

I was in Washington, D.C., for the inauguration of Lyndon B. Johnson in 1965 (with my high school youth group, handing out tracts in the crowd). I saw LBJ and watched him take the oath of office and deliver his inaugural address. If anyone asks me who assumed the presidency in January 1965, I would say it was Lyndon Johnson. Now consider the possibility of someone challenging my report: I'm only saying these things because I'm personally convinced that LBJ was president; maybe it was really Barry Goldwater. Yes, I am personally convinced that LBJ was president, but rightly so because I am going on all the evidence available to me. In short, there is nothing wrong with a "biased" report if the "bias" is based on the evidence (see the last chapter on historical methodology).

In the same way, if the Gospel writers all make the case that Jesus is God, maybe that is because Jesus really is God. Keep in mind that, for all practical purposes, their writings are the only evidence we have. There are only two options available: either close your mind to the evidence altogether, or consider the evidence as they presented it. Is it reasonable to believe that Jesus truly is God? This is the topic of the next chapter.

For Growth and Study

Mastering the Material

When you have studied this chapter you should be able to:

1. Tell why it is legitimate to treat the Gospels as historical documents.
2. List five criteria for assessing the historical reliability of the Gospels.
3. Defend the Gospels as records of people closely in touch with the events.

4. Make a case for how we can know what the original autographs of the Gospels said.
5. Defend the assertion that the Gospels do not report impossibilities.
6. Show why we can say that the Gospels are not so prejudiced as to be unbelievable.
7. Name three sources about Jesus outside of the New Testament and describe the information they contain.
8. Identify the following names with the contribution to which we have alluded in this chapter: Bertrand Russell, Tacitus, Josephus.

Thinking About the Ideas

1. Why do people sometimes have different standards of reliability for the New Testament than for other writings? To what extent can this be fair and unfair?
2. Is all biblical literature historical in nature? How can we decide?
3. Explore how textual criticism is applied in areas outside of biblical studies, such as in English literature or law.
4. Check out several modern English versions of the Bible. Look for references to different manuscripts in the margins or notes.
5. Research allusions to Jesus in classical literature other than the ones cited here.
6. Interact with the statement, "We can get reliable historical information from a document that may contain errors."
7. Research the issue of the complete truthfulness (inerrancy) of the Bible. What are the historical and spiritual issues? Can they be separated?

For Further Exploration

F. F. Bruce, *The New Testament Documents: Are They Reliable?* (Grand Rapids: Eerdmans, 1943).

Norman L. Geisler, ed., *Inerrancy* (Grand Rapids: Zondervan, 1979).

Gary R. Habermas, *The Verdict of History*, 2nd ed. (Nashville, Thomas Nelson, 1988).

Bruce M. Metzger, *The New Testament: Its Background, Growth, and Content* (Nashville: Abingdon, 1965).

11

Who Is Jesus?

Jesus Never Claims to Be God

Vignette 1: My brother and I had helped another youth group with a musical presentation about Christ and modern life. After the show we mingled with the audience. Eventually I wound up talking with a young man who identified himself as a serviceman on leave.

"I'm sorry," he apologized. "I'm really too drunk to follow everything everybody was saying. But it was good."

How does one respond to that?

"That's OK," I said. "The important part of the message was that Jesus wants to be your Lord and Savior."

"I appreciate that, but really, Jesus was only a man, so what can he do for me?"

"The Bible teaches that Jesus was not only a man, but that he was God. He said so Himself, you know."

"I don't believe that." My new acquaintance was adamant. "Jesus never claimed to be God."

The Resurrection as Superstition

Vignette 2: I was eighteen, caught up in the proverbial search for my identity. Somehow the superficial questions of life loomed large. How do I dress? How long can I let my hair grow? Should I try to grow a beard? Actually, I was secure in the more important matters: Jesus was alive and living inside of me.

One day I was talking to a family friend, a man who had been active in church all his life. He was obviously trying to relate to what he thought the "new generation" wanted to hear and believe.

"Of course, the church has done a lot of good in the world, like helping people and so forth; but this stuff about Jesus being God and being resurrected, that's all superstition."

Science Versus Christianity

Vignette 3: Quite a few years ago I was on the committee interviewing a potential biology professor. We chatted about various aspects of his position and were making good headway.

When it was my turn to ask a question, I asked, "In what way do you relate your Christian faith and your science to each other?"

"They don't have anything to do with each other," was his surprising reply. "They are different fields of inquiry with different methods and different conclusions. Was Jesus resurrected? According to Christian theology, yes. According to scientific facts, you can't even ask the question."

Cynical Youth Pastor

Vignette 4: As a college student I read some of the arguments for the Resurrection that I am describing below. That year, when Easter came around, I was in charge of the program for our Sunday evening college and career meeting. I shared with the group all that I had learned about evidence for the Resurrection.

When I was done, Ed, our youth pastor commented: "Well, that just goes to show: You can prove anything from the Bible if you try hard enough."

But is it true? Can we really believe that there was a man on earth approximately two thousand years ago who was God? How can one possibly establish such an assertion? We can do the following:

- Look at the historical records to see what this man claimed about Himself. If He did not claim to be God, that would be a serious lack of evidence on behalf of this hypothesis.
- Compare competing hypotheses to see which one is most in accord with His claim (assuming He made it).
- Evaluate further evidence to substantiate the claim.

This is the basic outline for this chapter. Our hypothesis is the following: *According to the historical records, the most plausible explanation is that Jesus of Nazareth was (and is) who He claimed to be, namely God.*

Did Jesus Claim to Be God?

It makes no sense to read this chapter in isolation. The case that I am making here is the result of a cumulative investigation. It is premised on the earlier conclusions that:

a. There is objective truth;
b. Truth can be known;
c. There is a God (as described by theism);
d. Miracles are possible and knowable;
e. We can ascertain truth from historical records;
f. The Gospels are reliable historical accounts about Jesus.

Take away these assumptions, and the case about Jesus in this chapter is not going to work. As a matter of fact, most discussions about the conclusions of this chapter usually wind up involving these earlier points. Discussions of apologetics rarely involve only one issue, and that is how it should be. People do their thinking in terms of worldviews, not isolated beliefs.

In the last chapter we established that by accepted historical method, we can use the Gospels to uncover reliable information about Jesus. They are good records about Him, and we can accept what they say. Thus our question now is: According to these records, did Jesus say that He was God?

This is a crucial question. It is one thing for the followers of a person to say that He must have been God. It is quite another for that man Himself to say that He is God. The latter severely limits the options of what He truly must have been. After all, being or not being God is not the kind of thing about which one can be casually mistaken. It is ridiculous to think that someone might wind up saying, "Whoops, I'm sorry. I thought I was God, but I guess I'm not. Please forgive me; it was an honest mistake." If Jesus claimed to be God and was not, a serious alternative explanation will be required. If He did not claim to be God, then later claims about Him as God lose their force, since the most important witness to His identity (Himself) never said such a thing.

So, did Jesus claim to be God? Of course He did. There are many places in the Gospel records where He did so, directly and indirectly. I am going to point out seven specifically, though many more are possible. The one thing that they all have in common is that in each case it is Jesus Himself who makes this claim.

John 8:58

In this passage Jesus is involved in a controversy with His Jewish contemporaries. The subject of the argument is Jesus' own identity. In the process, He states that Abraham was glad to see Him. This statement really confuses the people, and they question how He could possibly have been around at the time of Abraham. Jesus responds: "Before Abraham was born, I am" (NIV). The expression, "I Am" was not a phrase that pious Jews would ever use, let alone in reference to themselves; for it was the name of God (see Exod. 3:14), and it would have been considered blasphemous to use that name for oneself. In referring to Himself as "I Am," He was saying that He was God.

Does this sound far-fetched to you? Is it not possible that we are reading all kinds of weighty theological information into a simple statement Jesus made? Fortunately we are being given clear information on how to understand this saying. In the next verse, we see the people picking up stones to throw at Him—the traditional response to evident blasphemy. Christ's listeners got the message exactly as He meant it: He was claiming to be God.

John 10:30

This passage is even clearer. In another debate about Jesus' identity, He says: "I and My Father are one" (NKJV). Thus He declared Himself to be equal with God the Father.

Once again this is a self-checking passage. We could debate for a long time exactly what Jesus might have meant, but the next verse leaves no doubt about what He communicated to His immediate audience. They took up stones again. They knew that once again He had claimed deity for Himself.

Luke 22:70 and Parallel Passages in Matthew and Mark

Here Jesus is on trial before the Sanhedrin, the Jewish council. After some futile efforts to convict Him on various charges, the priest and his associates turn to Jesus directly and question Him. Eventually they ask Him, "Are you the Son of God?" Jesus responds, "Yes, I am." It appears that we have a double claim here. Jesus acknowledges that He is the Son of God and also uses "I am" in His response as recorded by Luke.

Some scholars have questioned of late whether the claim to be the "Son of God" really entails a claim to being God.[1] It is possible that at times the title was used simply to refer to the Messiah, but such an interpretation is impossible in this context. The reaction of the audience tells us exactly how we are supposed to understand what Jesus said and meant. Look at the next verse as well as the reactions reported in Matthew 26:63-66. It was not blasphemy to claim to be the Messiah, but it certainly was blasphemous to claim to be God, and that is exactly what Jesus must have done here.

John 5:17

Even Jesus' claim that God was His Father was a claim to deity. When Jesus said that His Father was at work in Him, He was not just expressing a sentimental attitude toward God. Once more His listeners sought to kill Him because He made Himself equal to God.

Mark 2:1-12

On some occasions when Jesus claimed to be God, He was a less direct; but by His *actions* He made it clear how He felt about His identity. One example is in this passage. Instead of healing the paralytic immediately, Jesus told him that his sins are forgiven. The scribes in the audience were appalled: "Only God can forgive sins." Reading their thoughts, Jesus then proves that He has the power to forgive sins by healing the man. And, of course, the scribes had it right all along. By forgiving sins Jesus showed that He was, in fact, God.

---

[1]Compare the discussion by Colin Brown, *Miracles and the Critical Mind* (Grand Rapids: Eerdmans, 1984), 294-99.

Matthew 7:22, 23

Any passage in which Jesus referred to Himself as judge on the last day constitutes a claim to be God. To His Jewish hearers it was a given that only God Himself would preside at the Last Judgment. Isaiah 33:22 says, "The Lord is our judge" (NIV). By making Himself Judge, Jesus was making Himself the Lord.

Mark 2:23—3:6

Have you ever wondered why the Jewish authorities got so angry with Jesus? For example, the verses here deal with Jesus' attitude toward the Sabbath; they end with the Pharisees' and Herodians' counseling to put Jesus to death. Were they that irate because Jesus and His disciples broke the Sabbath or because Jesus taught humanism and displayed a relaxed attitude toward the Sabbath? Surely not. In fact, Jesus was saying things some of the more liberal-minded rabbis had said already without being put to death.

The clue to this passage is in verse 28. Jesus called Himself *Lord of the Sabbath*. To understand the import of this title, we need to know how the Jews felt (and still do feel) about the Sabbath commandment. No other commandment was regarded as a blessing so much as the fourth: "Remember the Sabbath day to keep it holy." No other commandment was seen as expressing so well the intimate relationship between God and His people. The Sabbath commandment was seen as the closest expression of God's love for the Jews. When Jesus called Himself "Lord of the Sabbath," He applied to Himself that very special place that belonged only to God.

Jesus' subsequent relaxed attitude toward the Sabbath should be seen as an expression of this conviction. He could do with the Sabbath as He liked because He owned the Sabbath. What blasphemy in His listeners' ears! Only God owns the Sabbath. No wonder, given their perspective, that they decided to kill this blasphemer!

Did Jesus claim to be God? These representative passages make it very clear that He did.

The Alternatives

Just because someone said that He was God would not make Him God. Many people would say that Jesus was not God. Then who or what was He? Let us consider some of the alternative explanations and see if they are defensible.

Jesus Was a Mere Human Being Like You and I

We could begin by entertaining the possibility that there was nothing special about Jesus. He was a completely ordinary human being in all respects, no different from any other human being who ever lived, but there are some glaring problems with such an approach.

If there was nothing special about Jesus, there is no reason why the Christian religion should have developed as a form of belief in Him. This theory flies in the face of all the historical documents. Even the pagan sources make Him out to have been very exceptional. Most importantly, as we just saw, Jesus claimed to be God. That claim removes Him from the company of the rest of us ordinary mortals. As we said above, being God is not the kind of thing you can be accidentally wrong about. If you are God, then you are definitely special. If you claim to be God and are not, then you may be mentally ill or a deliberate liar. For now, the point is that someone who claims to be God can never be a purely ordinary human being. He must be in some way extraordinary.

Jesus Was Merely a Great Teacher

Many people believe that He was one of the great religious teachers of all time, though He was not God. For example, Thomas Jefferson claimed that in Jesus' teachings we have the highest expression of divine truth. Others may not go this far but may accord Jesus a place among the other great prophets and teachers of wisdom, such as Buddha, Muhammad, Lao-tse, and Splinter the Rat. He was a great teacher, but He was not God.

To evaluate this possibility, we need to keep some important points in mind: Jesus' teaching revolved around Himself. No matter what the topic under discussion was, He brought it down to His own person. "I am the way and the truth and the life. No one comes to the Father except through me" (John 14:6, NIV). Such assertions abound throughout the Gospels. In John R. W. Stott's fascinating phraseology, Jesus' teaching was self-centered. The focus was on Himself. Thus when Jesus claimed to be God, He was making a claim about the very core of His teaching.

Consequently, if Jesus was not God, as He claimed to be, He was mistaken about something that was at the core of His teaching. His claims about Himself were not a sidelight to the rest of His teaching. If these claims were wrong, then the very central message of His teaching was wrong.

Someone who is mistaken about the very core of the message he is teaching is not a great teacher. A great teacher could conceivably be mistaken about a peripheral issue to his message. For example, part of my teaching load includes a course in logic. I could one day accidentally commit a fallacy and still be a good teacher. If throughout the entire course I endorsed fallacies rather than valid reasoning, however, I would not be a good teacher. In the same way, if Jesus consistently taught that He was God (and He did!), and if Jesus consistently taught that His identity was at the core of His teaching (and it was!), whatever else He may have been, He could not have been a great teacher if He was wrong on this point. For that matter, at the risk of belaboring the obvious, the question of whether you are God or not can never be a marginal issue.

Thus the conclusion is that Jesus could not have been merely a great teacher if He was not also God. Of course I can say that He was a great teacher, but only if I accept that what He taught was true. And He taught that He was God.

The only way in which one can hang on to the idea that Jesus was a great teacher without being God is by doctoring up the evidence to eliminate His claims to deity. Many people do just that. They simply choose to ignore passages that do not fit in. This is precisely what Thomas Jefferson did in his revision of the Gospels, but Jefferson flew in the face of sound historical methodology. Jesus was not merely a great teacher; He was either more or less.

Jesus Was Mentally Ill

I have met some people who thought they were God. Their stories are very sad. They suffer from delusions of grandeur. If Jesus sincerely thought and taught that He was God, but was not, then He was suffering from mental illness.

Does such a diagnosis fit the evidence as we have it (which, you will remember, is the only evidence there is)? Clearly not. Aside from Jesus' claim (which is admittedly not a minor matter), there is no further evidence whatsoever for symptoms of mental illness. Most importantly, the reality of His miracles completely takes the steam out of any quick dismissal of Jesus as crazy. I tell my students that, if I should ever walk into class and claim to be God, the Creator of the universe and only Savior, they should gently direct me to the nearest therapist. If I make that claim and turn water into wine, heal many people with simple words, feed thousands of people with one boy's lunch, raise several people from the dead, predict my own death and resurrection and carry it out, then they need to take my claim more seriously. Whatever else I may be, I am not simply crazy. Jesus did all of these things and many more; He was not just mentally ill.

Jesus Was a Charlatan

There have been people who have deliberately deceived others into thinking they were God, but were not. We call these people charlatans. They are lying in order to collect followers along with the power and wealth such a claim could provide. Could Jesus have been such a person?

Once again the evidence does not support such an interpretation. Jesus did not get any tangible benefits out of His claim. He died deserted by even His closest followers, penniless, tortured by one of the cruelest methods ever devised by human beings. This fact makes the idea that Jesus deliberately deceived people for His personal benefit seem pretty fatuous.

Again the miracles are the biggest obstacle. Remember that the quotation from the Talmud, which had every intention of discrediting Jesus, nevertheless acknowledged that He did miraculous deeds (though it called them "sorcery"). The portrait of Jesus as the healer and miraculous helper is not that of a person deliberately deceiving others. In fact, the two are irreconcilable. Thus Jesus could not have been a charlatan.

Jesus Was Demonic

The refutation of the previous two alternatives rested to a large extent on the fact that Jesus performed miracles. As we saw, however, the Talmudic quotation accepted Jesus as a miracle worker, but not as God. These Jews saw Jesus as a demonic sorcerer who had probably come to test their faith in the true God. They did not deny that Jesus did miracles, but they thought that these miracles were evidence that Jesus was not of God, but of Satan. This is the interpretation given in Mark 3:22. Could Jesus have been demonic?

Again, the clear answer is no. The charge is groundless; it is based on an incomplete understanding of Jesus' teaching and actions. The best refutation of the charge is to point out the continuity between Jesus and the teaching of the Old Testament. Jesus was not an antagonist to the revelation of the Old Testament but the fulfillment of the prophecies.

It is possible to treat fulfilled prophecies as a particular kind of miracle. Among other prophecies, the Old Testament predicts the Messiah's birthplace (Mic. 5:2), the manner of His death (Ps. 22; Isa. 53), and even His resurrection (Ps. 16:10). No one can deliberately contrive to bring about such things; the fulfillment is miraculous. Nor can we lightly ascribe it all to coincidence. The probability of all prophecies having been fulfilled by coincidence alone has been estimated at 1 in 10 to the 157th power.[2] We are looking at a miracle.

Even more important, these prophecies and their fulfillment demonstrate continuity with the Old Testament. Again and again, as we see Christians debating with Jews in the early church, this theme became the focal point: Jesus is no evil competitor with the God of the Old Testament; He is the Son of the God of the Old Testament. The way in which

---

[2]Josh McDowell, *Evidence That Demands a Verdict* (San Bernardino, CA: Here's Life, 1972, 1979), 167.

He fulfilled the Old Testament prophecies proved that point. Jesus was not demonic.[3]

Jesus Was Who He Claimed to Be: God

Who was Jesus? We have established that He was not merely an undistinguished human being; He was not merely a great teacher; He was not mentally ill; He was not a charlatan; He was not demonic. We are out of options. The only possibility left is that He was exactly what He claimed to be, namely God.

Of course, this is not an easy statement to make. Anytime we want to assert that a particular individual is God, we should be sure of our facts. Sooner or later we must face the inevitable conclusion. Sherlock Holmes' dictum was, "When all the impossibilities have been ruled out, the improbable must be true." This saying applies here. The improbable, that God actually was a human being in Jesus of Nazareth, must be the truth because no other possibility fits the facts at all.

The Four L's

This whole argument has been condensed into a quick formula that is easy to remember. There are only four options with regard to who Jesus was.

- *Legend*. There never was a Jesus who claimed to be God. This option is contradicted by sound historical methodology.
- *Lunatic*. Jesus really thought He was God, but He was wrong. This option is contradicted by His character and miracles.
- *Liar*. Jesus deliberately deceived people (as a charlatan or as an agent of Satan). This option is contradicted by His miracles, the outcome of His life, and fulfilled prophecy.
- *Lord*. He was who He claimed to be.

---

[3]Every once in a while a student raises the objection that maybe the God of the Old Testament Himself was demonic, and it is all a fraud; but this objection is not possible to hold since it robs the words being used of all meaning. By definition, God is not demonic, good is not evil, and so forth. So, if Jesus is the Son of God, He cannot be demonic.

This formula is a good summary of the argument, but please do not treat it as a recipe for turning atheists into Christians. The argument is based on conclusions that we have fought for up to this point, but you cannot necessarily assume others will accept them in a conversation. These conclusions are that:

- There is truth and that it can be known.
- There is a God (as described by theism).
- Miracles are possible and knowable.
- It is possible to learn truth from history.
- The New Testament is a reliable historical source.

Without these facts established, the argument for the deity of Christ would not have a chance.

However, once we have established these presuppositions and have eliminated competing alternatives by means of the proper methodology, the result is in place. *The hypothesis that Jesus is God is the most plausible.*

The Two Biggest Miracles

One particular aspect of the foregoing argument that appeals to me personally is that it is strong enough to stand up without having to rely on two of the biggest miracles with regard to Christ's life: His virgin birth and His resurrection. Establishing these two events as real will put the final clincher on the truth of the hypothesis that Jesus is God.

The Virgin Birth

The Gospels of Matthew and Luke report that Jesus was born of a virgin, that is, by the power of God without benefit of a biological father. Is this report believable? For that matter, how could one possibly check out the truth of something like this? It is very possible that Mary, the mother of Jesus, told people, including Matthew and Luke, about this strange occurrence, but can one accept it as true without simply deciding to believe something unbelievable?

Many religions attribute miraculous births to their founders. For example, the ancient Chinese sage Lao-tse, sometimes called the founder of Taoism, was supposedly born at the age of seventy-two with wrinkled skin and white hair. It was inconceivable to his followers that anyone as wise as Lao-tse could possibly be born as a mere infant, so they invented this story about him in order to increase his stature. Is it not possible that we have the same phenomenon repeated with Jesus? Perhaps someone made up the story of the virgin birth in order to endow Him with greater glory.

The New Testament scholar J. Gresham Machen wrote a book in which he provided a powerful argument for the plausibility of the virgin birth.[4] Let us summarize his argument.

There is a basic fact for which we can supply two different hypotheses as explanations. The fact is that Matthew and Luke recorded a virgin birth. The two hypotheses are (1) it did happen and (2) it did not happen. How can one possibly decide between these two hypotheses?

The key lies in a corollary to hypothesis (2), that the virgin birth did not occur. If it did not, then Matthew and Luke—or their sources—made up the story. If this is true, they must have had plausible motivation to do such a thing. The upshot of Machen's argument is that no such plausible motivation can be found and that it is thus highly improbable that the story could have been invented.

The first point to consider in the course of this argument is that Matthew, and Luke's sources, would have been Jewish. They were God-fearing Jews who saw themselves in continuity with the Old Testament. Could such people have made up the story of the virgin birth? The answer is no. The very notion would have been considered blasphemous. There are plenty of miraculous birth stories in the Old Testament, of course; but there was always a biological father. The idea of making up a story in which God, through pure miraculous power, causes a child to be conceived without a father did not fit into Jewish thinking of the day at all. It is not at all believable that these Jews would have invented a story of a virgin birth.[5]

---

[4]J. Gresham Machen, *The Virgin Birth of Christ* (Grand Rapids: Baker, 1930).

[5]Someone might raise a reasonable objection: Would the Jews not have expected a virgin birth on the basis of Isaiah's prophecy in Isaiah 7:14: "Behold, a virgin shall

Because of the foregoing, most people seeking an alternative explanation do not propose the virgin birth as a Jewish invention but point to the evident pagan parallels. For example, there are various stories in which Zeus seduced a maiden and fathered a son by her. What the Gospel writers did, so it is claimed, was to borrow the idea of a virgin birth from these pagan myths. Machen pointed out two major flaws with this idea:

(a) The idea that Christians borrowed a piece of mythology from the pagans to enhance the standing of Jesus is wrong-headed. The whole point of Christian teaching was to set Christianity apart from paganism, not to assimilate it.

(b) There were no actual pagan virgin birth stories. All of these stories are incidents where gods seduced women and had offspring. The women may have been virgins before intercourse, but they most certainly were not virgins afterwards. The miraculous thing about the New Testament virgin birth story is that Mary was a virgin both before and after conception. This story could not have been copied from pagan parallels because it is not found in any pagan accounts.

This points out a serious problem in the second hypothesis. If the virgin birth did not happen, we have no plausible explanation for why it was ever recorded. Matthew's and Luke's sources could not have made it up, for no pious Jew would have invented such a story. They could not have borrowed the idea from pagan parallels because there are no true parallels. Thus the most likely explanation was that a virgin birth was reported because a virgin birth occurred.

The point here is not to show that all alternatives are completely impossible but that they are not so plausible as the hypothesis that the virgin birth was recorded because the virgin birth happened. Of course, this hypothesis can only be acceptable given our earlier conclusions: that there is a

---

conceive . . ."(KJV). The answer is, again, no. The word "virgin" in the Hebrew (alma) is capable of being translated as both "virgin," or, more simply, "young woman." As a Christian, I am convinced that the correct translation is "virgin," but the Jews in Jesus' day did not understand the passage that way. They would have seen it as referring to nothing more than a young woman.

God; that miracles are possible; that historical sources are sources for truth.

The Resurrection

The same pattern of argumentation can be applied to the resurrection of Jesus. It is not that we have direct deductive or empirical proof for it, but, given the information we do have, alternative explanations are not plausible. By resurrection we mean that Jesus was physically dead and was miraculously made alive again by the power of God.

There are two major lines of evidence for the Resurrection: the appearances of the resurrected Jesus and the evidence of the empty tomb. Understandably, the early church concentrated on the appearances. By way of parallel, imagine that I had been out with the flu and students are trying to decide if I am back on campus (the object being to see whether they have to attend my lecture or not). They could draw a good conclusion on the basis of circumstantial evidence: if my car is in the parking lot; if the light is on in my office; if my mailbox is empty. But that information would take a backseat to reports that I had actually been seen on campus. That would settle the issue. In the same way, reports by the disciples that they had seen Jesus took precedence over other lines of evidence. Thus, this is the line of evidence we ought to address first.

The Appearances

The earliest *written* report of the Resurrection is not in the Gospels, but in Paul's first letter to the Corinthians. In chapter 15, Paul gave an impressive list of those who saw the resurrected Jesus: Peter, the twelve disciples, five hundred brethren at one time, James, all the apostles (missionaries of the early church), and Paul himself. With regard to the five hundred, Paul emphasized that most of them were still alive at the time of writing. The implication was that since they were still alive, the readers could ask them.

Historical methodology demands that we consider the reports to be legitimate evidence. The question is, how do we explain them? One hypothesis is that Jesus was seen by the people because He was resurrected. A second hypothesis is that Jesus was not resurrected and that these reports must have another cause.

What could another cause be if Jesus was not resurrected? Why would so many people give these reports? There are two possible options.

One is that they did not see anything, but deliberately lied about it. This possibility becomes highly implausible in the light of subsequent events. The preaching of the early church centered on the resurrected Christ. The disciples were persecuted and eventually martyred for this particular message. It is not plausible that they gave their lives for a deliberate lie.

The second is that they were subject to some form of hallucination. It is a fact that at times someone who cannot cope with the death of a loved one hallucinates that he or she saw the deceased alive again. One could think that the Resurrection appearances were actually that kind of hallucination.

The problem with this theory is that, in the case of the Resurrection appearances, everything we know about hallucinations is violated. The appearances did not follow the patterns always present in hallucinations, for hallucinations are private and arise out of a state of extreme emotional instability in which the hallucination functions as a sort of wish-fulfillment. What occurred after the Resurrection was very different. The disciples had little trouble accepting Christ's departure; they decided to go back to their fishing. The appearances came as surprises while the disciples were intent on other things. Most importantly, the appearances came to *groups* of people, with each member seeing the same thing. That is simply not how hallucinations work. Thus the Resurrection appearances could not have been hallucinations.

In fact, the reports of the appearances could not have had cause other than that the people actually saw the resurrected Jesus. It is not possible that they would have all lied about it or that they were all subject to hallucinations about it. As historians we have to reckon with the fact that they actually met the risen Jesus.

The Empty Tomb

The second line of evidence is circumstantial. In essence it is that given the fact of the empty tomb, this fact can be explained only on the basis of the resurrection of Jesus.

If ever a fact of ancient history may count as indisputable, it should be the empty tomb. From Easter Sunday on there must have been a tomb, clearly known as the tomb of Jesus, that did not contain His body. This much is beyond dispute: Christian teaching from the very beginning promoted a living, resurrected Savior. The Jewish authorities strongly opposed this teaching and were prepared to go to any lengths in order to suppress it. Their job would have been easy if they could have invited potential converts for a quick stroll to the tomb and there produced Christ's body. That would have been the end of the Christian message. The fact that a church centering around the risen Christ could come about demonstrates that there must have been an empty tomb.

How did this tomb get to be empty? Just because there is an empty tomb does not mean that a resurrection has occurred. Once again we need to think in terms of competing hypotheses. The resurrection is one hypothesis; another hypothesis is that something natural, non-miraculous happened. Again we need to question whether a naturalistic hypothesis can account for the evidence.

Actually, a number of competing, mutually incompatible alternatives have been proposed by skeptics of the Resurrection. This fact in and of itself is already a good indicator of the weakness of all of those alternative theories. A good friend of mine remarked in his popular lecture on the Resurrection that actually the Christian need not bother refuting any naturalistic theories because each one of them is shot down by another naturalist whose theory is then demolished by a further naturalist.[6] None of their explanations work; all they have in common is that they try to avoid the conclusion that Christ was miraculously resurrected from the dead. Let us look at some of the better hypotheses.

---

[6]Gary Habermas has written widely on the Resurrection. See *The Resurrection of Jesus* (New York: University Press of America, 1984).

The disciples stole the body. This explanation was the first to be advanced, albeit in a form so unbelievable that it immediately revealed the desperation of those who were trying to circumvent the evidence. According to Matthew 28:11-15, the guards informed the priests of what had happened at the tomb; clearly they had no explanation of their own because one was provided for them by the priests. The priests bribed the guards and instructed them to tell anyone, "While we were sleeping, the disciples came and stole the body." As a piece of evidence, this testimony was fatuous. No one could say what happened while they were sleeping. It was a theory without any support.

Was this theory even plausible? The evidence is against it. First of all, we need to be aware that the guards were placed at the tomb precisely in order to keep the disciples from stealing the body (Matt. 27:62-66). It was late Saturday evening after the official end of the Sabbath. The authorities had gone to see Pontius Pilate. They specifically asked him to secure the tomb because they remembered Jesus' prediction of His resurrection and wanted to make sure the disciples did not commit a resurrection fraud. Thus Saturday evening the tomb was sealed and guards were placed in front of it as protection against a possible plot by the disciples. The guards' mission was clear: Keep the disciples from stealing the body!

Now we must remember a few other crucial points. First of all, rolling away the stone in front of a first-century Palestinian tomb was not the kind of thing you could do quietly and unobtrusively. The stone was a large disk running in a groove; it would have settled in a depression right in front of the door. Once it was firmly in place, it could only be moved with a great deal of effort, which would undoubtedly have caused a lot of noise. (Remember, the women on the way to the tomb had no idea how they were going to get the stone moved and were shocked when they saw it was out of place, because of its large size.) The idea that the disciples sneaked into the tomb area and then, while the guards were not paying attention, slid away the stone and stole the body, is not feasible.

Even if the guards had been sleeping, an attempt to move the stone would have awakened them, but it is extremely unlikely that the guards were sleeping. The text leaves it open as to whether these guards were Roman soldiers or Jewish temple guards, but at this instance the distinction is not relevant; they were there under the authority of Pontius Pilate and would have been subject to Roman law. Under Roman law, a guard sleeping on duty would be subject to immediate execution. This is the reason why the Jewish authorities reassured the guards after the bribery by saying, "If word of this gets to Pilate, we will take care of it." As a piece of historical inference, we have to assume that the guards stayed awake.

Finally we have to repeat a point we made earlier in connection with the question of whether the disciples lied about the appearances of Jesus. The disciples spent the rest of their lives preaching that Jesus was alive; they gave their own lives willingly for that belief. It is not plausible that they all would have died for a fraud they perpetrated themselves. Our conclusion is that whatever else may have happened at the tomb, it could not have been a matter of the disciples' stealing the body.

The women stole the body. Astonishingly, as implausible as it is, the hypothesis that the disciples stole the body is still the best of all of the alternatives. From here on, the alternatives get weaker. Consider, for example, the possibility that the women, who came to the tomb early on Sunday morning, stole the body. Everything we said against the previous theory applies here, only with even greater force. If it was not possible for the disciples to perpetrate a resurrection fraud, it would have been even less possible for the women. According to the evidence (which was written to people who were in a position to know how plausible such a claim could be), these women were not even capable, by themselves, of rolling away the stone. If the disciples did not steal the body, neither did the women.

The women went to the wrong tomb. Perhaps the women went to a different tomb, saw that it did not contain Christ's body, and began to proclaim the Resurrection. This theory is not plausible because the identity of the real tomb was known to Roman and Jewish authorities; the tomb was sealed by Pilate and under guard; when the disciples heard the women's report, they immediately verified it for themselves (John 20:1-10). Theoretically, it could be conceivable that the women might have made a mistake, but it is a mistake that is of such serious import that undoubtedly it would have been corrected at once.

Joseph of Arimathea moved the body elsewhere. The theory that Joseph of Arimathea for some inexplicable reason moved the body to another tomb fares no better than the idea that the disciples stole the body. He could not have stolen the body before Saturday evening because Pilate and the authorities would not have sealed and guarded an empty tomb. Afterwards he would have been in no better position than the disciples. He, too, would have been up against the guards who were placed there in order to prevent the moving of the body.

At this point it might be appropriate to mention the completely untenable idea that the Roman or Jewish authorities could have been involved in the removal of the body. Although this idea would explain some of the puzzles left by the other hypotheses, it is about as wrongheaded a theory as one can hold. We have no evidence for it whatsoever; all of the evidence points in the direction that the authorities were trying to suppress the idea of a resurrection, not to foster it. If historical methods have any meaning at all, it is unbelievable that the authorities took the body away (or assisted Joseph, the women, or the disciples in doing so).

Jesus never actually died. Some people have advocated a "swoon" theory, saying Jesus actually only went into a coma, but never truly died. Then, after some time in the tomb, He awoke, left the tomb, and presented Himself to the disciples as resurrected. To refute this theory all we need to do is look at the records of what Jesus suffered after His arrest: the multiple beatings, crown of thorns, and crucifixion. When the Roman soldiers checked Him on the cross, they were surprised to find that He was dead already; it was not a case of their simply assuming that He was dead, since they did not expect His death yet. Then, just to make sure, they pierced Him right through the pericardial cavity, so that both blood and water flowed out of His side. There can be no question, Jesus was dead.

Then Jesus was partially embalmed, wrapped in linen, and laid without any medical attention into the tomb. There He remained until Sunday morning. According to the hypothesis, He would have had to awaken suddenly, move the stone all by Himself, sneak past the guards, and then convince the disciples that He had conquered death. It would require a miracle for this hypothesis to hold up. It is simpler to stick to the record and believe in the miracle of the Resurrection than the miracle of the "swoon theory."

Jesus' body was consumed by a new strain of mutant bacteria. This hypothesis was proposed to me by a student during a class discussion. According to his theory, a new strain of bacteria mutated inside the tomb and totally devoured Christ's body, leaving the linen exactly in place. Thus the tomb was devoid of a body, and the disciples began to believe that Jesus had been resurrected.

There are some obvious flaws with this idea. It does not deal at all with the phenomenon of the rolled-away stone. According to Matthew 28:2, there was an earthquake, the angel of the Lord rolled away the stone and then sat on it. If Jesus' body had remained in the tomb without further special effects, no one would even have suspected a resurrection, no matter how fast the body might have disappeared. A sped-up decomposition process would not have given rise to belief in the Resurrection.

This theory gives us occasion to add an important word concerning alternative hypotheses. I do not doubt that, given enough fantasy, it would be possible to come up with much more ingenious theories that would be difficult to refute. For example, why not construe the whole event as having been brought about by an alien invasion? Perhaps it was extraterrestrial creatures who took the body, emptied the tomb, and then even caused the appearances of the risen Jesus.

The problem with the alien and bacteria theories is that they have no intrinsic plausibility. I have brought up this point twice in this book. First, in the second chapter, I argued that I do not need to defend my beliefs against objections that nobody would accept anyway. Then, in the discussion on miracles, I asserted that not all explanatory hypotheses are created equal. There is such a thing as a reasonable presumption as to which of several different explanations for an event are reasonable. Since we have made a case for God and the possibility of miracles, the possibility of a resurrection comes with a reasonable presumption. Because we have no evidence for mutant bacteria or alien invasions, these hypotheses cannot be seen as having reasonable presumptions in their favor. We are not trying to play a fantasy game but to find a plausible historical explanation.

Further alternative scenarios to the resurrection are possible, but only as combinations of the above. Consequently they would also suffer the fate of those hypotheses. Non-miraculous explanations of what happened at the empty tomb have to face a cruel choice: either they have to rewrite the evidence in order to suit themselves or they have to accept the fact that they are not consistent with present evidence. The only hypothesis that fits the evidence is that Jesus was really resurrected. Could the Man who predicted His death and resurrection, only to have it come to pass exactly as He had said, be anything but God?

As I am writing these words, the radio in my office is broadcasting an advertisement for yet another television show on aliens and UFOs, supposedly based on eyewitness reports. Of course, I am skeptical about these claims; but then, I have not yet examined the evidence. It would take a lot to convince me that these stories are based on fact, but we have to be open to the possibility that some things that strike us as very unlikely may turn out to be true.

Similarly, I would never expect someone to accept lightly the fact that Christ is God, but the evidence is in. We saw in this chapter that, given Jesus' claim about Himself, the only sound hypothesis that fits all of the facts is that He is indeed God. The evidence for the virgin birth and the Resurrection only bolsters that claim.

Once again we can close this chapter by addressing the vignettes.

Response to Vignette 1: "Jesus never claimed to be God." I showed above that He did. That ought to settle the argument. Sadly, it frequently does not, not because the evidence is not there but because it is ignored or eliminated.

Drunken soldiers are not the only ones who say such things. If it is announced from the lectern by an authority figure, such as a professor (who may actually know no more about it than the G.I. in the vignette), suddenly many people will believe him without considering the evidence any further.

Also, one runs into a circular argument on the topic. This argument simply denies that Jesus ever said these things; that the historical Jesus never claimed to be God, so all references to that effect must be later inventions of the church. How do we know that the church made up these sayings? Because Jesus would not have stated them. How do we know that Jesus did not state them? Because the church made them up later.

We have tried to show that a fair treatment of the historical documents shows that Jesus did make these claims about Himself.

Response to Vignette 2: I remember not saying anything in reply to this man, but feeling very sorry for him. Aside from his missing out on the truth, he was continuing to be active in the church, wasting his time on something he really did not believe. I have never been able to understand that phenomenon.

As I stated above, I am sympathetic with anyone not willing to embrace belief in the deity of Christ the first time he or she hears it. In my work with different religions, I constantly hear people make claims that I dismiss pretty quickly, but there comes a time when I need to consider the evidence. In the same way, persons who relegate the deity of Christ to superstition despite the evidence may think they are being modern and rational, but actually they are irrational.

Response to Vignette 3: There may be no approach to the Resurrection more dangerous than to remove it from the world of facts. Suddenly it becomes possible to believe something that may not be true according to any normal criteria of truth. I suspect that most people who take that approach believe deep down in their hearts that their beliefs are really false, that the Resurrection did not really happen.

This approach also makes the belief meaningless. A resurrection that did not occur in the normal space-time continuum of the world of facts is neither what the Bible teaches nor understandable. What is a resurrection that did happen, but did not happen? I do not know; this candidate did not know; and neither does anyone else. A flight into the irrational does not salvage faith; it sinks it.

Response to Vignette 4: Who knows how far the cause of Christ will advance, if ever those who claim to believe in Him will stop mouthing such cynical things, which are obviously false! If by "prove" you mean establishing facts rationally according to normal rules of evidence, you certainly cannot "prove anything" with the Bible. The criteria we have made use of in this chapter are the normal criteria for historical study. Ultimately they are based on common sense.

If the historical facts about Jesus were truly inconclusive, we would have a serious problem. In that case, you would lose the theological information as well. You cannot know that Jesus died on the cross for your sins unless you know that Jesus died on the cross. You cannot know that Jesus is your living Savior unless He was resurrected. These issues are of more than trivial interest. If Jesus is not who He claimed to be, then there is no point in Christianity. Conversely, we know that Jesus is God, that He did give evidence of His identity, and that He invites you to let His work set you free.

For Growth and Study

Mastering the Material

When you have studied this chapter you should be able to:
1. Summarize seven passages in which Jesus claimed to be God.
2. List the five alternative explanations to Jesus' being God; describe where they are flawed; and show how His being God is the best explanation.
3. Make a case for why it is plausible that the virgin birth did happen and why alternative explanations do not fit the facts.
4. Show why Christ's post-resurrection appearances could not have been hallucinations.
5. Refute six alternative hypotheses to the idea that the empty tomb was caused by Christ's resurrection.
6. Identify the following names with the contribution to which we have alluded in this chapter: John R. W. Stott, J. Gresham Machen.

Thinking About the Ideas

1. Can you find further passages in which Jesus claimed to be God?

2. Find an example of a contemporary person who has claimed to be God. Apply the criteria of this chapter to that case.
3. Find stories about miraculous births in other religions. How do they differ from the account of Jesus' virgin birth in the New Testament?
4. Imagine someone told you that they saw or experienced something very unusual. Keep track of your thought processes as you try to decide whether to believe the person. How do your thoughts apply to the reports of people who said they had seen the resurrected Jesus?
5. Find further alternative explanations people have given to avoid the idea of a resurrection. Show how they are refuted by the arguments of this chapter.
6. Trace the flow of the argument of this book from the possibility of truth to the fact of the Resurrection. To what extent is the interdependence of the arguments an asset or a liability?

For Further Exploration

J. Gresham Machen, *The Virgin Birth of Christ* (Grand Rapids: Baker, 1930).

H. D. McDonald, *Jesus: Human and Divine* (Grand Rapids: Zondervan, 1968).

Josh McDowell, *More Than a Carpenter* (Wheaton, IL: Tyndale House, 1977).

Frank Morison, *Who Moved the Stone?* (Grand Rapids: Zondervan, 1930).

12

From Christ to Christianity

Jesus Versus Christianity

Vignette 1: Let us locate once again inside a coffeehouse on a Saturday night. I was talking to a college student who was very interested in what we were doing.

"What's the purpose of this place?" he asked.

"There are several purposes," I replied. "To give people a quiet place to go; to help people communicate through informal conversation; to help people find Jesus Christ; to show people what Christianity is all about."

"Wait a minute!" the student expostulated. "You're mixing up two different things. First you said, 'Jesus'; then you said, 'Christianity.' Those are two different things."

"I don't think so," I allowed. "Christianity is the teachings of Jesus Christ."

He countered adamantly, "No, they are very different. Christianity has totally messed up Jesus' teaching. I want to follow Jesus, but I don't want anything to do with what is called 'Christianity.'"

Sin

Vignette 2: At the literature table in the student union a curious fellow student wanted to know what we were "selling." I shared the gospel with her, pointing out that Jesus died for our sins.

"Sins?" she reacted skeptically. "I'm not a sinner."

I took up the challenge. "Are you telling me that you have never sinned?"

"No. Never."

I did not give up. "Do you mean that you have never done anything that in any way hurt other people?"

Do You Need Faith?

Vignette 3: On a bike trip down the East Coast, at a little roadside restaurant, the management allowed us to hose ourselves down outside—a welcome relief in the 100+ degree Virginia heat. We were joined by Max, another bicyclist who had come all the way from California. After the usual comparisons and contrasts of our experiences on the road, the talk drifted to religion. Max shared with us that part of the reason for his long solo trip was to give himself time to think about his commitment to Jesus Christ. He was convinced that, if he tried hard enough, he could live a life of perfect obedience to Christ.

Jim, one of my fellow riders, started to probe a little.

"What about faith?" he asked. "Don't you need to have faith in Christ too?"

"No," Max replied. "Faith is a crutch. It is possible for me to follow Christ completely without escaping into faith."

"But Jesus taught that we need to have faith in Him. He died for our sins."

"Actually," retorted Max, "if you read the Gospels carefully, you'll find that Jesus Himself never taught such a thing. He wanted us to follow Him, not to avoid our responsibility by believing in His death."

Room for Faith

Vignette 4: It was the last day of the semester! Time for my last lecture, instructions about the final exam, and minor celebrations tempered by the prospect of having to read all those finals. A few students thanked me for a course they found helpful.

One student told me: "Last night some of us working in the dishroom were talking about your course. There were some mixed opinions about it."

"Oh?" I answered, not very intelligently. I got the feeling that always comes over me when I know that my humility is about to be enhanced.

"Yeah," he replied. "You know Matt who had your course last semester? He says that by the time you're done proving everything, there's no room left for faith."

We have shown in the last chapter that it is reasonable to accept that Jesus is God. From there it is but a short step to verifying those beliefs that make up the core of Christianity. By the "core of Christianity" I mean the list of beliefs that I am about to enumerate. These are not intended to be the dogmatic formulation of all essential truth; the phrasing and scope of much of what I am going to say may be subject to theological refinement. I am beginning with the hypothesis that genuine Christianity needs to accept these beliefs, however nuanced, as nonnegotiable. The question is, can we support them? Here are the five beliefs in question:[1]

1. The Scriptures of the Old and New Testament are the inspired Word of God.
2. Human beings are estranged from God due to their sin, and cannot restore themselves to a state of being acceptable to God.
3. By His death on the cross and His resurrection, Christ made provision for us to be reconciled to God.
4. To receive salvation from Christ, it is necessary and sufficient to have faith in Him.
5. The person who has been saved by Christ gives evidence of being saved by a righteous life.
   Are these beliefs supportable?

First Core Belief: The Bible as the Word of God

Our key question in this section will be the following: Did Jesus teach that the Bible is the Word of God?

If Jesus is God, then His teachings must be true. This is a very simple statement, but it is hard to see how it could be false. If this is true then whatever Jesus taught about Scripture must also be true. If Jesus believed that the Old Testament was inspired, it is incumbent on us to hold the same view. If Jesus guaranteed that the teachings of the apostles would have His own authority, then we need to accept them as such.

---

[1] We have already established a number of other beliefs without which there could be no Christianity: that there is a God, that Jesus existed as a historical figure, that Jesus is God, etc.

This is precisely the argument we want to put forward at this point. On the basis of Jesus' authority as God, we can conclude that the Scriptures, Old and New Testament, are the inspired Word of God.

Jesus Accepted the Old Testament as Inspired

Jesus consistently referred to Old Testament Scripture as having divine authority. Let us break this basic fact down into components. Jesus asserted that:

- *The law came from God.* He referred to it as "the commandment of God" and made a clear distinction between it and human laws and traditions (Mark 7:7-8).
- *The law is fixed and permanent.* He stated that not one jot or tittle of it would pass away until it would be completely fulfilled (Matt. 5:18).
- *Scripture is authoritative.* We see Jesus using Scripture in order to settle an argument. For example, Jesus defeated Satan with direct Scripture quotations when He was tempted (Matt. 4).
- *Scripture contains supernatural predictions.* On more than one occasion, Jesus stated that the Old Testament Scriptures referred to Himself. The only way this could be possible is if the Old Testament is a divine book containing supernatural predictions (John 5:46-47; Luke 24:25-27).

Thus we see that Jesus used the Scriptures as coming from God. Jesus considered the Scriptures as fixed and permanent, authoritative, and supernatural. We summarize these points with the phrase that Scripture is "inspired." In particular, this expression emphasizes that Scripture is writing that originated with God and contains God's authoritative message.

Did Jesus personally believe what He said about the Scriptures? Is it not possible that He used these writings in the way that He did only so that He could communicate with His Jewish audience? They accepted Scripture as inspired; so He used the same Scriptures in order to teach them. Thus He would not necessarily have been expressing His own convictions so much as accommodating Himself to His listeners.

Even though at first this accommodation theory seems to have a certain plausibility, it does not hold up on inspection. First of all, we are referring to the man who is also God. It does not make sense that this person was endorsing ideas that He knew to be false. If the Old Testament is in fact not inspired, then God would be aware of that fact; Christ's endorsement of the notion would be tantamount to His abetting a known falsehood. For mere human beings such a thing would be reprehensible; for God it is impossible.

Second, the idea that Jesus was merely accommodating Himself to the people is highly problematic. If there is one fact that stands out about Christ's ministry, it is that He steadfastly refused to compromise. We are talking about the Man who defended His disciples when they did not wash their hands in keeping with law and custom (Mark 7:5), addressed His audience as the offspring of the devil (John 8:44), broke Jewish customs Himself on many occasions, and essentially made it a point to alienate the authorities at every turn. The idea that He suddenly would compromise His own convictions in order to communicate does not fit this picture at all.

At that, a quick look at how and when Jesus used Scripture makes it even less plausible that He was accommodating Himself to His Jewish audience. For, invariably, He did so to confront, not to conciliate. His audience was wrong and had not treated Scripture properly. For example, He told them that, if they had believed what they read in the writings of Moses, they would now be able to believe Him (Jesus); their unbelief was due to an insufficient belief in Scripture. Jesus was calling them back to a deeper acceptance of Scripture and its message. This is the very opposite of accommodation. Thus the notion that Jesus only used Scripture in the way that His audience did is ruled out.

So we see that in the teachings of Jesus, the Son of God, Old Testament Scripture emerges as inspired writing from God Himself. Therefore, the early church also accepted Old Testament Scriptures as inspired writings. On the same authority, that of Jesus, so should we.

An important question in this context concerns which books belong in this collection of inspired writings. Given the above reasoning, the easy—and correct—answer is: those books that belonged to the Old Testament in first-century Palestine. For only those are the books that Jesus would have accepted as inspired. Around A.D. 90 a conclave of rabbis (Jewish, not Christian), meeting in the Palestinian town of Jamnia, gave their permanent endorsement to the list of books that the Jewish synagogues already accepted as Scripture. These rabbis never did consider adding any further books; they thought about deleting some but did not. Thus we have a clear standard of which books Jesus would have accepted as Scripture: the ones in the list of the rabbis. These books are exactly the ones that we call the "Old Testament," namely Genesis through Malachi.

There exists another group of books that have at times been included in the Old Testament writings, most notably by the Roman Catholic Church. These include 1 and 2 Maccabees, Tobit, Judith, Wisdom of Solomon, and others. These books are frequently referred to as the Apocrypha. "Apocryphal" means "doubtful," and it is indeed more than doubtful whether these books should be considered Scripture. They ought to be rejected as Scripture, not primarily because of their content (which is highly uneven) but because they do not come with the authority of first-century Judaism. They were not accepted by the rabbis; they were not accepted by Jesus. Thus we have no basis on which to accept them as inspired.

The New Testament Scriptures Rest on Christ's Authority

Obviously the argument for the New Testament books has to look different since they were not even written until many years after Jesus had ascended into heaven. In this case, the point is that Jesus authorized His disciples to record and continue His teaching. This teaching became a permanent record in the form of the New Testament.

The crucial statement by Jesus to this effect is found in John 14:26. In this verse Jesus promises His disciples that the Holy Spirit will bring all of His teachings to their minds after He is gone. Again, in John 15:26-27, Jesus states that,

through the Holy Spirit, the disciples will be His witnesses.
Other passages to the same effect are Matthew 28:19-20 and
Acts 1:8. The picture emerges of the disciples being called in
a special way to propagate Christ's teachings. They moved
from being "disciples," which means "followers and
learners," to being "apostles," which means "represen-
tatives." Hearing an apostle teach carried the same weight
as hearing Christ teach.

The collection of books we now call the "New Testament"
has to be seen as an extension of the apostles' teaching
ministry. Each of the books was written by either an apostle
or someone closely associated with an apostle—someone
whose teaching would reproduce the teaching of the apostle.
For example, Luke was known as Paul's associate, and Mark
as Peter's.

The process of recognizing these books as authoritative
began almost immediately. In 2 Peter 3:16, the apostle Peter
refers to the letters of Paul by classifying them with
"Scriptures." The word that is used here is a technical term
used only in reference to what was considered to be inspired
writings. Thus, by using this term of Paul's writings, Peter is
already acknowledging their inspired character.

The recognition of the New Testament proceeded at a
brisk pace. Contrary to a common misunderstanding, it did
not consist of many centuries of indecisive debate which was
finally settled by the arbitrary decision of a council. In fact,
this process of recognition was relatively smooth. By the end
of the second century after Christ, (a hundred years or so
after the last book had been written), most churches were
already using a collection of books very similar to our
present New Testament.[2] The official pronouncements of
councils came much later.

Of course, not all books were accepted by everyone all
at once. In fact, there was some pretty animated
discussion on whether to include a few books, such as
Hebrews and 2 Peter. During these debates the most
important question was about authorship, the very same

---

[2]We have some hard evidence in the form of a surviving list for this claim. See
"The Muratorian Canon" in Henry Bettenson, ed., *Documents of the Christian Church*,
2nd ed. (New York: Oxford University Press, 1963), 28-29.

issue to which we are pointing here: Was the book written by someone who was an apostle or directly represented an apostle? If so, it could be included; if not, it would have to be rejected.

Something else needs to be highlighted as we describe the process of selection.[3] There were no sudden surprises or last-minute additions. The books that were under discussion, and became universally accepted had been recognized by most churches all along. The churches merely reached a consensus on books they had been using for a long time.

The first *official* recognition of the New Testament canon came in A.D. 397 by the Synod of Carthage. It endorsed the same twenty-seven books that have continued to make up our New Testament. The only thing that this conference of bishops actually did was to pronounce its official approval on something that was already true in the local churches. Henry Chadwick, an eminent church historian, evaluates the whole process this way: "Sometimes modern writers wonder at the disagreements. The truly astonishing thing is that so great a measure of agreement was reached so quickly."[4]

Thus the argument for the authority of the New Testament rests on the following pattern: Jesus endowed the apostles with full teaching authority by the power of the Holy Spirit. The teaching of the apostles is perpetuated in the collection of their writings, which is the New Testament. Thus we receive the New Testament on the authority of Jesus Himself.

These considerations also make it clear that no new books can be added to the New Testament. From time to time someone raises the question of whether the canon is closed or whether we might need to add some more writings to the New Testament. Now, I would not want to say that the Holy Spirit can no longer inspire people to record new revelations. God is omnipotent, and He can certainly bring about such a thing. Nonetheless, any new

---

[3]The process is customarily referred to as "canonization," or the accumulation of the "canon." The Greek word "canon" means "ruler, measuring rod." Thus we are looking at the question of which books measure up.

[4]Henry Chadwick, *The Early Church* (Baltimore: Penguin, 1967), 44.

writings would not be produced by an apostle and would not, therefore, come with Jesus' authority. We would not be able to recognize them as inspired and authoritative for the whole church in the same way in which we recognize the New Testament.

We have taken the first step in moving from Christ to Christianity. Jesus Christ, the Son of God, endorsed the Old and the New Testament with His authority. Consequently we cannot coherently pledge allegiance to the teachings of Jesus without simultaneously recognizing the revelation of Scripture. We know that the Old and New Testaments are the Word of God because that is how the Son of God taught us to accept them. In our earlier discussion we made the case that the New Testament is authoritative as history; now we have shown that it is also authoritative as divine revelation. As an additional consequence, the discussion below of further topics can now make reference to not only what Jesus taught directly, but also to what the rest of the New Testament writers had to say.

Second Core Belief: Sin

Our key question in this section will be the following: Did Jesus teach that we are sinful? We have already stated that an essential ingredient of Christianity is the supposition of our sinfulness. We are so sinful that we need to be brought into a relationship with God through a saving experience. Did Jesus teach such a thing?

To be able to answer this question we need to have a correct understanding of the nature of Jesus' teaching and the nature of sin. If someone is going to look for a verse in which Jesus is saying, "You have committed sins and deserve to be condemned," he or she is not going to find it in those words. Nevertheless, Jesus' teaching about sin leaves no doubt on the matter.

First of all, we must place Jesus' teaching into the proper historical context. Almost all of it was directed to Jews, who were still living under the Old Testament law (which, as we just saw, Jesus Himself accepted as divinely revealed). Jesus' audience did not need to have the nature of sin spelled out to them; they knew it meant not living up to God's standards. More specifically, sin involved the breaking of particular commandments, but the act of breaking a commandment was seen as directly infringing on the God who had issued it. Consequently, in much of His teaching, Jesus lifted up God's standards of righteousness and demonstrated how impossible it is for us to live up to them. In the process, He issued a verdict every bit as potent as the statement: "You have committed sins and deserve to be condemned."

Let us look at a few representative verses. In Matthew 5:20 Jesus says: "Unless your righteousness surpasses that of the scribes and Pharisees, you shall not enter the kingdom of heaven" (NASB). Note first of all that the basic issue concerns entry into the kingdom of heaven, or being in the proper relationship to God. Second, observe that for all practical purposes Jesus closes the door on any human making it into the kingdom of heaven, for nobody was more punctilious in observing personal righteousness than the scribes and Pharisees. To be sure, in some places Jesus reprimanded them for sin and hypocrisy, but what makes these reprimands so poignant is that Jesus was showing up flaws in some of the most meticulously pious people on earth. If they could not make it, nobody could. The chapter closes with the amazing exhortation: "You are to be perfect, as your heavenly Father is perfect" (Matt. 5:48, NASB). Unfortunately, too many discussions on the Sermon on the Mount miss the point by watering down Christ's requirements. Jesus was *not* motivating us to try a little harder to become a little better. He was expounding an impossible standard of righteousness that leaves us with only two choices: (1) try to do the impossible and fail, or (2) rely on God to do for us what we cannot possibly do ourselves.

Similar observations must be made for many other teaching passages. Even the story of the good Samaritan (Luke 10:25-37), which is often understood as moral exhortation, must be understood first of all as condemnation. A quick look at the context shows that the parable comes up in response to a question involving salvation: "What shall I do to inherit eternal life?" (v. 25, NASB). Jesus then uses the parable to illustrate the idea that the Jewish legalistic framework does not suffice to merit eternal life.

Thus it is not surprising that Jesus made some sweeping statements about our alienation from God. In John 3:18—not nearly so well known as the preceding verses—He stated that the world (those who do not believe in Him) stands condemned already. In another passage, in which Jesus promised the coming of the Holy Spirit, Jesus said that the Spirit will make evident the world's condemnation (John 16:8-11). In short, given the fact that we cannot measure up to God's standards of righteousness, we are already in a state of condemnation. There is nothing we have to do to separate ourselves from God; we are separated already. We cannot remedy that situation by ourselves. Jesus said: "No one can come to Me, unless the Father who sent Me draws him" (John 6:44, NASB). Did Jesus teach that we are sinners in need of salvation? It is clear that He did.

Other New Testament authors emphasized this message. Jesus' original hearers were almost all Jews, but the New Testament authors wrote to both Jewish and gentile readers. For this reason, they were careful to point out human sinfulness. The apostle John stressed the fact that all people are sinners (1 John 1:8, 10) and that our sin and God's righteousness are incompatible (1 John 1:5). He also clarified that broken relationships among people are signs of a broken relationship with God (1 John 4:20).

The apostle Paul also stressed our sinfulness. In Romans 3:23 he taught that "all have sinned and fall short of the glory of God" (NASB). This pointed to the same concept that Jesus had been teaching. Sin is not merely a legal infraction, it is a violation of God's own purity. All that falls short of God's glory is sin. Thus "the wages of sin is death" (Rom. 6:23, NASB). It cannot be otherwise because the gap between God and us cannot be ignored. Finally, Paul made it clear that sinfulness is a permanent condition of being human, a natural characteristic of "Adam's race." We give evidence of this when we willfully violate God's law (Rom. 5:12).

Third Core Belief: The Cross

The key question in this section will be the following: Did Jesus teach that He would die for our sins?

Possibly no verse among Jesus' teachings has caused as much consternation of late as His claim in John 14:6: "I am the way, the truth, and the life; no one comes to the Father, but through Me" (NASB). He claimed to be, not only a way, but the only way.

This exclusive statement was also reaffirmed by the apostles. Peter said, "And there is salvation in no one else; for there is no other name under heaven that has been given among men, by which we must be saved" (Acts 4:12, NASB). Paul affirms, "For there is one God, and one mediator also between God and men, the man Christ Jesus" (1 Tim. 2:5, NASB). In a slightly weaker statement, John clarified that the work of Jesus is sufficient for the entire world—no other savior is needed (1 John 2:2).

It is crucial to note why Jesus made these exclusive statements. It was not because He was God, nor because of His power and wisdom. In each of the above verses, the reason for an exclusive claim is that *only Jesus died for our sins.* (Even John 14:6 comes directly after Jesus prophesied His death.) Whenever Jesus is held up as our only Savior, it is because He is the one who saved us. Thus the exclusive claims are not made out of arrogance or superiority; they are statements of hope. We are to understand that "there is no other way out of our sinful state. But rejoice! God has provided this one way through Jesus Christ."

Thus the cross of Christ is essential to understand His role as Savior. We observed in the last chapter how Christ's teaching was "self-centered." From the very beginning He made Himself the center of attention as God, as Judge, as Master, as the fulfillment of prophecy. Once His disciples grasped that reality, He added that His mission included His death on the cross. That is to say, once the disciples were sure that He was the Christ (Mark 8:29), He began to prepare them with predictions of His death and resurrection (Mark 8:31; 9:31; 10:33-34). In a private conversation, Jesus had already made clear to Nicodemus that His death was essential to our salvation (John 3:14-15).

This theme was frequently elaborated in the writings of the apostles. Paul wrote, "God commendeth his love toward us, in that, while we were yet sinners, Christ died for us" (Rom. 5:8, KJV). John wrote, "If any man sin, we have an advocate with the Father, Jesus Christ the righteous: And he is the propitiation for our sins: and not for ours only, but also for the sins of the whole world" (1 John 2:1-2, KJV). Peter wrote, "Ye know that ye were not redeemed with corruptible things, as silver and gold, . . . but with the precious blood of Christ, as of a lamb without blemish and without spot" (1 Pet. 1:18-19, KJV). Christ's death is the center of the Christian message. Paul summarized his message to the Corinthians: "I determined not to know any thing among you, save Jesus Christ, and him crucified" (1 Cor. 2:2, KJV).

Fourth Core Belief: Faith

The key question in this section will be the following: Did Jesus teach that we must have faith in Him?

In the first chapter we delineated several meanings of the word *faith*. There is an intellectual conception of faith (knowing faith) expressed with the statement, "I believe that . . . ." But there is also the notion of faith as trust or reliance, expressed as "I believe in . . . ." This form of faith is a kind of abandonment; you stop depending on anything else and rely on the object of your faith alone.

Faith as trust (as in saving and growing faith) manifests itself as commitment. Let me illustrate my intended point. I preach on Sundays at a country church, and occasionally students from my college come out to present special music. Most of them have never travelled that way before, and so I always warn them about a particular stretch of road: "When you go along here, it's going to seem like it's taking forever. After a while you're going to think you missed the turn-off, but don't worry. Trust me; you can't miss the turn-off once you get to it." Invariably, the students tell me afterwards that I was right. They say they had felt sure they must have missed the turn, but, because of what I said, they kept on going. They knew me, believed me, and trusted me. Their trust was not just an empty attitude of a frame of mind; it manifested itself in the fact that they did not turn around or ask for directions but kept on driving in the right direction.

Faith implies personal loyalty. Looking at the matter from the other direction, this kind of personal loyalty makes sense only on the basis of trust. Thus it would be a mistake to drive a wedge between biblical statements calling for faith in Christ and others calling for personal loyalty and obedience. They are not antithetical to each other; they are two sides of the same coin.

In short, when Christ calls for undivided loyalty to Himself or for total obedience to Himself, these demands must be seen as equivalent to requiring direct faith in Him. In many places Jesus first holds up to His audience the requirements of the Old Testament law, but the law is an impossible standard for us sinners to keep. Consequently Jesus turns from the law to Himself and explains that we can be saved only by exclusively clinging to Him. It is a serious mistake (which many people unfortunately commit) to interpret Christ as substituting a new and harder law for the older one. The change is not from one law to another, but from the law to personal loyalty to Christ.

Can we substantiate that this is what Jesus taught? Let one example illustrate that He did (Mark 10:17-22). A young man of high standing in the synagogue came to Jesus wanting to know what he must do to inherit eternal life. Jesus began by reciting to him a representative list from the Ten Commandments. The young man claimed that he had kept all of these; but note: the conversation went on! The man knew that what he had done was inadequate; otherwise he would not have come to Jesus to begin with. Jesus told him, "Sell all you have and follow me." Note something else important in this passage. Mark specifically pointed out that Jesus said these words to him out of love. In other words, He did not decide, "This guy is really arrogant; I'm going to lay a really burdensome commandment on him." No, Jesus showed him that salvation is found only in the kind of abandonment to Him that is willing to forego all attachment to worldly goods. Unfortunately, the young man was not yet ready for such faith.

Did Jesus teach that we must have faith in Him? Yes. Jesus taught that salvation requires personal loyalty and faith in Himself.

Clearly, Paul taught the same thing. In fact, he hammered away at it. The only way in which we can have salvation is through faith in Christ. Thus he wrote in Galatians 2:16 (NIV), "We . . . know that a man is not justified by observing the law, but by faith in Jesus Christ" (NIV). In Ephesians 2:8-9 he added, "For by grace are ye saved through faith; and that not of yourselves, it is the gift of God: Not of works, lest any man should boast" (KJV)

Paul went to great lengths to make the point that salvation depends on an exclusive relationship of trust in Jesus. In Galatians he counters the heretics who attempt to impose circumcision as a requirement on all people. Apparently these were the same persons who are quoted in Acts as saying, "Unless you are circumcised according to the custom taught by Moses, you cannot be saved" (Acts 15:1, NIV). So, in Galatians 5:3-4 Paul argued that "every man who lets himself be circumcised . . . is obligated to obey the whole law. You who are trying to be justified by law have been alienated from Christ; you have fallen away from grace" (NIV). These are strong words, and it takes a clear understanding of the nature of faith to appreciate them. One might be tempted to say that adding good works to one's faith only increases one's chances of becoming acceptable to God. At worst, one might be doing something meaningless, but where is the harm?

The answer is that faith is supposed to be an attitude of complete trust. Imagine the following situation. A student has accidentally walked out of an exam with her test. An hour later she shows up at my office claiming that it was a pure accident; she just found the test and is turning it in exactly the way she finished it during the exam time. What if I said something like this: "It's not that I don't trust you, but I'm going to have to ask you to take the whole test over again"? That would be a lie. People say these kinds of things all of the time, but they cannot be true. If I really trusted the student, I would not ask her to retake the test. Real trust implies that I would accept her word for what happened and let it go. As soon as we say, "I trust you, but . . . ," we do not really trust. In the same way, if we say to Christ, "I trust You for my salvation, but I will make sure of it by adding some of my own good works," we do not really trust Christ. Thus Paul emphasized Jesus' teaching that faith is an act of unreserved trust. This kind of faith is not a barrier but the only way in which we do receive salvation as a gift from God. Faith is not only necessary for us; it is also sufficient.

Fifth Core Belief: Righteousness

The key question in this section will be the following: Did Jesus teach that a righteous life is the result of being saved by Him? Does the fact that saving faith rules out cooperation with good works mean that good works are irrelevant to the believer? No, Jesus taught at many different times and places that those who stand in proper relationship to God will have evident works of righteousness. He said of false prophets that "by their fruits ye shall know them" (Matt. 7:20, KJV). Of His disciples He states, "By this shall all men know that ye are my disciples, if ye have love one to another" (John 13:35, KJV). Those who know Him are expected to confess Him before others (Matt. 10:32), be prepared to forsake their families (10:35-37), carry their own cross (10:38), and in many other ways demonstrate their allegiance to Christ. Even the most cursory reading of the Gospels makes it clear that it is inconceivable for someone to have a relationship to Jesus without strong evidence for it in a life of righteousness.

To understand this point, it is necessary to distinguish between a *condition* (or cause or prerequisite) and a *consequence* (or effect or result) of salvation. Good works cannot be a prerequisite, but they are a result of salvation. They are neither condition nor cause, but they are the consequence and result of being saved.

Consider the following illustration of this pattern. The only way to have chicken pox is to catch the virus that causes it. Once you are infected, you will break out in an itchy, bumpy rash (and, if you are a child, your parents—who are not itching—will forbid you to scratch it). You cannot give yourself chicken pox by making yourself break out (say, by eating something to which you are allergic). If you do have the virus, you had better also have the bumps on your skin if you expect anyone to believe that you have the disease. Thus, once you have salvation through the "virus" of faith, you should break out into the "rash" of good works. Good works cannot "infect" you with salvation, but once you have the "disease," you should show the "symptoms" of a righteous life.

Surely this kind of pattern is what James had in mind when he wrote that faith without works is dead (Jas. 2:17). The crucial statement in this passage is verse 18, where he proclaims, "I will shew thee my faith by my works" (KJV). In other words, the kind of faith that saves an individual is the kind of living faith that manifests itself in good works.

The same point is made by Paul on various occasions. In Ephesians 2:8-10, Paul insisted that we are saved by grace through faith alone. In this same paragraph he added that our salvation has a deliberate purpose: we are "created in Christ Jesus unto good works" (v. 10, KJV). Paul reiterated that message three times in Titus 2:11—3:8. The third time is the clearest. Once again Paul protested that our salvation is due entirely to the acts of God—"not by works of righteousness which we have done, but according to his mercy he saved us" (3:5, KJV). The section concludes with the exhortation that "they which have believed in God might be careful to maintain good works" (3:8).

The apostle John argued for the same point, but in a different context: "If anyone says, 'I love God,' yet hates his brother, he is a liar" (1 John 4:20, NIV). That is, you cannot have a relationship with God and not have your life show it.

Yes, Jesus taught that people who are saved by Him give evidence of their salvation by a changed life. The rest of the New Testament concurs.

We began this chapter by pointing to five items as the core of Christianity: the Bible, sin, the cross, faith, righteousness. In the course of previous chapters we have shown that we need to recognize Jesus as God. Now we can conclude that if we accept Jesus for who He is on the basis of the historical evidence, then we need to also accept the truth of these core items in Christianity. Therefore, we have completed the project we began in the first chapter. We asked ourselves: But is it true? Now we can say: Yes, on the authority of God Himself, it is true.

In the last chapter we will address the question of how this truth speaks to the needs of our culture. First, though, we can return to our opening vignettes.

Response to Vignette 1: Christ, but not Christianity—is such a thing possible? In part, the answer to the question depends on how one defines Christianity. A person who makes such a statement may actually be thinking of some external aspects of the culture associated with Western Christianity. The Christian faith can prosper without buildings with steeples and pews in which people go through a pre-established set of acts of worship once a week; although the Bible does enjoin Christians to meet together on a regular basis. The cultural side of Christian life is certainly not obligatory, but that is not how we have defined Christianity. Instead we pointed to some essential beliefs having to do with a person's relationship to God. What we tried to show was that Jesus Himself taught these beliefs, which were then also corroborated by His appointed teachers, the apostles. Thus to acknowledge Christ means to accept His teachings (what else could it mean?). His teachings are precisely what constitutes Christianity.

In the light of what we showed in this chapter, the only way it is possible to accept Christ, but not Christianity, is to revise what Jesus actually taught to suit our preconceptions. As human beings, this is a very natural tendency for us. Since we have already demonstrated the historical reliability of the New Testament, however, there is no factual basis for doing such a thing.

Response to Vignette 2: Sin is something much more serious than having hurt other people somewhere along the line. Jesus did not die, and you do not need to be redeemed, because you made your little sister cry when you were five years old. The nature of sin has to do with a broken relationship with God, which then also manifests itself in broken relationships with people.

Thus I have included this vignette as another item under the heading of "things I wish I hadn't said." As I recall the conversation, the girl said something like, "Oh sure, but that's not sin. That's just being human." Now I was stuck, and I needed to explain to her what I should have said in the first place, namely that we are by our very nature already alienated from God. Of course many people reject this notion, but, as this little example shows, to minimize the nature of sin in order to get people to acknowledge their sinfulness does not help either.

Response to Vignette 3: This vignette is not that different from the previous one. Once again it concerns the need to help people see that they are in a state of sin from which they need to be redeemed. I have included it in order to make one simple point: Jesus taught this very thing. To strip sin and redemption from Jesus' teaching is to do violence to it. Christ's teachings make it apparent that we need to be saved from our sinful condition.

Response to Vignette 4: In chapter 1 we outlined three types of faith, one of which is knowing faith. In this rubric we "believe that" something is true. Frequently it consists of accepting a belief as true simply on the basis of authority apart from evidence. Even though it is not possible to dispense with this kind of faith, for purposes of this study we set ourselves the task of seeing whether we can know Christianity to be true on the basis of evidence. If we have succeeded in doing so, why should that be a fault?

I hear this kind of objection often these days, and I must say that I am a little nonplussed by it. What are people asking for? Should I slip in an invalid argument every once in a while? (I could come up with a few.) Should I tell people, "Even though there is pretty good evidence, I want you to ignore the evidence and believe on the basis of my say-so!"? I cannot bring myself to believe that such a move would advance the cause of truth.

Yes, faith is essential for Christianity, but true faith does not ask us to believe an apparent falsehood. True faith is willing, not only to assent to certain truths, but also to stake all of our being for eternity in an act of trust on the one we have shown to be the Truth.

For Growth and Study

Mastering the Material

When you have studied this chapter you should be able to:
1. List five beliefs which are at the core of Christianity.
2. Show how our acceptance of the Old Testament as the inspired Word of God is grounded in the authority of Jesus.

3. Show how our acceptance of the New Testament as the inspired Word of God is grounded in the authority of Jesus.
4. Make a case for how Jesus and the apostles taught that we are sinful.
5. Summarize what Jesus and the apostles taught about His death on the cross.
6. Show what Jesus and the apostles taught about faith.
7. Defend Paul's contention that faith cannot be supplemented by works.
8. Show how, in the teachings of Jesus and the apostles, good works are presented as a consequence of faith.
9. Identify the following name with the contribution to which we have alluded in this chapter: Henry Chadwick.

Thinking About the Ideas

1. We have set up a list of five core beliefs of Christianity. Make a case for deleting from or adding to that list.
2. In the light of the discussion, construct a sound argument against including further new books in the Bible.
3. Why is the concept of sin such a crucial factor in understanding the nature of Christianity?
4. Compile New Testament passages that treat the effect of Christ's death on the cross. What kind of a picture emerges?
5. Why is faith not even a minimal kind of work? Why, then, is faith linked to obedience in the New Testament?
6. Some people argue that by expecting good works as an effect of faith, we reintroduce salvation by works. Why is this not the case?
7. Pull together a short summary of Christianity, complete with Scripture verses, as taught by Jesus and the apostles.

For Further Exploration

Winfried Corduan, *Handmaid to Theology* (Grand Rapids: Baker, 1981).

Paul Enns, *The Moody Handbook of Theology* (Chicago: Moody Press, 1989).

Robert H. Stein, *The Method and Message of Jesus' Teachings* (Philadelphia: Westminster, 1978).

John R. W. Stott, *Basic Christianity* (Downers Grove, IL: InterVarsity, 1958).

13

Truth and Our Culture

Is It Arrogant to Say You Are Right?

Vignette 1: As a graduate student I frequently found myself defending a conservative point of view during seminar discussions. To their credit, my professors usually permitted me to present my beliefs as long as I allowed myself to be challenged by differing perspectives. During one such discussion, a point of comparison was brought up between a Christian and a Hindu understanding of a certain issue. Without any lengthy reflection, I made a remark to the effect that we needed to make the assumption that the Christian view was correct and that the Hindu view false.

My professor fixed me with a stare. "Are you so arrogant as to believe that you alone are right, and everybody else is wrong?"

Why Be Moral?

Vignette 2: While teaching Introduction to Philosophy as an adjunct at a state university, my class came to a unit on ethics in which we had lively discussions on principles of moral decision making.

One evening I challenged the class. "Imagine you have shown a person the right thing to do. Then he says, 'I don't care if it's right or wrong; I will just do what I want to.' How do you respond?"

I looked at blank faces and listened to silence. So I rephrased my question. "On what basis should someone even want to be a good, moral person? Where can we look if someone really doesn't care about being moral?"

I was hoping that one of my students would say something about self-esteem, religion, humanism, evolution, anything to answer the question. Finally a student hesitantly broke the silence by suggesting, "It's whatever way you were brought up, isn't it?"

Art

Vignette 3: I was in Washington, D.C., at the Museum of Modern Art, a branch of the Smithsonian. I was viewing a work entitled, "White Painting," by Robert Rauschenberg. The painting was unframed; it consisted of five panels of canvas covered uniformly with white oil paint—nothing more. Adjacent was a similar production, except in black, entitled "Black Painting."

What made the moment so memorable was that a boy, about sixteen years old, was standing in front of the white panels with his mother. Apparently she had just made a disparaging remark about the work.

"You just don't understand, Mom," he protested. "There's actually a lot of deep meaning here."

But is it true? We have shown over the course of the last twelve chapters that, yes, Christianity is true. One final investigation is helpful. It seeks to contrast the Christian commitment to truth with the presuppositions of our culture. Let me clarify the purpose of this chapter by first stating what I am not trying to do.

1. My primary purpose is not to write a quick expose of modern culture with an eye toward condemning its sinfulness. Although some of these themes are implicit in what I am going to say, my aim is not to condemn but to point to the self-destructiveness of our culture in order to make the case for the need for Christian truth.

2. This discussion is not intended to be a practical guide to witnessing. I hope that the information conveyed here (as well as that of the entire book) will help those who share their faith in Christ with others, but the point is not simply to provide ammunition for evangelistic conversations. This chapter, like the others, requires thought; it does not simply provide formulas.

This chapter will look at three major human concerns: *truth, goodness, and beauty*.[1] For each of these we will show that the understanding provided by our culture is inadequate and potentially disastrous. We will then make it apparent that Christianity will meet precisely that need in our culture.

What Is Culture?

A word needs to be said about what I mean by "culture." An anthropologist might define culture as "that complex whole which includes knowledge, belief, art, morals, law, custom, and any other capabilities and habits acquired by man as a member of society."[2] In other words, culture colors our environments, our lives, and how we think about them. In many ways our cultures are as close and as permanent a part of us as our bodies. Much of the time we do not even notice them unless there is something wrong with them.

Consequently, the perspective I bring to this look at culture is already culturally skewed. It represents the culture of a white middle-class American, although—and this is also a part of the skew—I have been immersed in other cultures by way of origin and travel. Further, the very nature of American culture today is influenced by multicultural awareness due to living together with clearly identifiable ethnic subcultures such as African-American, Hispanic, and Chinese. The point of this observation is that to be dogmatic about what *the culture clearly says* would be to go far beyond the feasible. Still I am quite sure that by drawing carefully qualified generalizations, I will be able to speak, not only of myself, but also about what most Americans will recognize as broadly American culture.

Implicit in our definition of culture is the fact that it is impossible to divorce yourself from it completely, and it is not at all clear why anyone would want to do that. *All* cultures have flaws; yet *all* human beings live within a

---

[1]Philosophers, at least since Plato, have seen these three areas as major concerns. Plato himself thought that "the true," "the good," and "the beautiful" were real by themselves. See *Republic* 6, 507B.

[2]Edward B. Tylor, *Primitive Culture* (London: Murray, 1871), 1.

culture. Thus, from the point of view of a critic of a culture, the only possible—and desirable—thing to do is to criticize the culture from within the culture with an eye toward redeeming it, not to attempt the impossible and discard it. (See the study of system-dependent thinking in chapter 4.)

Christmas Lights in October

As I have been thinking about how to characterize our culture, a particular image has persisted in my mind. Driving home one evening around the middle of October, we passed a house on the outskirts of town already decorated fully for the Christmas season with the lights blazing. Halloween lights? Not likely, not with the red and green bulbs glowing. Nor was it a business (we are all familiar with the chocolate Santas starting to stale on supermarket shelves from September on). It was a private house; apparently the folks living there enjoyed Christmas so much that they decided to start to celebrate a good two months before the event.

I am not offended by premature Christmas celebrations; there is no moral issue here, but this image can guide our observations on contemporary culture in several ways.

1. The image stems from the ordinary lives of ordinary people in a midwestern town that bills itself as "Smalltown, USA." The cultural patterns we seek to describe are not the latest ruminations of some avant garde theater company. They are what shapes the lives of people in the living rooms of America, forged by many popular influences.

2. We see a pattern of instant gratification in this image. It is certainly not immoral to have Christmas lights at times other than in December. They are not an issue in itself (in fact, they were pretty), but they point us to an assumption that governs our lives: *whatever we want, we are entitled to have, and we should have it now.* Consequently, we are a culture saturated with never-ending opportunities for amusement. For example, through cable television my family receives about twenty-five channels. Yet there are nights when "there is nothing much on." So we can supplement our TV diet with the fare offered at about a dozen movie theaters within easy driving distance, some of which offer ten or more features at one time. In addition we have sports events, musical shows, video games, parks, and recreational facilities—and we do not even live in a big city.

One characteristic of our culture is that we not only demand instant gratification for our desires, we are accustomed to getting it. If our paychecks are adequate, we can procure for ourselves what we want. If we do not have the money, we feel that we are being deprived of what we are entitled to. In other words, we not only expect instant gratification, we believe we are entitled to it.

As a result, in our society nothing is "special" any longer. We are sated and glutted, looking for more. Nothing is left beyond our reach, except in terms of quantity. Here we come to the heart of the image: because nothing is special, *nothing really matters any longer.* Below we will examine how this attitude works out in terms of truth, goodness, and beauty. For now, let us affix a label to this phenomenon: *nihilism.* We can define nihilism as *the attitude that nothing carries any ultimate worth, that all things are equally meaningless.* Sadly, as I look at our contemporary culture, what I see as the philosophy that underlies our lives, increasingly, is nihilism. In the mid-1960s a number of Christian writers argued that a contemporary non-Christian has but two alternatives: despair or irrational escape.[3] We referred to this argument in chapter 5 in our discussion of atheism. We said that

- The person without God has no rational basis for obligatory values, yet needs them to live by (the "lower story");
- The only way in which such a person can hold on to obligatory values is by an irrational escape by grabbing something that is actually contradictory to his or her worldview (the "upper story").

What we are now seeing as a part of our culture is the reaction of living in the upper story too long. People realize that the values by which they live are only irrational escapes; they are not objectively derived. Consequently your escape is as good as mine; they are all irrational, so it does not even make sense to ask which one is right. In one sense they are all right; in another sense none of them is. Nothing really matters. Christmas lights in October are more than an

---

[3]One of the most popular treatments was Francis A. Schaeffer, *The God Who Is There* (Downer's Grove, IL: InterVarsity Press, 1968).

innocent, enjoyable decoration: they are also a profound symbol for a culture that has lost its bearings. Let us now see what more specifically happens to truth, goodness, and beauty in this context.

Truth

This entire book has been devoted to the study of truth, from its possibility to its method to its application to Christianity. We have argued that (a) it is possible to have truth and that (b) we can show that Christianity is true. We now return to take a closer look at the question of how truth is treated in our culture.

In broad terms, the most popular approach to truth today is *relativism,* which we already analyzed in chapter 2. Relativism teaches that there are many valid religious truths. Christianity might be true, but so could religious traditions that contradict Christianity. Here is a quote by Marcus Bach to that end: "I feel that the great religions should be viewed as different dialects by which man speaks to God—and God to man."[4] This statement implies that there is a fundamental reality, described with the term "God." Various religions, with their concepts, images, myths, and languages are all different ways of relating to this God. This kind of statement (pacesetting when it was first penned in 1961) can serve as a rallying point for what has become conventional wisdom approaching the twenty-first century. It is a particular instance of relativism, which we can call inclusivism. Yet there are serious problems with inclusivism.

1. Inclusivism cannot include an exclusive religion. Some religions claim to be the only way to God. One such religion is Christianity. Jesus said, "I am the way and the truth and the life. No one comes to the Father except through me" (John 14:6, NIV).[5] There are only two logical options in view of such a statement: (1) Christianity is false or (2) Christianity

---

[4]Marcus Bach, *Had You Been Born in Another Faith* (Englewood Cliffs, NJ: Prentice-Hall, 1961), ix.

[5]Remember that in the last chapter we showed that this exclusive claim is an essential part of Christianity. Christ is our only access to God because Christ alone made atonement for our sin.

is exclusively true. Christianity cannot be true alongside other religions that are equally true. For if Christianity is true, then it must be true in accord with what it claims to be—the only way to God. If this claim is false, however, then it can no longer be said that Christianity is true. Something cannot be false and true at the same time. Of course something very much like Christianity could still be true, namely a Christianity that has been purged of all exclusive claims. This would not be biblical Christianity, but a Christianity reduced to suit the thesis of inclusivism.

If one wanted to change Christianity to accommodate it to inclusivism, one should have some good reason to think that inclusivism is true. Let us look at its possible support.

2. *There is no evidence for inclusivism.* What could conceivably count as evidence for Marcus Bach's statement? How could we know that we are actually referring to the same reality? One answer to this question could be the principle of the identity of indiscernibles; we used this principle in chapter 6 to show that there can be only one God. The way in which we stated the principle was that if two things share all of the same properties, then they are identical; they are one and the same. If we can show that God as conceived in any religion always has the same properties, then the principle would lead us to posit that all religions worship the same God.

Nothing, however, could be further from the truth. As I am writing this, I am thinking back to a day in Singapore a few months ago. In the morning a group of students and I attended a staff meeting of Youth for Christ. We sang hymns, prayed, and listened to an exposition of James. In the afternoon we attended a Hindu temple for the Taipusan festival, a local celebration to the god Muruga.[6] We stood in the temple and watched devotees of Muruga pierce themselves with skewers with heavy weights (the "kavadi") attached, and we saw them drive skewers through their

---

[6]Muruga is known by many different names (and spellings). He was probably worshiped in South India before becoming absorbed into the Hindu pantheon. He is now identified with Kartikeya or Skandar, the Hindu god of war. In Hindu mythology he is seen as the son of Shiva, the Destroyer, and Shiva's wife, Paravati. His brother is Ganesha, the elephant-headed Remover of Obstacles.

cheeks and tongues. They then walked along the street to the accompaniment of chants, many of which celebrate "vel," the spear of Muruga. As I observed the proceedings, I contemplated the contemporary slogan, "We all worship the same god; we just give him different names." I could not get over how implausible this slogan is. The differences between the Christ whom I worshiped in the morning and the Muruga worshiped by my Hindu acquaintances are insurmountable. Jesus carried the cross and was pierced on our behalf; Muruga demands that we carry the "kavadi" and are pierced to appease him. There may be analogies on a trivial level (both are gods, both are being worshiped), but there is hardly any significant similarity at all, let alone the kind of similarity required by the principle of the identity of indiscernibles. Thus the principle does not bear out inclusivism.

Yet Bach does not appeal to the principle of the identity of indiscernibles. He makes his statement at the beginning of a book in which he shows how religions function in the lives of people belonging to many different faiths. His thesis seems to be that since all religions function in the same way in people's lives, there must be a common reality behind them.

The premise of this argument, that all religions occupy a similar role in people's lives, can only be ascertained experientially. Bach's experience leads him to assert it, though my experience leads me to question it, except in terms so broad that they are almost empty. Even within one religion, adherents are involved for drastically different reasons: to insure material benefits or to compensate for not having material goods, to work towards forgiveness of sins or to express gratitude for having been forgiven, to be motivated to change the world or to escape from it, etc. I do not believe you can stick to the particulars of what people say about their religion and claim that they all function in the same way.

Even if Bach's premise were true, the conclusion would not follow at all. Imagine two men, Fred and Ricky, who are married to two women, Ethel and Lucy. Presumably Ethel functions in Fred's life roughly the way Lucy functions in

Ricky's. Still that is no reason to think that Fred and Ricky are married to the same woman, and that "Ethel" and "Lucy" are simply two different names for one female reality. The only way it could be so is if they shared all of the same properties (including occupying the same space at the same time), but they clearly do not. In the same way, it does not follow that if all religions function in similar ways, they refer to the same reality. The assertion simply begs the question, for they surely do not all have the same properties (as we have seen). Thus experience does not support inclusivism.

What could then count as evidence for inclusivism? Let us look a little closer at Bach's statement. He does not actually refer to *all* religions, just the "great religions." His statement is not totally inclusive for it leaves room to escape if the evidence makes it necessary. If I could show, for example, that a specific religion cannot be accommodated to this view, then Bach still would have the possibility of taking recourse to the idea that this religion must not be a "great religion." Thus evidence can ultimately be putty in his hands.

Look a little closer. The statement is made apart from evidence anyway. Bach says, "I feel that . . . ." He is not asserting a conclusion ultimately based on evidence but an assumption with which he approaches the evidence. Our question of what could possibly count as evidence for the assertion is really irrelevant. In the light of the initial assumption, the evidence is not all that important.

3. *Inclusivism leads to nihilism.* We have taken this close look at an inclusivist statement and lack of evidence in order to make a point as clearly as possible. Contemporary religious inclusivism (and the relativism on which it is based) is not the conclusion of scholarly inquiry, for there is nothing in the data to support it. Inclusivism is a dogmatic assumption, plain and simple. The dogma is this: all religions are equally true. All points of view are equally true. Differences and issues of plausibility do not really matter.

Thus we have arrived at the nihilistic outcome of the matter. It is acceptable to be religious. It is acceptable *not* to be religious. Whatever religion one chooses is acceptable. In the final analysis, it just does not matter. Thus relativism leads to nihilism.

4. *Nihilism leads to authoritarianism.* This progression does not stop with nihilism. As paradoxical as it sounds, a nihilistic approach to truth leads to an authoritarian approach to truth. The logic of this thesis is simple. We saw that in a scheme based on relativism there is no objective truth; there is no way to establish truth by appealing to objective facts. As we said in chapter 2, people cannot live that way. We need to live by truth-as-opposed-to-falsehood. Where can such a truth come from? The only source that is left is that truth becomes arbitrarily defined. In the case of a whole culture or society, truth would have to be defined by whoever is in a position of authority. This can happen through church, academics, or media, but ultimately through political authority. When the prerogative to decide truth (that is to decree, not to discover) is left in the hands of a group of people with enough power to enforce their decree, we are well under way towards an authoritarian society.

In chapter 2 we alluded to the fact that a lot of people with good intentions embrace relativism because of a misunderstanding. They believe that to hold to an objective understanding of truth leads to intolerance and persecution. A look at the dynamics of history shows that this is not the way in which authoritarian societies have developed. Intolerance is first and last a function of power; the understanding of truth involved really plays no role. If someone is truly committed to objective truth, they have nothing to fear from free inquiry and representation of opposing viewpoints. The fact that an authoritarian society resorts to suppressing opposing viewpoints demonstrates that such a society is not based on objective truth, but on the opinion of those in power.

We can clinch this case—and in the process lodge a public protest—by exposing a fashionable contemporary myth. It is frequently pointed out to me that I, as an evangelical teacher who holds to an objective view of truth, am contributing to the rise of intolerance in the world. Then I am asked instead to embrace relativism, supposedly an eastern view of truth that engenders tolerance. Aldous Huxley, for example, blamed the intolerance that has at times characterized European history on an objective view of truth and commended a mystical, intuitive approach, as exemplified in Indian thought.[7] Such commendations, as well-meaning as they may be, simply have no basis in fact. The traditional Hindu society with its caste system is nothing if not institutionalized racism. Some of the bloodiest battles over religion in the twentieth century have been fought on the Indian subcontinent. My point is not to cast aspersion on India or the Hindu religion, but to point out that an eastern view of truth is no hedge against intolerance. Intolerance is simply not the consequence of a particular view of truth but of the power struggles of human beings. When relativism turns into nihilism, it prepares the way for such authoritarianism.

How can we tell if we are on the way to an authoritarian society? Here are some tell-tale signs:

- When people try to impose their point of view on others through force rather than debate and reason.
- When people feel it is necessary to rewrite history to conform it to their point of view.
- When people look to governmental authorities such as the Supreme Court or state legislatures to decree what is true.
- When schools establish a curriculum and select textbooks for political reasons more than educational goals.
- When information is evaluated on the basis of how well it promotes political goals, not on whether it is true.
- When it becomes apparent that people would rather be comfortable with a known lie than uncomfortable with the truth.

As I am writing these points, I can think of examples across the political spectrum for each of them. Thus it is not clear whether the "left," "right," or "middle" will ultimately come out ahead. That these dynamics are in motion in our

---

[7]Aldous Huxley, *The Perennial Philosophy* (New York: Harper & Row, 1944), 140-141.

culture is evident. Twenty-five years ago various writers
warned that if we did not return to an objective view of
truth, the result would be chaos. Chaos is here. The next
step could be an authoritarian society.

Goodness

One Thursday afternoon in November of 1990, an NBA
basketball player was arrested on prostitution charges,
booked, jailed, and released to report late to the game his
team was playing. When he walked into the arena, the
spectators (who were aware of the news reports) gave him a
rousing ovation, then gave him another ovation when he
entered the game. Basketball players, like all people
everywhere at all times, are fallible, but the reaction of the
crowd is telling for our culture. It is doubtful that they
particularly condoned what the player had done; with their
reaction they were saying that it did not matter. This is
precisely what was expressed by a teammate in a newspaper
statement.[8]

This example illustrates the fact that our culture is on the
verge of nihilism in regard to morality as well. We no longer
have clear standards of right and wrong; but we feel that we
no longer need them either. It just does not matter.

This is not to say that our culture promotes immorality.
Such a notion is easier to support from the pulpit than in real
life. Preachers who say that there is no morality whatsoever
on television any longer probably do not watch it. We can
summarize a code of ethics of sorts that most contemporary
situation comedies (at least) seem to endorse most of the
time:

- Always be true to yourself.
- Always be loyal to your friends (unless it violates the
  above).
- Always be accepting of other people and their
  convictions. Who is to say that in the end they may
  not turn out to be right?

---

[8]*Los Angeles Times*, November 16, 1990.

- Children, recognize that your parents are only human and be prepared to forgive them for their selfish and thoughtless behavior (a complete reversal from the days of Theodore "Beaver" Cleaver!).
- Sex is very special. You should never go to bed with someone unless you really like him or her. Do not be judgmental toward those who have not yet attained this level of moral sophistication.

Of course this gruel is so thin it would not even be served in a Charles Dickens orphanage! Yet it largely represents where we are, in terms of moral consensus in this culture. There is no moral consensus, and so we hide behind moral and relational platitudes that mean nothing. When it comes down to particulars, not much can be said; but then, it does not really matter so long as you were "true to yourself."

This is the message with which we are bombarded day in and day out. It shows up in sugar-coated ways in television shows, popular music, and newspaper editorials. It is hammered out relentlessly in the music geared to the present youth culture. One rock group, Metallica, declares a position of caring for nothing but yourself and asserts that "nothing else matters."

A society cannot survive in complete moral chaos. To ensure that society will continue to function, sooner or later a moral code or policy must be found. If there is none, one will be imposed. We will wind up with a government-sponsored social morality. *Moral nihilism also leads to authoritarianism.*

This claim appears paradoxical because the idea of ethical relativism is to be tolerant. In fact, it seems that tolerance is the only universal value left. All people should respect the values of all others at all times. Unfortunately the commitment to tolerance is much more ambiguous than that. Only a person who believes that right and wrong are based on something other than human preference (such as divine will) and that judgment is not of human doing can be truly tolerant.[9] The person who believes that right and wrong are

---

[9]This is not to say that someone who believes in God as the source of ethical values is necessarily tolerant. A lot of people professing Christian morality are extremely intolerant.

based purely on one's own decisions and that it is up to him or her to enforce that decision cannot be tolerant. From a purely logical perspective, he or she can be tolerant only up to a point, namely until their personal preferences are infringed on. Consequently, when people espouse the ultimate virtue of tolerance, they can only mean tolerance within what is acceptable to them. If a moral judgment opposes their own preference, they are shown to be as intolerant as anyone else.

Sadly, then, we conclude that moral chaos is upon us. Behind a thin veneer of moral platitudes there lies a wasteland in which nothing is wrong and ultimately nothing is completely right either. Unless our culture returns to an objective foundation of morality, the specter of authoritarianism as a way out of the morass could be just around the corner.

Beauty

An important aspect of a culture is the art it produces. Traditionally art expresses what is considered to be beautiful in a culture. What do we find beautiful in our culture? Many people would consider the very question either meaningless or even offensive. Everyone knows that "beauty lies in the eye of the beholder"—don't they? Surely no one is entitled to speak dogmatically about what is supposed to be beautiful. When it comes to this issue, even Christians have drunk deeply at the fountain of nihilism, and say that standards of beauty either do not exist or do not matter. As long as somebody finds something pleasing, that is all that counts.

The statement that "beauty is in the eye of the beholder" is highly ambiguous. It could be taken to mean one of two things:

- *It takes a beholder to recognize beauty where it is.* The identification of beauty is dependent on there being somebody who sees it. This meaning would be the case, for example, when a jeweler recognizes the beauty of an as-yet-uncut diamond.

- *Beauty is whatever somebody wants it to be.* The beholder decides what is beautiful to him or her with no further reference to any objective standards of beauty.

Our culture understands the nature of beauty in this second sense. There are no standards for what constitutes good art. Anything a person may want to produce is as good as anything else. One person's appreciation begins and ends with pictures of red barns and porcelain cats; another person (a former art teacher of mine) frames a piece of tar paper he found along the road as great art. It is all the same. There are no standards. Nothing matters.

Does it matter? It matters because *art is not neutral.* A work of art is a piece of communication. With his or her creation the artist communicates something about his or her experience of, attitude towards, or vision of the world. A serious artist does not simply make a pretty picture. He or she shows us something about how the world could be seen. Art makes statements; consequently, it does matter.

This sort of discussion made the news recently in connection with the works of Andres Serrano and Robert Mapplethorpe. Serrano caused offense with his "Piss Christ," a crucifix immersed in a container of his own urine. The Contemporary Art Center in Cincinnati was prosecuted for obscenity for displaying the homoerotic and sado-masochistic photographs by Mapplethorpe (who had died of AIDS previously). The verdict in that trial was "not guilty"; the jury became convinced that, even if art is offensive, it is still art and, consequently, beyond any moral standards. *Cincinnati Enquirer* art critic Owen Findsen rejoiced in the verdict inasmuch as it showed that "evil existed in the eye of the beholder."[10]

This is aesthetic nihilism, and it is just as problematic as nihilism in truth and morality. Art does not have to be beautiful and realistic. It can be challenging and disturbing, but it should not be destructive. Serrano's celebration of bodily fluids[11] and Mapplethorpe's depictions of men abusing each other in the worst imaginable ways destroy human dignity and reduce humanity to meaningless physical organisms. These artists were making statements; and, ultimately, these

---

[10]*Art News* 89 (December 1990), 10.

[11]See *Art News* 89 (April 1990), 163.

statements were self-destructive. If nothing matters, the artist does not matter either. By destroying reality, the artist destroys him- or herself.

This is not a discussion of censorship—though it oftentimes turns into one, as we shall see below. It is first a discussion of the meaning of art and the fact that art is not neutral. We will have come a long way in this discussion if people realize that a nihilistic message about life and morality is being propagated in many contemporary art works. Mapplethorpe did not just happen to come across his scenes with his cameras. He planned, staged, and arranged his photographs deliberately in order to make his points.

Unsurprisingly *nihilism in art also bears the seeds of authoritarianism.* The Serrano/Mapplethorpe controversy broke out because both of their works had received extensive federal funding. There was an outcry for strict government censorship of art receiving government money. The art community responded by insisting on their right to freedom of expression and creativity. Let no one think that art is politically neutral. Today art is heavily pressed into service on behalf of many political interests. This is the logical outcome of nihilism. If in art neither content nor method matter, then one can use it to further one's own ends with impunity. As a result, it becomes the bearer of the artist's political agenda and is evaluated accordingly. A quick survey of the art section of a popular news magazine will confirm the fact. It is hard to escape from at least an implicit political message: environmentalist, feminist, reactionary, and so on.[12] This phenomenon is really a sign of the nihilistic attitude that makes art nothing more than the function of human whim. Art is laid open to the whim of whoever is in power. One of the first acts of any authoritarian government has been to bring art in line with its aims. Since there are no standards, the only way in which art is evaluated is by whether it contributes to the goals of society or not. The only

---

[12]To reassure myself on this point I turned to the issue of *Newsweek* I had just received in the mail and found the following: "The Far Side of Eden: In a new photography show, the mythical American landscape looks frayed," a careful discussion of excellent pictures—with heavy political overtones. *Newsweek*, June 1, 1992, 66-67.

defense against that move is the conviction that art has an integrity of its own.

Let me summarize this section. The chaos in our culture surrounding truth and morality is also reflected in our art. We have adopted a nihilistic approach to art that says that ultimately there are no standards; nothing matters. This approach is self-destructive; for it ultimately leads to the destruction of the artist and renders the art meaningless. Thus art can become the tool of authoritarianism.

An Objective Foundation

Our culture's chaos with regard to truth, goodness, and beauty represents the consequence of attempting to build worldviews apart from an objective foundation. Christianity, as defended in this book, provides such an objective foundation.

Truth: We begin with reality and describe as true what conforms to reality. This includes God who has revealed Himself in Scripture and in Christ.

Goodness: God is good, and what He commands is good. The basis for morality becomes God's nature as it is expressed in God's will.

Beauty: God created a reality that is objectively beautiful. The artist explores the nature of reality within the terms of his or her subjectivity, but he or she cannot encounter reality without encountering God's standards of beauty and goodness.

We need to be clear on the correct logical relationship. Christianity is not true because it fills the void of contemporary culture. Rather, it fills the void because it is true. Christianity does so, not by limiting all truth to Christian religious truth, but by providing an assumption of the world from which all truth, goodness, and beauty can be explored.

We have shown that Christianity is true. We have also shown that Christianity responds to a human void as exposed in our culture. Thus the bottom line of this entire discussion is a personal response. The matter is not merely intellectual. If our arguments have been successful, then we cannot simply acknowledge philosophical truth and philosophical error. We need to respond personally to the claim presented by Christianity. This means placing our faith in Jesus Christ Himself.

Intellectual arguments are important, as we have emphasized throughout, but intellectual arguments are not an end in themselves. They are essential only because they point us to the one who is our personal redeemer. Jesus Christ said, "Ye shall know the truth, and the truth shall make you free" (John 8:32, KJV). Now we can take one last look at vignettes.

Response to Vignette 1: I trust that I am not arrogant in my adherence to the truth. If I am, that is sinful on my part, and I need to let God work on my attitude. As we discussed extensively in chapter 2, to hold to truth is not necessarily arrogant. In fact, it is essential. Having truth, no matter how humbly received, implies that whoever holds a contradictory view, is in error. Christian theism and Hindu pantheism are mutually exclusive, as are the beliefs and practices of many other religions. The inclusivist thesis simply cannot be true, as we showed above. With all due respect and humility towards the overwhelming majority of humanity, we are allowed by God's grace to have the truth that they need to hear. Let us not forget that this is not a matter of religious imperialism but of redemption through the only way God has provided.

Response to Vignette 2: A number of my students in that class never did understand what I was after, even after another half hour or so of discussion. They had been completely ingrained in the current dogma that morality is no different from choosing coffee over tea or pepperoni over anchovies; that is to say, done purely on the basis of personal preference. The idea that you could have an objective basis for deciding right and wrong was inaccessible to them.

That episode was fascinating because some of the students had been among the most vigorous debaters when we had considered moral case studies. They had eagerly and enthusiastically defended their point of view, even though they could not even understand the notion of having a basis for their moral judgments.

This occasion was a good reminder for me to look beyond what people are saying to their presuppositions. People still use the language of morality; they still talk about right and wrong. Yet they may mean nothing more by it than whatever appeals to them subjectively.

Response to Vignette 3: In one sense the boy was right. There is a deep message in the white painting, but it is a message of nihilism. The message is that these white panels are just as much art as whatever else is in the museum, be it the large collection of Picasso's or Andy Warhol's soup cans.

A Christian is not committed to one particular style of art. My own personal taste runs past the realistic and representational, but a Christian can never say that it does not matter. In a universe created by God, all forms of expression matter.

For Growth and Study

Mastering the Material

When you have studied this chapter you should be able to:
1. Define nihilism.
2. Show how and why nihilism is becoming increasingly characteristic of our culture.
3. Describe inclusivism for religion and show why it is not a plausible thesis.
4. Demonstrate how nihilism exists behind a superficial contemporary morality.
5. Illustrate how nihilism is true in the world of art.
6. Show how nihilism in truth, goodness, and beauty leads to authoritarianism.
7. Identify the following names with the contribution to which we have alluded in this chapter: Marcus Bach, Andres Serrano, Robert Mapplethorpe.

Thinking About the Ideas

1. What changes in our physical and economic environment have caused current cultural and intellectual trends?
2. The claim that there can be no exclusive truth is clearly self-defeating, for it is itself a claim to exclusive truth. Why do people continue to advocate it anyway?
3. How do you represent an objective moral code within a political system based on pluralism? Is there a place where

freedom leaves off and the concern for the moral welfare of
society picks up?
4. "Standards of art" is a very ambiguous concept. How many
layers of meaning can you find in this idea? Which ones are
legitimate expectations one can place on an artist?
5. Current controversies have centered around the option of
deciding whether a work is either art or obscene. Is this an
appropriate range of choices? Can a work be legitimate art and
yet be obscene?
6. What is the proper role of government in promoting truth,
goodness, and beauty?
7. If Jesus Christ is the answer to the questions left unanswered by
our culture, why do so many people go out of their way to avoid
Him?

For Further Exploration

Carl F. H. Henry, *Twilight of a Great Civilization* (Westchester, IL:
Crossway, 1988).

H. R. Rookmaaker, *Modern Art and the Death of a Culture* (Downers
Grove, IL: InterVarsity, 1970).

Francis A. Schaeffer, *Escape from Reason* (Downers Grove, IL:
InterVarsity Press, 1968).

Helmut Thielicke, *Nihilism* (New York: Schocken, 1969).

Names Index

271

Scripture Index

Subject Index

275

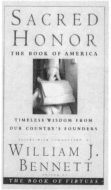

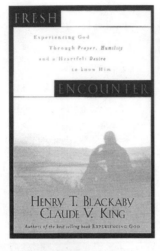